ACPL ITEM
3 1833 02529 38
350 R31
S0-CBH-590

BUS
STO

Research in public
administration

◄ ◄ ◄ ◄ ◄ ◄ ◄

Research

Adm   ion

DO NOT REMOVE
CARDS FROM POCKET

ALLEN COUNTY PUBLIC LIBRARY
FORT WAYNE, INDIANA 46802

You may return this book to any agency, branch,
or bookmobile of the Allen County Public Library.

DEMCO

The American Society for Public Administration

The American Society for Public Administration (ASPA) is a nationwide nonprofit educational and professional membership organization dedicated to excellence in public management and the promotion of public service. The Society seeks to achieve these objectives through:

- the advancement of the science, art, and processes of public administration,
- the development and exchange of public administration literature and information, and
- advocacy on behalf of public service and high ethical standards in government.

With more than twelve thousand members and subscribers, ASPA represents a broad array of professional interests and disciplines from all levels of government, the nonprofit and private sectors, and the academic community, both in the United States and abroad.

ASPA has provided national leadership in the areas of public administration and management since its inception in 1939. The Society and its members have been involved and influential in virtually every significant development in the theories and practice of public administration for half a century.

Though its networks of 126 local chapters, 20 national special-focus sections, individual and agency members, and organizational supporters, ASPA promotes recognition of public service achievements, develops a substantive dialogue on relevant issues, and enhances the professional development of its membership. To further its mission, ASPA

- communicates the importance and value of public service,
- promotes high ethical standards in public administration,
- speaks out in support of public service and seeks to improve the public's perception of government and to restore confidence in public servants,
- develops positions on significant public management and public interest issues,
- publishes a prestigious journal, *Public Administration Review,* an issues-oriented newspaper, *PA Times,* and other special books and publications, and
- recognizes excellence in public service through annual awards for special accomplishments in the literature of practice of public administration.

For additional information or membership materials, contact:

American Society for Public Administration
1120 G Street, NW
Suite 700
Washington, DC 20005
(202) 393-7878   Fax: (202) 638-4952

Research
in
Public
Administration

Reflections on Theory and Practice

Edited by

Jay D. White
Guy B. Adams

SAGE Publications
International Educational and Professional Publisher
Thousand Oaks   London   New Delhi

Allen County Public Library
900 Webster Street
PO Box 2270
Fort Wayne, IN 46801-2270

Copyright © 1994 by Sage Publications, Inc.

All rights reserved. No part of this book may be reproduced or utilized in any form or by any means, electronic or mechanical, including photocopying, recording, or by any information storage and retrieval system, without permission in writing from the publisher.

For information address:

SAGE Publications, Inc.
2455 Teller Road
Thousand Oaks, California 91320

SAGE Publications Ltd.
6 Bonhill Street
London EC2A 4PU
United Kingdom

SAGE Publications India Pvt. Ltd.
M-32 Market
Greater Kailash I
New Delhi 110 048 India

Printed in the United States of America

Library of Congress Cataloging-in-Publication Data

White, Jay D.
    Research in public administration : reflections on theory and
  practice / Jay D. White, Guy B. Adams.
        p. cm.
    Includes bibliographical references (p.   ) and index.
    ISBN 0-8039-5682-7 (cloth) — ISBN 0-8039-5683-5 (pbk.)
    1. Public administration—Research. I. Adams, Guy B. II. Title.
JF1338.A2W49   1994
350—dc20   94-7505
                                                       CIP

94 95 96 97 98   10 9 8 7 6 5 4 3 2 1

Sage Production Editor: Diana E. Axelsen

This book is dedicated to past, present, and future doctoral students in public administration and to Bayard L. Catron, mentor, friend, and wellspring of practical reason.

Contents

Foreword
Research Ideals and Realities

Chester A. Newland

Discipline and disciplines of civilization are about the struggle for knowledge: how to gain, expand, understand, and use it responsibly; how to maintain a balance of humility, hope, and informed self-confidence in the processes involved; and how to channel the efforts creatively to facilitate transformational achievement. That ideal and contrary realities are central to the subject of this book.

Research in public affairs and administration is an especially hard struggle for several reasons. First, the subjects are too vast to be defined as a discipline. This is an enormous field, and those in it employ discipline to draw on many disciplines and even other fields. Second, because it is a field that deals with people and their creations, inquiry into it must contend with human purposes and ways to accomplish them. Both the ends and means are the contentious stuff of struggle over civilization: whether and, optimistically, how people can lift themselves to transforming dreams and accomplishment of enhanced human dignity and reasonableness or whether and how, pessimistically, they condemn themselves to transactional struggles for transient power. Third, research takes time and other resources, and in public affairs time is often an impatient master, with many demands for prompt actions that acquaint most practitioners and many academicians with their fleeting mortality; getting resources for objective public affairs inquiry or even for instrumental advocacy research often seems to require a reach beyond the mortal. Fourth, only partially to make the point that the field is more complicated than the tripartite division of ancient Gaul, users of research-based knowledge in public affairs and administration are often amateurs, both well-intentioned and otherwise. Frequently, users of research are experts, some devoted to and skilled in substantive and procedural high mindedness and disciplined methods that are consistent with constitutional democracy and disciplined inquiry. Others are scoundrels, dedicated to self-serving ends through whatever means are available.

The struggle in recent decades to advance public administration knowledge through research has been highlighted more in the *Public Administration Review* (PAR) than in any other publication. The articles collected in this book draw chiefly on that rich resource. They reveal issues, passionate and reasoned debates over them, combatants, collaborators, and referees, among others, in an ongoing, often rough-and-tumble search. They demonstrate that public administration is not simply professionally introspective, but also a passionately self-conscious enterprise.

The greatest struggles have been over theory bases and research methodologies. Passions have been highest when methodology appeared for some—to some others—to be elevated to *the* preeminent theory or even to the only basic concern. These struggles were especially vital following World War II in the search for a science of public administration. Long before and during that war, professionals had engaged the positivist view that value propositions, although of enormous importance, are not subject to scientific demonstration. Efforts then grew to advance pure science by testing empirical propositions about specific subjects of human knowledge. Earlier, the field had been almost exclusively applied, based in part on scientific knowledge but drawing heavily on interpretation of experience and critical analysis of past, present, and future realities and ideals. Decades later, public administration remains largely an applied field, and the search for scientific verifiability remains important but not dominant.

In retrospect today, the classic debates in PAR over applied and pure research lend a quality of caricature to the field. Leading figures come across as both bigger and smaller than human, sometimes coincidentally in a single person. The Herbert Simon debates, for example, were and still are mind-stretching and gut-wrenching: Simon versus Dahl, Simon versus Waldo, Simon versus Argyris. These cut not only constructively to substantive and procedural dimensions of disciplined inquiry but also forcefully to the bone and the quick of professional endeavor. The earlier Finer and Friedrich dialogues and Carl Friedrich's sustained concerns about positivism reached well beyond PAR and the articles in this book, but some of the more recent articles republished here revive the debates, not so much in images of caricature but in refinement of longer-tested argumentation and accumulated knowledge.

The accumulation of substantive knowledge and methodologies in public administration, while often inadequate to needs and expectations, is now relatively so enormous that one may reasonably long for another time of overdrawn sketches: self-governing people, consistent with fundamentals of popular sovereignty and limited government; democratic leaders, attuned to "best practices," including public service, not personal aggrandizement and pandering to hero worship; and easy acronyms of leadership and management principles drawn from experience.

Today's problems that lead to such nostalgia are basic. The larger problem of the field is not that present concerns are so complex or that many early conclusions from experience and limited research were overdrawn in the past. It is rather that earlier work and even parallel inquiry of today is often ignored in research. An exaggerated caricature reveals that considerable inquiry in public affairs and administration skips about among current issues, often in ignorance of past experience and research, producing a dense hodgepodge as a large part of today's accumulated products. During my more than six years as editor of PAR, the hardest struggle beyond facilitating dialogue between and among practitioners and academicians was to encourage research by almost any methodology building on earlier theory-based inquiry. Research subjects and methodologies became a rare example of disciplined follow-up work, as demonstrated in the many articles republished here. But beyond such self-conscious exploration of the field's bellybutton (about which many practitioners expressed doubts), examples of sustained follow-up research were and still are few.

With respect to research, the most neglected, important subject may be the users of knowledge and the methodological mechanics and technicians who serve them. Leaders such as Herbert Simon, among advocates of enhanced discipline seeking a larger measure of pure science, understood and accepted the central importance of normative values, even when they seemed to dismiss experience and humanistic studies as sources of knowledge about them. Likewise, leaders among realists, such as Karl Llewellyn, sought clarity about who actually gets what, when, where, and how, precisely because of the importance of ideals and discrepancies from them as revealed by both sophisticated research and careful, objective observation. The brutal grasps of power-hungry dictators in the 1930s and 1940s, along with lesser realities of political and administrative debasement—precedent-bound judges who ignored terrible outcomes in cases and pocket-picking politicians with toothy grins—cried out for attention with questions: why and how? Power and what it got were important answers, but thoughtful advocates of science and realism did not embrace naked power as an ought. They held on to other ideals, while continuing to test them and methods associated with them, along with old and new hypothesized alternatives.

Yet it is only fair to say that the humanities came to be neglected by some advocates of scientific discipline in public affairs. Dwight Waldo and other distinguished students of history and philosophy struggled thoughtfully for balance. But, by the 1950s, some users, undisciplined by ideals of constitutional democracy and rigorous scientific methods, took the conclusions and methods of science and realism in directions that greatly altered the discipline of political science and the field of public administration. And what realists, both humanists and scientists often found—self-aggrandizement and raw accumulation and exercise of power—became *the* purposes of politics for many of these abusers of research. As Marshall Dimock often lamented, political science in the 1950s shifted focus to explanations and justifications of pressure groups and pursuits of power because these activities were thought to be realistic. In disciplines related to public administration, mechanics and technicians in polling and other crafts of getting and using power nearly displaced both humanists and scientists for more than a generation. Both political science and economics as disciplines turned away from concerns with institutions and other deep interests of earlier political economy, the one engaged in here-and-now power pursuits with few more penetrating concerns than how to win, and the other recast in untested certainty in supposed "universals" of economic "knowledge." Both fields escaped much of that narrowness by the late 1980s.

All of this is to say, through use of only slight exaggeration, that the subject of this book—research—not only probes the basics of the field, but also crucially defines them, often in rugged struggles. The articles that follow provide more detached and graphically complete histories and commentaries than this sketch allows. These studies support one common conclusion: In the field of public affairs and administration, methodologies and understandings of and about them—by researchers and users alike—make enormous differences in knowledge and what is done with it.

Preface

The quality and character of research in an academic field is widely thought to bear importantly on that field's status as a discipline or profession. Moreover, research is the chief ingredient of knowledge and theory development within a field. Numerous recent articles in public administration discuss various aspects of these important issues. Some of that research has examined dissertations and journal publications to determine the type of research that has been conducted, assess its quality, and prescribe approaches to research. Other research has addressed philosophical issues about knowledge acquisition and theory development in a field that strives for both basic and applied knowledge. As the Foreword by Chester A. Newland makes clear, these issues have enjoyed a long and rich tradition of debate and discourse within public administration.

The discussion of these issues has seen renewed and heightened interest in the past 10 years. Some have compared research in public administration to mainstream social science research. They have concluded that research published in the major journals in the field is basically applied, noncumulative, conceptual, nonempirical, suspect in terms of methodological rigor, and lacking institutional support. The methodological rigor of doctoral dissertations has also been called into question, along with the relevance of the dissertation topics. Assessed against the standards of mainstream social science, much public administration research falls short, according to these analyses.

The mainstream social science standards, in turn, have been questioned, with several authors suggesting that alternative methods of inquiry such as interpretive, critical, systems theoretical, or postpositivist are also legitimate for research in the field. Yet little research appears in journals or dissertations that systematically uses an alternative method such as ethnomethodology or grounded theory. Others have argued that practitioners possess their own type of knowledge fundamentally different from that produced by science. Such knowledge is considered to be more relevant for professional decision making. Unfortunately, the legitimacy of practitioner knowledge has been masked by a bureaucratic, engineering mentality that permeates organizational hierarchies. Still others have placed questions about research into a historical and epistemological context in the hope that scholars and practitioners will see the consequences of research that is atheoretical, ahistorical, and of poor quality.

In an attempt to develop a more comprehensive view of research in public administration, we have collected most of the recent reflections on research in this book. We were motivated by two additional concerns. First, these reflections appeared in issues of the *Public Administration Review,* connected by only a few statements and citations. Their common concern for improving academic research and professional practice recommends that they be collected in one place. Our hope, and our second motivation, is that this volume will generate the critical mass necessary to advance further the discourse and dialogue about appropriate methods, standards, and epistemologies for research in the field. The rationality of scientific knowledge is predicated on practical discourse, that is, discussion, debate, deliberation, and argumentation over what is true or false, good or bad, right or wrong, and what should be desired (White, 1990). Certainly, the same can be said for methodological and philosophical reflection in the field.

The breath and depth of concern about research in public administration may be captured in a series of questions.

- Why is there so little mainstream social science research being done in the field?
- Is the field too varied to develop a cumulative body of knowledge? If so, should there not at least be enclaves of cumulative knowledge?
- Are the methodological standards of mainstream social science appropriate for research in the field?
- Are the truly important questions in the field approachable only from alternative methodological frameworks?
- Why is the methodological rigor of doctoral research questionable?
- Why are many of the topics of doctoral research relatively unimportant to knowledge and theory development in the field?
- Why do so few recipients of doctoral degrees go on to publish anything at all in scholarly or even in professional journals?
- Is theory really unrelated to practice?
- Is there something inherently different about knowledge acquisition and use in an applied, professional field?
- Is the type of knowledge that practitioners use different from scientific knowledge or even common sense?

Taken together, the contributors to this volume offer answers to these questions, but not every contributor would agree with a particular answer.

So these questions remain as unresolved issues that must be consciously addressed and debated.

Efforts to address these issues raise deeper historical and philosophical questions.

- What are the societal consequences of adopting technical rationality and its chief constituent, the scientific-analytic mind-set, as the sole approach to knowledge development and use in the field? If we do not like these consequences, what alternatives are available?
- What ontological and epistemological assumptions are at the foundation of our attempts to develop theory and knowledge and to use them in the field?
- Is inattention to the philosophical assumptions of research at the center of unsuccessful, low quality research?

These issues have also been addressed by the contributors, although the answers they give would certainly be questioned by some who are concerned with research, scholarship, and professional practice in public administration. Yet there is some common ground. All agree that research, scholarship, and professional practice in public administration need to be improved.

The contributions in this book should be of considerable interest to all students of public administration. How research and knowledge development are conceived goes far to define the boundaries and parameters of a field. What are the areas of research emphasis? Are they the most significant problems in the field? for society at large? What progress has been made in building knowledge and theory in the field? Do we know more now than we did 50 or 100 years ago?

These questions, of course, assume even greater centrality for doctoral students and the faculty who direct their research. The chapters portray problems and pitfalls that might be avoided in doing a dissertation. Also, possibilities and opportunities for research of major significance to the field are framed in several discussions of methodology and philosophy. Professionals in the practice of public administration, especially those who pursue advanced study in the field, should also find the research issues and questions important. All the issues bear on the troubled relationship between theory and practice, surely one of the most crucial questions within the field of public administration.

Researchers, scholars, and professionals in related fields such as management, planning, criminal justice, social work, and education should find these reflections on research of interest. Although specifics about public administration research would not weigh heavily on the minds of these people, the philosophical and methodological issues raised here are pertinent to research and professional practice in any practice-oriented field.

We have grouped these reflections into four parts, each with its own brief introduction. Part 1 addresses broad philosophical and historical issues regarding the acquisition, development, and use of knowledge in the field. Part 2 presents three critical examinations of published research in public administration. Part 3 presents two examinations of doctoral research in public administration and a critical inquiry about the nature of doctoral education in a practice-oriented field. Part 4 offers an argument in support of the much maligned case study approach to research, a postpositivist conception of knowledge acquisition and use, and two arguments showing how alternative kinds of knowledge are employed in professional practice. The references at the end of the book must be mentioned as a significant resource in themselves, constituting a comprehensive collection of writings on social inquiry, the contemporary philosophy of science, social science research, and methodological approaches of all kinds.

In Chapter 1, which represents our own original contribution to this discussion, we attempt to place the research issues in public administration into a broader philosophical and historical context that includes:

- an analysis of the limits of technical rationality and its deleterious effects on practical discourse;
- a discussion of how professionalism moved from craft to technique and in doing so lost its voice of advocacy and reform;
- an examination of how public administration reflects our postmodern condition in its inability to develop a grand narrative of meaning;
- an analysis of postmodern theories of knowledge that threaten theory development with relativism in all domains of inquiry; and
- a discussion of how interpretive and critical reason can rescue theory building from postmodern thought.

We argue that no single approach to research and knowledge development can sustain the range of inquiry demanded by the nature of the field and its larger social context. We agree that the quality of research of all kinds needs improvement, but assert that many approaches to knowledge and theory development must be utilized; we call this making sense with diversity.

We have many individuals, and one association, to thank for their help on this book. Starting with the association, the American Society for Public Administration made this volume possible, through the efforts of the ASPA staff—in particular:

- Sheila McCormick, director of communications; John Larkin, production specialist; and John Thomas, executive director;

- the publications committee and its chair, Marc Holzer, and acquisitions editor Darrell Pugh; and
- the *Public Administration Review,* and its editor-in-chief, David Rosenbloom, and managing editor Mel Dubnick.

The contributors, who authored the chapters herein, produced scholarship of the highest quality, as evidenced by its appearance in the *Public Administration Review,* widely considered to be the journal of record in public administration. We greatly appreciate the support of our colleagues at the University of Nebraska at Omaha, B. J. Reed and David Hinton; and at the University of Missouri-Columbia, Michael Diamond, John Forrester, Sheilah Watson, and Dale Swoboda. We also appreciate the high quality work that Nancy M. Krzycki provided in producing the manuscript. Carrie Mullen, public administration editor at Sage Publications, has been a complete pleasure to work with. She saw immediately the potential for this collection, and worked unflaggingly and with remarkable speed to move this through the appropriate channels at Sage. Our respective spouses have shown great understanding and support during a time when it must have seemed that our chief endeavor was to enhance this year's telephone company earnings and to burn the E-mail circuits with great regularity.

Jay D. White
Guy B. Adams

1

Making Sense With Diversity: The Context of Research, Theory, and Knowledge Development in Public Administration

JAY D. WHITE

GUY B. ADAMS

The discussion of research, theory, and knowledge development in public administration has been carried on, for the most part, with little sense of the historical context of the issues at hand. Most critics of research in the field have not placed their methodological and philosophical reflections in the context of modernity—Western society's current, dominant historical consciousness. Modernity is characterized by a powerful faith in science and technology to free us from the physical and social constraints on our existence. Modernity, although it has other antecedents in the history of ideas, is a product of the 16th-century Enlightenment.

The philosophers, social theorists, and later, scientists of the Enlightenment era dreamed of a society in which there would be universal truth, justice, goodness, prosperity, and beauty. This would be accomplished in the domains of science, law, economics, government, and art by adherence to a combination of the scientific-analytic mind-set and technological progress, which we call *technical rationality*. The state became the fulcrum for achieving this dream for the other domains. Over the years, a large governmental apparatus was built to enforce and adjudicate laws, regulate economies and markets, fund scientific discovery and technological innovations, and support the arts. In much of Western society, these tasks could not be accomplished by legislative bodies and courts alone. An executive-dominated administrative state resulted. Thus modern public administration was conceived of a dream dating back hundreds of years.

The Enlightenment dream has been realized, but only to a limited extent. The natural sciences have had successes in controlling nature and freeing humankind from physical constraints, but not without some unintended consequences such as the creation of world-threatening environmental problems. The application of science to the conduct of human affairs has not been as successful. Although a body of knowledge about our social existence has been accumulated, the social sciences have not, in the main, succeeded in describing, explaining, or controlling human affairs.

More generally, the dream of modernity has not been realized. There is no apparent universal truth, justice, goodness, prosperity, or beauty—certainly not in the material world of science and technology. Instead, society is fragmented, hedonistic, disobedient, narcissistic, and lacking in social identification, as has been recognized for a number of years (Bell, 1976). An ever-increasing public sphere defines our lives in terms of anonymity and impersonality, while an ever-decreasing private sphere narrows our opportunity for intimacy, meaning, and self-identity (Berger, Berger, & Kellner, 1973). Science, morality, law, art, and religion have all been institutionalized, separated from our life-world experience, and placed under the control of technical experts (Habermas, 1970). Many differing symbolic universes have flourished, creating conflicts among different value and belief systems. Technical rationality invades our private lives and leads us to make decisions about politics, the family, education, and even leisure activities blind to any sense of history and consequently meaning. These features of society have become known as the *postmodern condition* (Lyotard, 1984).

Why did this very different picture of modernity emerge? Three reasons stand out. First, technical rationality narrowly defined reason to be the coordination of means to given ends, leaving little space for rational discussion of the ends themselves. Second, technical rationality narrowed our understanding of professionalism, severely diminishing the capacity of the professions for social advocacy and reform. Third, too much faith was placed in supposedly universal and objective grand narratives of history (e.g., Marxism or capitalism) to provide meaning for our lives. These grand narratives have fallen by the wayside except for one—the tacit, grand narrative of technical rationality, defined as the combination of the scientific-analytic mind-set and the belief in technological progress. The diversity of local narratives that have emerged in the last century all rest on the foundation of this tacit, grand narrative, with the exception of those postmodern "narratives" (discussed below) that deconstruct all knowledge.

In this chapter, we first address these three historical topics: technical rationality, professionalism, and the grand narratives of postmodernism. Next, we examine six local narratives that have emerged within the field of public administration during this century. These are all partial narratives that have in common the foundation of the tacit grand narrative of technical rationality. Then we take up how this tacit grand narrative has established itself within the field down through the decades of public administration history. The postmodern threat to knowledge is the next topic of consideration; the fragmentation and chaos of postmodernism question the very foundations of reason as a ground for knowledge and theory development. We argue that an expanded conception of reason can still serve as a basis for inquiry in public administration and elsewhere, and we then discuss three modes of research, which follow from our more expansive characterization of reason. We close with a discussion of the implications of our analysis for research in public administration in which we emphasize both diversity and quality, as well as a vision of the field that sees its mission in part as addressing larger social issues.

Before doing so, we must be clear about what we mean by technical rationality and its chief constituents—the scientific-analytic mind-set and the belief in technological progress. Technical rationality is not to be equated with science per se, or with the tangible products of technology. Rather it has three dimensions that transcend science and technology to become a normative ideology (Habermas, 1971). First is a faith in the power of science and technology to liberate us from the natural and social constraints on our development; a faith that is blind to the detrimental effects of relying on the scientific-analytic mind-set and technique alone. Second is the mistaken belief that one's research or professional practice is rigorous and objective only to the extent that it is "scientific," that is, it follows a *procedure* understood as scientific. Third is a lack of regard for nonscientific but otherwise equally legitimate ways of knowing and acting. A peculiar feature of technical rationality is that it can be both explicit and tacit. On the one hand, it is the explicit framework informing the research of many in the academy (Smith, 1990). On the other hand, it is an unexamined and tacit set of beliefs very widely held in society at large. Indeed, one philosopher of science has suggested that it represents the first universal culture of humankind (Vanderburg, 1985).

Technical Rationality and Instrumental Reason

Modernity, though a child of the Enlightenment, coalesced in the United States only in the last 150 years. Developments in the latter half of the 19th century resulted in the powerful combination of science, instrumental reason, and technological progress that is the hallmark of technical rationality in the modern age. During this time period, technical rationality was applied to the social world and placed on the political agenda. A torrent of ideas and practices was unleashed into the social and political world as a result of what

Wiebe (1967) has characterized as the "search for order" (pp. 145-163). Technical rationality became the avenue of progress in the social and political world and prompted professionals—including managers, social scientists, and industrial psychologists—toward a worldview in which human conflicts and passions appeared as problems fit for engineering solutions (Bendix, 1956; see also Ellul, 1954).

Technical rationality employs instrumental reasoning. It is the coordination of means to ends in the domains of thought and action. Thinking is rational to the extent that it follows the rules of deductive inference to calculate the correct means to a given end. Action is rational when it follows a prescribed set of rules to coordinate means to given ends. Both dimensions of rationality are based on the deductive logic of scientific inference (Horkheimer, 1947).

This type of reasoning is particularly useful when technique is paramount—finding the one best way of accomplishing something. It is also the logic of the rational model of decision making found in economics, political science, sociology, and administrative theory. The rational model of decision making has been central to public administration. It is wholly consistent with the idea of politically neutral decision making in the sense that the ends of administrative action are prescribed, or given, by the political system, which is responsible for normative policy decisions. It is also consistent with the bureaucratic model of organization, which is predicated on the very idea of instrumental thought and action. As an institution, public administration has perpetuated instrumental thought and action within the broader context of society.

Instrumental reason paints a very narrow picture of how people behave economically, politically, socially, and administratively (White, 1990). Herbert Simon (1983) sees both the advantages and disadvantages of this type of reasoning: "We see that reason is wholly instrumental. It cannot tell us where to go; at best it can tell us how to get there. It is a gun for hire that can be employed in the service of whatever goals we have, good or bad" (pp. 7-8). Simon's observation points to the structural limits of instrumental reason. There is nothing within the logic of instrumental reason that allows one to break out of an endless means-ends chain to question the efficacy of the ends themselves in the broader context of one's life and its meaning. From the perspective of instrumental reason, the ends of thought and action are assumed to be given. There is no rational basis for determining what the appropriate ends might be. The same can be said for means. They are merely assumed to be available. Instrumental reason provides no explanation of how means are discovered or envisioned.

Decisions about ends are matters of political, moral, or even aesthetic judgments. Such decisions fall in the domain of practical as opposed to theoretical discourse (White, 1990). Practical discourse involves discussion, debate, deliberation, and argumentation over what is good or bad, right or wrong, and beautiful or ugly. It is a type of discourse that answers the question "What should be desired?" not "How should it be achieved?"

Because practical discourse is not driven by instrumental reason, it is considered to be nonrational at best, irrational at worst, and definitely noncognitive and nondescribable. Science and instrumental reason have so diminished practical discourse that little is remembered about the logic of political, normative, moral, or aesthetic decision making (Arendt, 1958). Indeed, science and instrumental reason would not recognize any type of logic in this type of decision making. Later we will show how practical discourse has a logic of its own. It is supported by interpretive and critical reason that provide an equally rational grounding as theoretical discourse.

Professionalism: From Craft to Technique

Professions gradually grew out of the earlier craft guilds. The practice of a craft carried with it a very different gestalt of professionalism than the one that would emerge with the more specialized, more scientific version of professionalism that developed by the early part of the 20th century. The evolution of professional associations in the latter half of the 19th century, as well as during the Progressive Era (1896-1916), reveals much about the current state of public administration as well as other fields and disciplines. Put simply, technical rationality, and its chief constituent, the scientific-analytic mind-set, won out over aspects of the former gestalt, which included centrally reform and advocacy (Furner, 1975). Advocacy and reform, although in widely differing versions, were an integral part of the ethos of most professions until the turn of the century. This meant that professions understood themselves as connected, as in a web, to the society at large, that their mission was to improve that society (through reform and advocacy, not through aggrandizement of the profession itself), and that this commitment was not merely rhetorical.

Thomas L. Haskell, in *The Emergence of Professional Social Science* (1977), traces the history of the old American Social Science Association, founded in 1865, as it confronted what he calls a "crisis of professional authority" (p. vi). Reform and advocacy coexisted, albeit somewhat uneasily, with science and objectivity during most of the latter half of the 19th century within the ASSA, a generalist organization of both practitioners and academics. But the tensions grew, and eventually choices had to be made. Haskell places the crucial turning point during the "watershed decade" of the 1890s.

In his founding address to the American Economic Association in 1886, Richard Ely (1982) attempted to preserve both science and reform, yet he called prominently for the scientific study of economics. The founding AEA Platform captured the ambiguity as well:

> We regard the state as an educational and ethical agency whose positive aid is an indispensable condition of human progress. . . . We hold that the doctrine of laissez-faire is unsafe in politics and unsound in morals. . . . We hold that the conflict of labor and capital has brought to the front a vast number of social problems whose solution is impossible without the united efforts of Church, state and science. (Ely, 1982, p. 282)

The formation of the AEA in the 1880s, along with the American History Association and the American Statistics Association, was indicative of both the growing specialization of academic social science and of the fatal contradiction in the ASSA. By the time the American Political Science Association and the American Sociological Association were founded in 1903, it was clear that the demise of the ASSA was imminent. Franklin H. Giddings of Columbia University made it clear to the ASSA as early as its 1894 meeting that social science, as the association had conceived it, was dying, and its heir was to be scientific sociology (Haskell, 1977, p. 204). The comments of Albion W. Small (1916, p. 729), the founding editor of the *American Journal of Sociology* and chair of the sociology department at the University of Chicago, about the ASSA are representative: "It represented humanitarian sentiment more distinctly than a desire for critical methodology."

Outside the academy, a similar process was occurring in a variety of professional associations formed in the 19th century, including dentists (1840), doctors (1847), pharmacists (1852), architects (1857), civil engineers (1867), lawyers (1878), and accountants (1887). The American Medical Association, reorganized in 1903 under the banner of scientific medicine, is representative. The AMA's Council on Medical Education, relying on visits to medical schools by Abraham Flexner, set about to insure the conformity of medical education to the principles of "scientific medicine." This process was characterized by Larson (1977, p. 163) as "the same general principles that guided the general movement of reform in the nineties and in the first decades of the [20th] century: centralization, consolidation into larger units, efficient management by experts, and the inevitable accent on technology." Reform became equated with science and technical expertise. Flexner's conclusions— "fewer and better doctors"—were firmly and colorfully stated (Larson, 1977, p. 163): "The privileges of the medical school can no longer be open to casual strollers from the highway." Flexner operationalized this dictum by recommending that the 131 medical schools in the United States be cut down to the 31 that could teach on the "modern, scientific bases" (Larson, 1977, p. 163).

Parallel developments were occurring within the university. First came graduate schools and then the proliferation of professional schools around the turn of the century. It was crucial for aspiring professions to legitimize their "scientific" base by securing a place within the modern university (Larson, 1977). By the mid-20th century, the academy had evolved into what William F. May (1980) has called the "positivist university," that is, a university that mirrors the specialized, compartmentalized disciplines and fields of the professions and of technical rationality. Older notions of "liberal" education, which had emphasized the development of general knowledge and critical thinking, in important part toward the betterment of society, degenerated into "general education," seen as a set of requirements to be met before the more useful, specialized training in one or another of the professional schools began.

As the Progressive Era drew to a close, professionalism had come to mean predominantly the increasing reliance on technical rationality and the scientific-analytic mind-set, and the growing specialization and expertise of the professions. It also meant the sloughing off of advocacy and reform as a trademark of professionalism. Their loss left a technically expert, but morally impoverished professionalism (Adams, 1993), and a positivist university, divided into departments that could promote the development of disciplines, but which were poorly organized to speak to larger social and ethical issues.

The Postmodern Condition

Jean-Francois Lyotard (1984) points out that the Enlightenment brought with it "grand narratives" of meaning: Hegel's dialectic of the spirit, Marx's emancipation of the working class, Adam Smith's moral philosophy of capitalism, and, most enduringly, the belief that science would free us from natural and social constraints on our development. These narratives were supposed to provide a stable, universal, overarching framework to which all members of a society might appeal to make sense of themselves and of society as it progressed toward the Enlightenment dream.

It is now widely acknowledged that all versions of grand narratives have failed in the project of establishing a unitary culture. In their place, groups within society weave their own local narratives to give meaning to their lives. Local narratives help members of a community make sense of themselves for themselves and for others. They define who the players are, the proper positions they may take, the roles they may perform, the beliefs they may hold, the feelings they may have, and ultimately the actions they may take. Nevertheless, they are only legitimating narratives for the interested group or community.

Although local narratives are necessary for the members of a group, community, society, or profession to make sense of one another and themselves, they can be debilitating because most of us live with several narratives. For example, as professors, we must use three distinct languages within our own profession: the language of academia when speaking to colleagues, the language of bureaucracy when speaking with in-career MPA practitioners, and the language of "Beverly Hills 90210" when speaking with younger, more traditional students. Learning to speak within different narrative frames of reference can be difficult, but it is necessary given our diversity of narratives.

The dark side of the postmodern condition is the conflict that ensues when narratives collide and the confusion that results when narratives fall apart. Local narratives can compete with one another, causing conflict between groups. For example, prochoice and prolife groups have their own distinct narratives or stories to legitimate their beliefs and guide their actions. Those narratives seem to be incommensurable. Although the parties are speaking the same basic language, differing beliefs keep the parties from attaining a common ground of mutual understanding. Carried to the extreme, *incommensurablity* means the creation of a narrative to separate one group from another in what might otherwise be a common culture. Consider the case of street gangs. They weave their own stories to distinguish themselves from society and from other gangs. They have also created their own language to define themselves as being different from the rest of society.

Confusion arises when local narratives fall apart. Examples would be the debates over the North American Free Trade Agreement and national health care reform. Traditional definitions of Democrat, Republican, conservative, and liberal have shifted, in some instances almost beyond recognition. To complicate matters, incipient narratives such as "centrist politics" and the "United We Stand" movement have been offered up. When local narratives break down, it is hard to know what to believe and who to believe, let alone how to act. In the eyes of many citizens, government is understood as "out there," disconnected from the people—literally, no longer "of the people." It either lacks a convincing story to legitimate its existence, or the narratives people share about it—especially the relentlessly cynical narrative of the mass media—tell a story of inefficiency, ineffectiveness, corruption, and distrust.

The Partial Narratives of Public Administration

As a self-conscious field of study, public administration has characteristics similar to postmodernism. Since the turn of the century, at least six local narratives have been offered up to give meaning to our professional lives. All rest on the foundation of the tacit, grand narrative of technical rationality.

None adequately embraces the full meaning of the field, yet they all capture some of its essence. Each will be outlined here to show how public administration stands on the brink of the postmodern condition.

First, some have looked to the Constitution and the founding period for a narrative to legitimate public administration (Rohr, 1986). Although little direct justification for public administration is found in the Constitution, there is at least an implied grounding for the field. Although the framers of the Constitution saw the need for an executive function, they did not envision a large administrative structure capable of making relatively autonomous policy decisions that affect the lives of citizens. The Constitution provides some justification for public administration in attempts to explain to others what the field is all about and why it should exist, but it requires an interpretive leap.

A second legitimating narrative is the dichotomy between politics and administration, certainly a part of Woodrow Wilson's (1887) vision of the field. Although it may sometimes hold true in practice, this dichotomy is largely a fiction. The idea that elected officials make policy while politically neutral career government workers merely carry out the policy in a competent way fails to adequately guide professional practice. A stated belief in the dichotomy masks the reality of the daily practice of administration. Career government workers must, many times, make policy as they interpret the meaning of legislative or executive mandates. They may also selectively choose to enforce a policy or to ignore it. An appeal to the dichotomy as a legitimating narrative does not make sense of what a public administrator does, though it aligns well enough with the notion of a science of public administration and with the idea of neutral bureaucracy.

The third narrative is the scientific study and practice of public administration. As mentioned, it fit well with the dichotomy between politics and administration. Science was seen as value neutral and the use of scientific technologies was certainly instrumental. Yet science alone does not explain what public administration is all about. The stated purpose of the American Society for Public Administration is to "advance the science, process, and art of public administration." The existence of the words *science* and *art* in this statement represents a long-standing tension in the field. Public administration is more than just science. It is also an art form. As C. P. Snow (1964) argued in his "two cultures" essays, science and art are difficult to reconcile. Conventional wisdom says that they seem to proceed according to very different logics; one rational, the other nonrational. Later we will explain how their logics may be quite similar, if not identical.

The fourth narrative is the belief that theory informs practice. However, the relationship between theory and practice has been called into question many times with the often heard phrase "That may work in theory, but not in practice." A gulf exists between those who study public administration and those who practice it for linguistic (read "narrative") reasons. As Richard Box (1992), a practitioner turned academic, puts it:

> Theory is often found to be unrelated to practice. If so, it is because it is written in a language that serves as a code of communication for academicians. This code is not easily accessible to nonacademicians; often there is little attempt to connect theory to practice through the use of examples, case studies, etc., or the use of complex statistics confuses and alienates all but the technician before the punchline is reached. (pp. 65-66)

The language of scientific theory is clearly not the language of practice. This raises the question of whether or not science has much guidance to offer to practitioners.

The fifth, and perhaps most overt attempt at creating a legitimating narrative was the first Minnowbrook Conference held in 1968. The attendees responded to failed narratives by setting out an agenda for a "New Public Administration." It included an emphasis on enhancing the value of social equity, encouraging citizen participation in policy making, making the study of public administration more relevant to practitioners and citizens, and, to some extent, a rejection of positivism. However, the narrative of the New Public Administration was never really adopted by a broad spectrum of academics and practitioners as a legitimation of the field (O'Toole, 1984). The New Public Administration was seen by some as a grand attempt to create a paradigm switch; an attempt that failed (Marini, 1992, p. 7).

The second Minnowbrook Conference held 20 years later in 1988 may represent the culmination of the partial narratives discussed so far. If a new agenda (or a new paradigm, or even a new grand narrative) was hoped for from the conference, it was not realized. About the best that could be said about Minnowbrook II was that the participants agreed that the problems facing public administrators today are interconnected. They must be addressed as such, realizing that if you tinker with one problem, you are likely to trigger another. Mary Ellen Guy (1989) expressed a feeling of "constrained hopefulness" in government's ability to solve such problems. Reflecting on the conference, Mary Timney Bailey wrote, "The conferees left Minnowbrook in 1988 with a sense of incompleteness." Then she asked, "Was this the best that could be done?" (Bailey, 1989, p. 224).

A sixth narrative, one that is still emerging, reexamines public administration themes and images using the concept of gender. Arguably, the most interesting and groundbreaking work currently underway in the social sciences has been associated with feminist theory. Although much of this work is critical of science (sometimes seen as a product of patriarchy), it nonetheless joins the debate in the terms provided by the tacit, grand narrative. Some of the earlier work from this perspective was primarily critical of public administration thinking and practice (Ferguson, 1984). But recent work has begun a more systematic reconstruction of public administration history and concepts (Stivers, 1993). Stivers has shown that women reformers during the Progressive Era were far more instrumental in developing the institutions and practices of the administrative state than previous historical analysis has admitted. Still, it remains to be seen whether this narrative will develop into a comprehensive view of the entire field of public administration or whether its contribution will be primarily to correct deficiencies related to gender.

It should be clear by now that public administration has tried to offer up several self-understanding narratives, all of them partial at best. Most of them are local, and each persists today in the minds of some scholars and practitioners. Each represents only a partial view of what the field was and what it is today. Perhaps the best that we can hope for is a multiplicity and diversity of local narratives to legitimate public administration in our own eyes and in the eyes of other scholars, not to mention citizens. Nonetheless, if public administration can be thought of as a subculture within a larger society, it must examine its own postmodern condition.

The Tacit Grand Narrative

Underlying all the partial narratives discussed above is the tacit grand narrative of technical rationality. For some researchers, technical rationality is the local narrative of choice, one that informs their research. But for all, because of powerful social forces of enculturation, technical rationality acts as a tacit grand narrative. For most, the scientific-analytic mind-set has to be almost "unlearned" before other, alternative ways of knowing can be grasped. The very fact that we call these other ways of knowing "alternative," and very advisedly so, is itself revealing of the pervasiveness of technical rationality.

Technical rationality is the one narrative that seems to persist for public administration, but it is a confused one. Some people believed, and some still do, in the possibility of a science of administration; others believe in the possibility of the scientific practice of administration; others argue against science in either research or practice; and some say that their research is scientific when in fact it is not. Technical rationality forms the ground for all these perspectives, diverse as they may be.

Woodrow Wilson's article "The Study of Administration" (1887) is often cited as marking the beginning of the academic field of public administration.

Condemning the "poisonous atmosphere of city government, the crooked secrets of state administration, the crooked confusion, sinecurism, and corruption ever and again discovered in the bureaux at Washington," Wilson called for a science of public administration "which shall seek to straighten the paths of government, to make its business less unbusinesslike, to strengthen and purify its organization, and to crown its duties with dutifulness" (cited in Waldo, 1953, p. 67). Wilson clearly hoped that science and its attendant methods might be employed in governmental reform movements.

The call for a science of administration was echoed 50 years later in *The Science of Administration* (Gulick & Urwick, 1937). These authors believed that science might provide universal principles to guide administrative action. In many respects aligned with Frederick Taylor's scientific management, they thought public administration might be made more efficient and effective. Considerable faith was placed on "science-in-the-practice" of public administration.

Not everyone in those early years believed that science should or could be placed in the service of administration. In his opening remarks in an address before the Annual Conference of the Governmental Research Association in 1939, Charles A. Beard recalls:

> The word *science of administration* has been used. There are many who object to the term. Not long ago one of the most distinguished British writers on government and politics ridiculed the idea in my presence. He said that there is no such thing as a science of administration, that trying to teach it is folly, and that the very notion of training anybody in it is ridiculous. (Waldo, 1953, p. 76)

Perhaps this distinguished but by now unknown British scholar believed that the practice of administration was more an art than a science. Nevertheless, Beard went on in his address to advocate a science of administration.

In the years since, there has been considerable reflection on the nature of research in the field. The scientific study of public administration has, from time to time, been criticized for failing to develop a cumulative body of knowledge comparable to the natural sciences (Caldwell, 1968; Dahl, 1947; Honey, 1957; Mosher, 1956). More recently, a flurry of empirical assessments and logical arguments has been put forth in support of scientific research in the field (Bailey, 1992; Cleary, 1992; Houston & Delevan, 1990; McCurdy & Cleary, 1984; Perry & Kraemer, 1986; Stallings, 1986; Stallings & Ferris, 1988). Arguments have also been made against a narrow scientific approach to research in the field (Catron & Harmon, 1981; Denhardt, 1984; Harmon, 1981). These latter arguments share a common theme: Science is limited in what it discloses about our political and organizational lives, and much of what it obscures is important in understanding political and organizational life. More recently, several arguments have been made in favor of alternative approaches to research in the field (Daneke, 1990; Hummel, 1991; Kelly & Maynard-Moody, 1993; Schmidt, 1993). There have also been a few attempts to put the research issues in a broader historical or epistemological context (Adams, 1992; Box, 1992; White, 1986a).

The critiques that point out the limitations of science and those that offer alternative approaches to research in the field show that technical rationality cannot continue to serve as a grand narrative for research in the field. Although it is still the most widely accepted one, there are a variety of local narratives to support a diversity of approaches. It seems that there are many ways of making sense of public policy and administration. It is not clear, however, to what degree all these ways are legitimate and whether they share anything in common other than a desire to understand public administration and to improve its practice.

There is a final sense in which technical rationality emerges as a narrative for research in the field, but it does so in three peculiar ways. First, much of the dissertation and published research seems to be prescientific. It is research that conceptualizes or delineates problems or variables for further research (Houston & Delevan, 1990; McCurdy & Cleary, 1984; Perry & Kraemer, 1986; Stallings & Ferris, 1988; White, 1986b). Much of the research does not culminate in hypothesis testing, nor does it result in conclusions that would contribute to an existing body of knowledge following the logic of scientific inquiry. Second, much of the research is problem-oriented or practice-oriented rather than theory-oriented. Problem-oriented research is "applied" rather than "basic." This is also true for practice-oriented research that tends to focus on policy or administrative experience in the field (McCurdy & Cleary, 1984; White, 1986b). As Perry and Kraemer (1986) point out, "Problem-oriented research tends to reduce the chances that the conditions for sound theory will be met" (p. 219). The same can be said for practice-oriented research (Stallings, 1986). Third, much of the research was not done very well. These peculiarities make more understandable the flurry of recent calls for greater scientific rigor in the field.

At times, the critiques of research, knowledge, and theory development seem in keeping with the postmodern characterization of public administration and society in general. Those who advocate a greater reliance on mainstream social science employ a narrative that is quite different from the ones used by those who argue for alternative approaches to research in the field. On the surface those critiques seem to be irreconcilable and perpetually at odds with one another. The discussion of epistemological issues that follows shows the common ground upon which the critiques of research tread.

The Postmodern Threat to Knowledge

The arguments of several postmodern theorists pose a threat to all forms of knowledge development and use. Playing off the common theme of the linguistic basis for knowledge, they argue that all forms of knowledge in the humanities and the sciences are unstable, relative, and lacking in rational justification. They portray knowledge development to be just as fragmented and irrational as postmodern society. Although focused more on the humanities and the human sciences, their critiques of knowledge apply equally to the natural and social sciences (White, 1992).

Frederic Jameson (1984, 1985) argues that narrative is more than just a literary form. Rather, it is the fundamental epistemological category that enables us to have any type of knowledge of the world and our existence in it. This is not the simple notion that people make up stories about the world to make sense of their existence in it, which they do. It is the more radical position that whatever we experience about the world comes to us fundamentally as stories. Foundationally, it is not possible to think about something without having a story to frame it in order to make sense of it. Consequently, all types of knowledge are basically narratives or stories.

Jameson's philosophical argument is paralleled by Jean-Francois Lacan's (1978a, 1978b) psychoanalytic argument that culture comes before the body in determining the existence of the subject. Freud argued that the human subject (or psyche) was determined in part by biology (or the body). Lacan turned this around, arguing that it is impossible to have any sense of the body without a language (and the culture embedded in it) to determine it. Thus one must speak a language, even a primitive one that a child might speak, to have knowledge of the body and ultimately of the world. In this sense, the subject, the psyche, is constituted primarily by language, not the body. In order for the subject to develop psychically, humans must use language to develop a story about themselves and the world around them, and in the case of a very young child, a primitive story, but a story nonetheless.

From this linguistic constitution of the subject, it follows that culture comes before the body in determining the subject, because language is the vehicle for culture. Culture—not nature—and, ultimately, language becomes the basis for all the world's knowledge, social and natural. In this view culture becomes the basis for determining the truth, goodness, or beauty of the stories that give meaning to our lives. To the extent that culture is postmodern—that is, fragmented and irrational—it offers no standards for assessing truth, goodness, or beauty.

Perhaps the most devastating critiques of the stability of knowledge come from Lacan and Jacques Derrida (1973, 1976, 1978). They attack the structuralist theory of language (Saussure, 1974). In that theory, language is viewed as a collection of signs. Each sign comprises a single signified and a single signifier. The signified is a concept—for example, *table*—while the signifier is the sound image made by the word *table*. In this theory of language, the signified determines the signifier in the sense that there can be only one true signifier for each signified. This means it would be wrong to call a table a chair. The dominance of the signified and the one-to-one correspondence between the signified and the signifier ensures that language conveys true and stable meaning.

Lacan (1977) attacks the structuralist theory of language by speaking of "the incessant sliding of the signified under the signifier" (p. 154). Thus the signified can take on a variety of signifiers. In other words, a table could take on several signifiers. This means that the concept of a *table* could have the sound images of "desk," "bar," "counter," or "stand." Thus the process of signification is never complete, nor is it ever stable. Getting at the true meaning of something becomes increasingly difficult as the chain of significations grows unchecked.

Derrida takes an even more radical position than Lacan. He speaks of signifiers and signifieds as continually breaking apart and reattaching themselves in new and different combinations. Thus the meaning of signs radically changes over time. For example, at one point in time it would be appropriate to call a table a table, while at another point in time it would be equally appropriate to call a table a chair.

Changed meanings of signs becomes the basis for Derrida's deconstruction of literary texts. Colin Campbell (1986) offers a clear sense of what deconstruction means:

> To "deconstruct" a text is pretty much what it sounds like—to pick the thing carefully apart, exposing what deconstructors see as the central fact and tragic little secret of Western philosophy—namely, the circular tendency of language to refer to itself. Because the "language" of a text refers mainly to other "languages" and texts—and not to some hard, extratextual reality—the text tends to have several possible meanings, which usually undermine one another. In fact, the "meaning" of a piece of writing—it doesn't matter whether it is a poem or a novel or a philosophic treatise—is indeterminate. (p. 23)[1]

E. B. White once said, "Humor can be dissected, as a frog can, but the thing dies in the process." This is what deconstruction does. It kills the meaning of a text.

The structuralist theory of language is literary criticism's brand of positivism. It is logically parallel to the positivist correspondence theory of truth that maintained a one-to-one correspondence between the concepts in a neutral observation language and the facts themselves. Much like structuralism, this theory of truth has been discredited.

Although focusing primarily on the humanities, Lyotard's critique of knowledge may be applied to the natural and social sciences by way of his reliance on Wittgenstein's (1953) notion of a language game. Language games are composed of rules of grammar that enable speech and action. Implicit rules of language stand behind all attempts to make sense of what is going on; they make understanding possible. Lyotard argues that postmodern society is composed of a multiplicity of language games that parallel the multiplicity of local narratives. Language games are the basis for multiple forms of life through which we experience the world and make sense of it and ourselves.

Lyotard believes that language games are incommensurable. Each has its own set of rules, and the rules differ across language games. The rules are contractual, not standard or universal. Players merely agree to abide by them. Because the rules are contractual and are often made up as the game is played, Lyotard concludes that there can be no rational justification of the rules. In other words, no rational criteria exist outside of the game to justify it. This clearly remains a relativist position.

The arguments of Jameson, Lacan, and Lyotard leave us in an extreme relativist position. This relativism, they would claim, merely reflects the postmodern condition of fragmentation, conflict, and confusion. Ultimately, the relativism of postmodernism leaves us quite literally groundless, free-floating in an atmosphere of nihilism. Bernstein (1992) refers to this position as the rage against reason. Postmodernism is the Dark Ages redux.

Given the linguistic foundation of experience and knowledge development, we agree that all forms of knowledge are fundamentally narrative. We do not believe that these "stories" must be relative. A broader conception of reason has the potential to support different but equally legitimate types of knowledge that lend some degree of stability to our natural and social existence. We share this position with the German social theorist Jurgen Habermas (1983, 1987), who is critical of the technical rationality of the Enlightenment, yet unwilling to settle for the void of postmodernism. Like him, we look to an older, more expansive understanding of reason as a constitutive ground for knowledge and theory development.

Three Modes of Research
and Why Two Are Ignored

Three general types of research are available in the social sciences (Fay, 1976; Habermas, 1971). Explanatory (or positive) research seeks to control social events through prediction that relies on explanation. Interpretive research seeks an understanding of social events and artifacts in an effort to expand the meaning of our lives. Critical research questions the efficacy of our beliefs and actions in an attempt to enable our self-development. The philosophical foundations of these three types of research have been partly outlined for public administration (Denhardt, 1984; White, 1986a). Here we will add to that outline by explicating the modes of reason predominantly employed in each type of research, thereby showing how knowledge can be guided by reason—albeit a more expansive and older understanding of reason than the one currently in vogue. We will also indicate why interpretive and critical reason are largely ignored by the positivist tradition.

Within positivism, theoretical discourse is defined by the deductive logic of scientific inference. The classic model of scientific reasoning is Aristotle's syllogism in which a minor premise (e.g., "Socrates is a man") is subsumed under a more general premise ("All men are mortal") to arrive at a logical conclusion ("Socrates is mortal"). Although inductive reasoning is acknowledged as the source for the premises in a logical deduction, it is the deductive argument that gives science its explanatory and predictive power. It explains why something happened. Knowing why something happened presents an opportunity to predict if it is going to happen again and under what conditions. Logical deduction is the hallmark of explanatory research.

Human beings engage in at least two other forms of reasoning: interpretation and criticism. Like Mary Schmidt's (1993) "alternative kinds of knowledge," they have been largely ignored by scientists and positivist philosophers of science (Abel, 1948-49). Consequently, interpretation and criticism were relegated to the domain of practical discourse where normative judgments are made, a domain most surely beyond the scope of science.

Interpretive reasoning is employed when we wish to understand something. It is a referential and circular reasoning process rather than a linear deduction. Palmer (1969) explains interpretation's referential nature: "Understanding is basically a referential operation: we understand something by comparing it to something we already know" (p. 87). The circular nature of interpretive reasoning is captured in the hermeneutic circle. Theodore Kisiel (1972) explains how the circle works:

> When we read a book or view an abstract painting, a survey of some of the parts gives us an initial sense of what the whole is about, and this anticipation of the whole in turn determines the significance of the parts. In and through this shifting emphasis between parts and whole, we gradually develop an interpretation of the whole in terms of its parts, and the parts in terms of the whole. (p. 276)

This is the logic of interpretation that everyone uses to develop a primitive sense of what is going on and more generally to understand the meaning of things. Sir Geoffrey Vickers (1965) argues persuasively that this same logic underlies decision making, with his notion of the appreciative system.

Critical reasoning is used when we judge things to be true or false, good or bad, just or unjust, beautiful or ugly. The logic of critique involves self-reflection. It is the ability to see one's self in relation to one's situation or point of attention, be it a material object, another person, or a concept (White, 1990). This self-reflective turn allows one to see one's self in relation to one's object of attention. Both the self and the object are viewed together. In this way, the truth or desirability of one's relationship to things, persons, or events in one's environment may be judged for their significance.

Judgments of significance can lead to actions that change the relationship between a person and something else, such as a person, concept, artifact, or object. For example, it is not possible to say that the design of an automobile is beautiful or ugly without making a self-reflective turn that enables someone to say, "That car is ugly. I wouldn't be caught dead in it." Such critical judgments require a person to see him- or herself in relation to something else. In doing so, a person can judge the significance of the relationship between the self and the object. Thereby the person may decide to change that relationship. For example, it could lead one to say, "I can't see myself driving that car, so I won't buy it." In this case a potential relationship was altered.

As noted, the role of interpretation in science has been largely ignored by scientists and philosophers of science. The same can be said for criticism. This results partly from the fact that these modes of reason have historically been associated with the humanities, which were thought to follow logics of inquiry different from science; logics that at worst were thought to be irrational, at best nonrational.

This ignorance of interpretation and criticism also results partly from the fact that philosophers of science reconstructed the logic of scientific inquiry too narrowly, missing the role that interpretation and criticism play in scientific inquiry. For example, positivists such as Ernst Nagel (1961) admitted that something like interpretation might enter into the "context of discovery" but that it had no place in the "context of logic of validation," which is strictly deductive. He was partly correct. The logic of validation is deductive inference. This distinguishes explanatory research from interpretive and critical research, but defining scientific inquiry solely in terms of deductive validation gives a narrow and inaccurate picture of what scientific inquiry is all about.

The context of validation is almost meaningless without interpretive and critical reason. A conclusion drawn from a deductive inference is simply that—a conclusion. Its meaning and its significance are what count. Does the conclusion make sense within the context of existing theories? Does it confirm or deny previous conclusions? Will it alter existing theoretical knowledge? These questions cannot be answered by deductive reasoning alone. Interpretation makes sense of conclusions. Criticism decides if new conclusions confirm or deny existing ones.

Researchers must employ interpretive reason to make sense of conclusions or findings. They must understand a new conclusion by referentially comparing it to what is already known. They must use the logic of the hermeneutic circle to place a new conclusion (a part) within the greater context of an established body of knowledge (the whole). Understanding the meaning of a deductive inference calls for shifting between a new conclusion and a larger theory. In other words, shifting between parts and wholes.

Any potential change in a theory brought about by the introduction of a new conclusion requires critical reasoning. Researchers must place themselves and what they know about existing theory into a picture that also contains the new conclusion. Only when they see the relationship between what they themselves already know theoretically and the new conclusion can they judge whether the new conclusion is consistent with established theoretical knowledge.

So far our argument tries to show how interpretive and critical reason are evident in a broader logical reconstruction of inquiry. This is not intended to be a one-way street to shore up the logic of explanatory research. The street also goes the other way. There is no a priori reason to believe that interpretive or critical research cannot use deductive reasoning. Although interpretive research might rely primarily on the logic of the hermeneutic circle, deductive inferences may be brought into that circle to make a point. The same can be said for critical research. Moreover, interpretive research might also employ criticism, while critical research might use interpretation. In the end, it seems that the difference among the types of research rests with the mode of reason that is predominantly used.

Explicating the logic of the three types of research stands against the irrationalism and relativism of the postmodern critiques of knowledge. All three types of research and, consequently, knowledge are rational because they employ modes of reason that may be logically reconstructed from the nature of inquiry.

Making Sense With Diversity

We are persuaded by the weight of historical and epistemological evidence that no single approach—even if accorded the highly positive label *science*—is adequate for the conduct of research in public administration. If research is to be guided by reason, a diversity of approaches, honoring both practical and theoretical reason, seems necessary. Thus we want to suggest that knowledge and theory development in public adminstration should proceed in many ways, including hypothesis testing, case studies, analyses of administrative or policy processes, historical interpretations of the field or parts of it, deductive arguments, philosophical critiques, and personal reflections on administrative experiences. If Jameson's (1985) view that narration is the fundamental epistemological category is correct, then no matter in what form knowledge comes to public administration, it is narrative. Logically, each of the diverse ways that knowledge and theory can be developed should be accorded equal status. None of the approaches discussed should be arbitrarily dismissed in theory building or knowledge acquisition.

At the same time, we are in agreement with many commentators on the field of public administration (Cleary, 1992; Perry & Kraemer, 1986) that, regardless of the research approach chosen, a higher—in some cases, far higher—degree of quality in the conduct of research needs to be achieved. If calls for greater rigor in public administration research are calls for higher quality research, we certainly support those calls. Those who choose to follow the logic of mainstream social science, with hypothesis testing, experimentation, and the use of descriptive and inferential statistics, should do so well. Many have observed that case study research has an unusually prominent place in public administration research (McCurdy & Cleary, 1984; White, 1986b). Mary Timney Bailey (1992) has advanced a strong argument for the validity of case study research. However, we would like to see those pursuing case study research adhere much more closely to Bailey's standards of rigor for this approach.

In research guided by interpretive and critical reason, quality standards are equally important. The logic of knowledge development and use understood as narration needs further articulation. Methodological principles are needed to guide narrative research in the field. Attention must be paid to what counts as a good story. Discussions of appropriate standards and criteria for narrative knowledge are sorely needed. Acceptable rules for denotative, prescriptive, and technical language games must be uncovered and examined for their appropriateness for research. Too often others—namely, philosophers—reconstruct the logics of research. At times, their reconstructions may bear only partial resemblance to the practice of a field. Indeed, philosophers too rarely pay attention to public administration. We public administrationists must get into the business of reconstructing research logics.

Our advice is surely more easily given than taken, however. Social theorists have long emphasized that culture is a social construction and, as such, is a product of human interaction over time; they caution against reifying culture—that is, treating it as though it were a phenomenon of nature, a part of physical reality, or otherwise an object arising from nonhuman sources

(Berger & Luckmann, 1966; see also Harmon, 1981). No one, however, should leap to the conclusion that culture is therefore easily malleable or readily amenable to new constructions. On a smaller scale, consider the finding that children of abusive parents are more likely than children of nonabusive parents to abuse their own children. Certainly most who abuse their children do not intend to be like their parents; one can imagine them in a focus group, for example, agreeing that such behavior is reprehensible. Nonetheless, pushed to some limit, they find themselves acting just as their parents; such socially constructed practices can and do reverberate down through the generations of family systems.

Our culture is a culture of modernity, perhaps poised on the brink of postmodernity. A scientific-analytic mind-set and technical rationality are part and parcel of the modern age. They represent a part of the "first language" of American culture (Bellah, Madsen, Sullivan, Swidler, & Tipton, 1985). This first language makes other ways of thinking and acting difficult in the American cultural context, a point given strong emphasis here. Other images of research and theory development are available, though not easily articulated, within most academics' experience. These may be thought of as a second language, which can be remembered—albeit with some difficulty—and spoken, but cannot be as "natural," as much "second nature," as one's first language, the language of the tacit grand narrative of technical rationality. Second languages which offer us different versions of public administration research are certainly available, but the difficulty of displacing one language with another is not to be underestimated.

As difficult as it may be to develop new narratives for research in public adminstration, we believe the role of public administration in society must also be addressed. A profession that limits its chief concerns to the degree of scientific rigor of its research is too narrow. Even a profession that strives for high quality research using a diversity of approaches is too narrow. Public administration must attempt to remember ("re-member") itself as a profession measured by its contribution to the good of the social order. The field bears some responsibility for the administrative state as it presently exists and for the sustenance and perpetuation of the tacit grand narrative of technical rationality.

What changes are needed in the practice and study of public administration in light of the postmodern condition? There have been a variety of suggestions made in this direction (Adams, Bowerman, Dolbeare, & Stivers, 1990). Perhaps most noteworthy among these efforts is Terry L. Cooper's (1991) vision of a new professionalism for public administration based on citizenship. Understanding public administration as a practice, following MacIntyre (1984), Cooper argues for a more public-centered version of public administration, one that strongly emphasizes the tradition of democratic citizenship.

Whatever trajectory one prefers, we believe the following question must be addressed: What good are we as a field if we cannot make some constructive contribution to the great problems of our time?

Note

1. Copyright © 1986 by The New York Times Company. Reprinted by permission.

PART 1

The Nature of Research
in Public Administration

Taken together, the chapters in Part I address the major problems and issues facing theory development and knowledge acquisition in the field of public administration. Here the preeminent focus is the larger social and political context in which the research enterprise occurs. These chapters are concerned with historical and epistemological analysis, rather than the particular methodologies used in the conduct of research (although these are discussed to some extent). With the framework provided by the chapters in this section, it becomes much easier to understand and assess the critiques of various methodologies and research approaches that follow in Parts 2 and 3. Part 1 begins with a look at the historical context of knowledge and theory development in public administration.

In Chapter 2, Guy B. Adams addresses the impact that the "culture of modernity" has had on the field of public administration. He contends that the American cultural preoccupation with modernity has shaped the study of public administration into an ahistorical and atemporal field that stresses technical rationality and has limited capacity to address critical questions facing society. This approach to public administration puts its emphasis on professionalism and the "scientific" and "rigorous" study of the field. Adams calls for greater attention to history, which could produce a genuinely open inquiry in the field.

Concerned that the critiques of research in public administration might direct research in the field onto the narrow path of mainstream social science, in Chapter 3 Jay D. White outlines the philosophical foundations of interpretive and critical research. While recognizing that explanatory research has its place in theory building and professional practice, he shows how interpretive and critical research are equally legitimate paths to knowledge development and use in an applied professional field. He also shows how practical reason is the common ground for all three modes of inquiry.

In Chapter 4, Gregory A. Daneke takes note of the critiques of research in the field and the efforts of some to provide alternative approaches to research. He offers an advanced systems theory paradigm. It recognizes the limits of logical positivism without completely relying on relativistic notions or critical or phenomenological theories. It encourages the maintenance of rigorous methodologies, while allowing for increased equality and integration between quantitative and qualitative research. Advanced systems theory has the ability to embrace emerging conceptual advances from other domains (such as chaos theory and applied quantum logic), and it is particularly useful as a basis for purposeful action.

Richard C. Box, a practitioner turned academic, lends critical insight in Chapter 5 to the debate over research in public administration. Box questions the critics of research for holding up a narrow style of scientific writing as the only standard for methodological rigor. He points out that the critics assume that research in the field is inferior to the mainstream social sciences without their having looked at the research in those sciences. He also notes that no comparisons are made between public administration and other practice-oriented fields such as law, planning, architecture, and business administration. The critics of published research hold to an ideal model of scientific inquiry and theory building borrowed from the mainstream social sciences. The question then becomes: Is this ideal model appropriate for a practice-oriented discipline?

2

Enthralled With Modernity: The Historical Context of Knowledge and Theory Development in Public Administration

GUY B. ADAMS

"A Century of Progress"
TITLE OF THE 1933 CHICAGO WORLD'S FAIR

"Science Explores, Technology Executes, Mankind Conforms"
MOTTO OF THE 1933 CHICAGO WORLD'S FAIR

Much has been written in the last decade on knowledge and theory development in the field of American public administration (Box, 1992; Hummel, 1991; McCurdy & Cleary, 1984; Perry & Kraemer, 1986; Ventriss, 1987; White, 1986a). Although beneficial, none of these analyses has taken a self-consciously historical approach to questions of knowledge and theory development in public administration.[1] This article seeks to place this discourse in its historical context.

The most important aspect of the historical context is the culture at large within which American public administration is practiced, researched, and taught. Today, the culture at large may be characterized as one of modernity (Turner, 1990; also Bauman, 1989; Bernstein, 1985; Rabinbach, 1990). Modernity is the culmination of a centuries-long process of modernization. Intellectual strands of modernity reach back to the 16th and 17th centuries, but as the defining characteristic of our own culture, modernity coalesced only within the past century. Modernity describes a social, political, and economic world increasingly characterized by "secularization, the universalistic claims of instrumental rationality, the differentiation of the various spheres of the life-world, the bureaucratization of economic, political, and military practices, and the growing monetarization of values" (Turner, 1990, p. 6).

Our culture of modernity has as one of its chief constituents technical rationality (Barrett, 1979). Technical rationality is a way of thinking and living that emphasizes the scientific-analytical mind-set and the belief in technological progress. In the United States, the cornerstone of technical rationality was laid down just before and during the Progressive Era (1896-1920). A confluence of two streams occurred during this period that unleashed a flood of ideas and practices into the social and political world (Wiebe, 1967, pp. 145-163). One of the two streams emerged from the then recent history of epistemology in Western culture. This first stream was the scientific-analytical mind-set that was the legacy of 17th-century Enlightenment thinking. The second stream was the product of the Great Transformation of the 19th century and comprised the technological progress characteristic of this period of industrialization with its unparalleled succession of technological developments.

In this article, I examine the state of historical scholarship within the field of public administration. The development of technical rationality, along with professionalism and the emphasis on science and efficiency are closely examined. I suggest that the belief system of technical rationality accounts for the persistent atemporality of social science in general and public administration in particular. The implications of atemporality for knowledge and theory development in public administration are discussed. In spite of considerable historical research, the field of public administration continues to echo themes of technical rationality in repeated calls for professionalism and for more "rigorous" and "scientific" research. The identity question of public administration is linked to the culture at large as comprising both a political dimension and an epistemological dimension. Given the historical context of modernity, a context of technical rationality, the prospects for knowledge and theory development in public administration are discussed, and ways in which historical analysis can offer a renewed, critical perspective on the field of public administration are suggested.

Historical Scholarship in Public Administration

Attention to the historical roots of public administration has ebbed and flowed in the last half century. Dwight Waldo's *The Administrative State* (1948) is clearly the seminal work on the larger cultural context of American public administration. Well into the post-World War II era, those looking to public administration history found little enough beyond Leonard White's four volumes (1948, 1951, 1954, 1958) on the development of public administration institutions, although Paul Van Riper's *History of the U.S. Civil Service* (1958) appeared in the same year as White's last volume. The decade of the 1960s saw the publication of Frederick Mosher's *Democracy and the Public Service* (1968), along with two historical studies of the civil service (Aronson, 1964; Hoogenboom, 1961). The benchmarks of the 1970s were David Rosenbloom's *Federal Service and the Constitution* (1971) and a pair of articles, one by Lynton Caldwell (1976) and the other by Barry Karl (1976), in the bicentennial issue of *Public Administration Review*. An important book by Stephen Skowronek, *Building a New American State* (1982), appeared early in the next decade but received spotty attention in the public administration literature. Later in the same decade, Ralph Chandler's *A Centennial History of the American Administrative State* (1987) represented a significant contribution.

Some of the more recent research on the historical development of public administration has focused on the founding period, which is one of the key periods for the understanding of contemporary public administration.[2] John Rohr's (1985, 1986) work on the constitutional basis for public administration is a prominent example. Some have appropriately focused attention on the writing of Alexander Hamilton, who stands out among the founders for his attention to matters related to public administration and certainly for his relevance to the later development of public administration (Caldwell, 1990; Green, 1990).

The tension between democracy and administration, both as they were construed in the American founding and as their meaning has altered through time, has powerfully affected how the public sector in the United States has evolved. A recent article by Laurence O'Toole, Jr. (1987), illustrates how this tension manifested in the doctrines of separation of powers beginning with the founding period and later in the Progressive Era in the politics-administration dichotomy. The linkage between the founding period and the Progressive Era has also been emphasized in two pieces by Jeffrey Sedgwick (1986, 1987), which focus on similarities in the theories of administration between the founders and Woodrow Wilson. Both of these articles show clearly the relevance of these historical periods for contemporary thought in public administration. The focus here on modernity suggests further discussion of the period just before and during the Progressive Era.

THE PROGRESSIVE ERA:
A SECOND HAMILTONIAN SYSTEM

The dominant image of the Progressive Era, the period from 1896 to 1920, is perhaps still that of the age of reform (Hofstadter, 1955). The Progressive

Era was a time of popular outrage against the depredations of big business, social ills, and exploitation of all kinds. The result was a wave of progressive reform: child labor legislation, minimum wage, women's suffrage, direct election of senators, income tax, trust busting, as well as eliminating patronage, instituting clean government, and regulating industry. The image obscures as much as it reveals.

The Progressive Era saw Jeffersonian language emphasizing a laissez-faire, limited government used by conservative businessmen (especially small businessmen) (Weinstein, 1968). The reformers, on the other hand, used Hamiltonian language, promoting an active, assertive national government in the service of not just economic aims but also social principles. The Progressive aim was a Hamiltonian national government in the service of Jeffersonian ideals. In many instances, this was altered in practice to become a Hamiltonian national government with Jeffersonian rhetoric in the service of commercial interests. Gabriel Kolko (1963) aptly called this age of "reform" the "triumph of conservatism."

Clientele agencies such as the Department of Commerce, which was formed in 1913, straightforwardly served their "clients'" interests. Regulatory agencies, created in response to public outcry, often became, to all intents and purposes, client agencies of the regulated (M. Nelson, 1982).

THE PROGRESSIVE ERA LEGACY
FOR PUBLIC ADMINISTRATION

Considerable attention has been paid in the public administration literature to the Progressive Era (Caiden, 1984; Chandler, 1987; Karl, 1987; W. Nelson, 1982; Stever, 1988; Stillman, 1991; Ventriss, 1987). This period of time is widely acknowledged as the beginning of public administration as a field of study, with Woodrow Wilson, a prominent Progressive himself, almost universally cited as the founder of modern public administration (Link, 1964; Walker, 1990). However, the 20-year period before the Progressive Era (1877-1896) when the civil service reformers were active must also be included as central to the development of modern public administration (Rosenbloom, 1971). The civil service reformers set the stage for important developments that came together later in the Progressive Era. Two of the strongest historical analyses (Skowronek, 1982; Wiebe, 1967) use 1877 as a beginning date and 1920 as an end date. There is no inclination here to conflate long-term historical trends definitively within the 20-year bounds of the Progressive Era. The end of the Reconstruction period in 1877 and the close of World War I in 1920 represent about as clearly defined boundaries as one can achieve with historical analysis.

With some noteworthy exceptions, however, most contemporary public administration literature leaps immediately from Wilson's time to the New Deal era of the 1930s or to the World War II period, when, it is thought, institutions and practices that most closely resemble the present ones came together (Henry, 1990). Most often in the contemporary literature, a ritual mention of Wilson is followed by a jump to the present time with no historical analysis at all.

The legacy of the period before and during the Progressive Era for contemporary thought in public administration is considerably greater than is generally acknowledged. Laurence O'Toole, Jr. (1984), persuasively argues that basic reform principles and practices endemic in the public administration literature date from the Progressive days. The "new public administration," he states, rather than springing de novo from the ethos of the 1960s, shares the same ideology of reform that was elaborated at the turn of the century. I contend that the fundamental trajectory of knowledge and theory development in public administration also dates from the 1877-1920 period.

The broad structural and ideological outlines of the modern welfare liberal state came together in the Progressive Era, rather than much later as the conventional wisdom has it. As Weinstein (1968) puts it, "the political ideology now dominant in the United States, and the broad programmatic outlines of the liberal state (known by such names as the New Freedom, the New Deal, the New Frontier and the Great Society) were worked out and, in part, tried out by the end of the First World War" (p. ix). A similar argument, made in part by Skowronek (1982; also Lustig, 1982) holds for public administration. The basic parameters and trajectory of the field became visible during the period just before and during the Progressive Era, and the evolution of public administration since that time, both in practice and in thought, has not deviated significantly from that framework.

Skowronek analyzes the reconstitution of the federal government during this period, reaching back to the end of reconstruction in 1877 for the beginnings of this process (see Higgs, 1987). This transformation began as patchwork efforts to repair first one area and then another, often in response to the political pressure brought to bear by one or another socially powerful group. These efforts often went awry (M. Nelson, 1982). After the watershed presidential election contest of 1896 between Bryan and McKinley, however, a more systematic reconstruction was undertaken. Thus the federal government, according to Skowronek, was reconstructed during the Progressive Era to serve new goals and interests that were growing more and more important. The themes of this reconstruction were (a) the promise of a new democracy, (b) the embrace of corporate conservatism, (c) the lure of professionalism, and (d) the quest for administrative rationality (Skowronek, 1982, p. 18).

TECHNICAL RATIONALITY
AND PROFESSIONALISM

The scientific-analytic mind-set and technological progress that combined during the Progressive Era unleashed a powerful current of technical rationality and professionalism. Impressed by the tremendous achievements of science and technology in the physical world, the Progressives naturally wanted to apply them in the social and political world to achieve science-like precision and objectivity in these spheres as well (Bendix, 1956; Graebner, 1987).

Technical rationality led irresistibly to specialized, expert knowledge, the very life blood of the professional, and then to the proliferation of professional associations in the latter half of the 19th and early part of the 20th centuries (Larson, 1977). Without the legitimacy derived from specialized knowledge, the professional could not have gained the social status nor the autonomy and control over the practice of the profession, which are the ultimate goals, even if sometimes unstated, of every profession. The compartmentalization of knowledge demanded by technical rationality also inevitably led to a contextless, or timeless, practice (e.g., witness the lack of historical consciousness across the professions and disciplines). The practice of a profession with little or no sense of context has precluded meaningful engagement with the larger ethical and political concerns of a society (Guerreiro-Ramos, 1981). That is to say, professionalism, fed and nurtured by technical rationality, led inexorably to a naked public square. This is the antipolitical dimension of modernity (Arendt, 1954).

It is important to note that the Progressives and the civil service reformers who preceded them were not uniform in their thought (Noble, 1958, 1970; White, 1957). Many differences in their thinking were interwoven in their debates. James Stever's (1986, 1990) work, for example, points to the tension between organic idealism and scientific pragmatism, which is visible both in Woodrow Wilson's (1887) writing and Mary Parker Follett's (1918) work, among others. Nonetheless, technical rationality, with its emphasis on the application of scientific method and procedure, won the day (Miller & O'Leary, 1989).

The modern model of professionalism was conceived and tried out in the period just before and during the Progressive Era as well. The development of professional associations of all kinds began in the mid-19th century, at first more rapidly in England and then in the United States (Larson, 1977, p. 246). The characteristics of professions, which were fully visible around the turn of the century, include a professional association, a cognitive scientific base, institutionalized training (usually within higher education), licensing, work autonomy, colleague control, and a code of ethics (Larson, 1977, p. 208). Larson emphasizes the connection between the development of professionalism and the broader process of modernization, "the advance of science and cognitive rationality and the progressive differentiation and rationalization of the division of labor in industrial societies" (p. xiii).

Modernity and Technical Rationality

In the context of modernity, technical rationality is the convergence of the scientific-analytical mind-set and technological progress (Turner, 1990). Beginning in the Progressive Era, it was applied to the social world and placed on the political agenda. Technical rationality is quite similar to "functional rationality" as described by Karl Mannheim (1940). Mannheim saw functional rationality as the logical organization of tasks into smaller units, originally in the interest of efficiency. Mannheim contrasted this with "substantive rationality," the ability to understand the purposeful nature of the whole system of which a particular task is a part. Technical rationality is also closely akin to the notion of "instrumental reason" discussed by Max Horkheimer (1947). Instrumental reason is the narrow application of human reason solely in the service of instrumental aims. Until the modern era, reason was conceived as a process incorporating ethical and normative concerns as well as the consideration of merely instrumental aims. In the public administration literature, similar points have been made by Alberto Guerreiro-Ramos (1981).

RECENT HISTORY OF EPISTEMOLOGY

To understand how technical rationality became pervasive in the social and political world, and therefore in the public administration world as well, a brief look at the recent history of epistemology may help. By the time of the 17th-century Enlightenment, science, as physical science, had emerged on the scene and had begun to exert a powerful influence. Epistemology became preoccupied with a quest for the stubborn and irreducible facts of existence. By the 18th century, the split between European and Anglo-American epistemology and philosophy had begun to be visible (this split has blurred considerably more recently). European philosophy may be represented as a series of attempts to resuscitate epistemology and metaphysics from the problems posed by science and its method of empiricism (Hegel, 1965; Heidegger, 1977; Nietzsche, 1956). Anglo-American philosophy, in contrast, may be represented as a series of attempts to reconstruct the concerns of philosophy according to the insights of science and its method (Whitehead & Russell, 1910; Wittgenstein, 1922). In our culture, the scientific-analytical mind-set captured the way we thought, and the study of epistemology was largely reduced to commentaries on the history of science. The scientific-analytical mind-set, then, represents one part of the confluence that occurred in the Progressive Era; technological developments composed the other.

THE CONFLUENCE OF SCIENCE AND TECHNOLOGY

The astonishing succession of technological developments during the Great Transformation of the 19th century provided the physical, tangible embodiment of the sheer power of scientific thinking. What could have been more convincing? What could have been more plausible than to apply technical rationality to the social world in order to achieve science-like precision and objectivity? Frederick Taylor found a ready audience for the notion of scientific management during the Progressive Era (Haber, 1964; Merkle, 1980; Noble, 1970). Technical rationality became the vehicle of hope in the social and political world and created a wave that before World War II prompted new professionals, managers, behaviorists, social scientists, and industrial psychologists toward a worldview in which human conflicts appeared as problems fit for engineering solutions (Bendix, 1956; Ellul, 1954). By the present time, as William Barrett stated (1979),

> It would be silly for anyone to announce that he is "against" technology, whatever that might mean. We should have to be against ourselves in our present historical existence. We have now become dependent upon the increasingly complex and interlocking network of production for our barest necessities. (p. 229)

The Persistent Atemporality of Public Administration

The tendency to ignore and downplay history and context is not unique to public administration. This impoverished historical consciousness is found across the professions and academic disciplines and, more broadly, is deeply embedded in the culture at large (Smith, 1990). That part of the belief system of modernity that finds expression in technical rationality is fundamentally atemporal. Borrowing its approach from turn-of-the-century physical science, social science remains dominantly committed to the notion of developing knowledge or certainty through atemporal causality (or the closest available approximation thereto) (Faulconer & Williams, 1985). Human action is to be explained through the development of general laws and models independent of time and space. There is, in this view, no need to include history and culture in accounts of human behavior.

This somewhat bald and radical statement of method is only rarely the overt, stated methodological or epistemological perspective of current-day researchers in social science and in public administration (McCurdy & Cleary, 1984, p. 50). However, it remains deeply embedded in the culture at large. Although there may be impediments and some accommodations may be needed, the application of scientific method should yield up certain knowledge (or at least knowledge as certain as possible). This belief represents a root assumption of modernity within American culture and helps account for public administration's persistent atemporality, which logically entails a diminished place for historical analysis, an approach concerned fundamentally with time.

DIMINISHED HISTORICAL CONSCIOUSNESS IN PUBLIC ADMINISTRATION

I do not wish to suggest that the scientific method was adopted within public administration at the turn of the century and little has changed since then. There have been large differences within the practice of research as to what "science" and "scientific method" have meant. What has remained constant is the scientific-analytic mind-set, the attachment to application of scientific method, however defined, as the best way to knowledge by most researchers in the field. At the turn of the century, doing science meant in part the application of the new method of statistics.[3] Richard Ely (1982, p. 282) in his founding statement in 1886 for the American Economic Association, called for the application of statistics, while William Allen (1907) exalted the role for statistics further:

> At first glance there is hope in the far-reaching remedies suggested: universal education, referendum, manual training, proper home surroundings, opportunity for child play, wholesome recreation, civil service reform, woman suffrage, municipal ownership, Christian spirit, prohibition of the liquor traffic, doing good, electing good men to office, etc. But important as each remedy may be, we have abundant testimony that none is adequate of itself. . . . There is one key—statistical method—which offers to trusteeship . . . a prompt record of work accomplished and of needs disclosed. (pp. 11-13)

The emphasis on statistics was no accident. In the classical formulations of the 17th-century Enlightenment, science meant a grand explanation of some aspect of nature. By the Progressive Era, science came to mean the application of scientific method: "Science had become a procedure, or an orientation, rather than a body of results" (Wiebe, 1967, p. 147). For many Progressives, this view of science had its parallel with politics, which also came to be viewed increasingly as procedural. Woodrow Wilson and Charles Merriam are but two examples of Progressives who saw a harmonious link between the proceduralism of science and that of politics (Karl, 1974; Rabin & Bowman, 1984; Van Riper, 1990).

Politics, especially in its democratic versions, also had to undergo considerable revision in order to be made compatible with this new emphasis on science and procedure. Herbert Croly's (1909) writing is particularly revealing of this resolution. The new requirements for professionalism, the demands for expertise, the growing calls for a politics-administration dichotomy, and the adage that there is "no Republican way to build a road" all rendered the greater democratic involvement of people in politics more and more problematic (Hanson, 1985). This tension between a meaningful democratic politics on the one hand, and a professionalized, scientized, expert administration on the other, has commanded attention in the public administration literature since the turn of the century. It was central to Waldo's *The Administrative State* (1948), and indeed, to most of his later writing. It has been noted more recently by Barry Karl (1987), among others (see Caiden, 1984; O'Toole, 1987; Redford, 1969), and has a central place in the recurring and persistent discussion of the identity of public administration (Adams, Bowerman, Dolbeare, & Stivers, 1990).

THREE EXAMPLES OF MODERNITY IN PUBLIC ADMINISTRATION

One of the central tenets of modernity, along with technical rationality, is the notion of progress (see the motto at the beginning of this article), which suggests the first example. One influential version of public administration history views the development of the field as occurring through five successive stages (Henry, 1990). The period of primary focus in this article, the Progressive Era, is labeled the politics-administration dichotomy. This period was then superseded by the "principles of administration" in the 1930s, followed by public administration as political science and public administration as management in the 1950s, and, finally, the culmination since 1970 of "public administration as public administration." This progression is characterized by the increasing professionalism of public administration and by its increasing development of the characteristics of an academic discipline with a scientific base. In this version, public administration has a history, but its origins, less than 100 years ago, are outmoded and have been superseded.

The 1960s, which offer the second example, saw the development of an apparently significant force in the field, the so-called new public administration (Frederickson, 1980; Marini, 1971). Ironically, the new public administration writers, many of whom explicitly saw themselves as constructing an alternative to technical rationality, were at the same time following in line with one of modernity's other central tenets, the progressive development of knowledge (O'Toole, 1984). New public administration was seen as a clear break with the orthodoxy of mainstream public administration. However, as O'Toole so usefully points out, this "break with orthodoxy" was entirely compatible with the tenets of reformism as developed in the Progressive Era. According to O'Toole, the development of public administration may best be viewed "not as successive efforts of apolitical experts to superimpose an artificial rationality on a pluralistic world, but as a continual, tension-filled struggle on the part of those who are deeply committed to some vision of democracy but who see the seeming inevitability of large-scale government bureaucracy" (p. 149). Even the new public administration, which saw itself as departing from technical rationality in its "antipositivist" stance, ironically remained well within the confines of modernity. Perhaps more tellingly, the new public administration seems almost quaint from the perspective of two decades later, given the occurrence of recent, repeated calls for greater professionalism and for greater rigor in the application of scientific method in the field (McCurdy & Cleary, 1984; Perry & Kraemer, 1986).

A third example comes from the characterization of public administration offered by Orion White, Jr., and Cynthia McSwain (1990). They characterize contemporary society, as well as public administration, as dominated by what they call the "technicist episteme," roughly what I call here technical rationality. They see the technicist episteme as characteristic of modern public administration, which they date as beginning after World War II, and they contrast modern public administration with "traditional" public administration, which occurred during the 1930s and 1940s. While their analysis of contemporary public administration and its predicament is insightful and important, their historical analysis, I would argue, is flawed.

The central tenets that they ascribe to the technicist episteme did not emerge and develop after World War II; rather they emerged as the dominant (but not the monolithic) ideology from the Progressive experience at the turn of the century. This is not to deny the important differences with technical rationality (or in White's and McSwain's terminology, the technicist episteme) exhibited by the "traditionalists." Much like the later new public administrationists, the traditionalists in part attempted to think their way out of technical rationality. Most important among these differences expressed by the traditionalists were those beliefs that emphasized the political and social context and connectedness of public administration.

White and McSwain do not call for a return to "traditionalism" in public administration; rather they investigate how traditionalist ideas can be reconstructed in ways relevant to present conditions. This proposed reconstruction is anything but sentimental, relegating a reconstituted public administration to agency "enclaves." They see very clearly the predominance of technical rationality and the difficulties of thinking and acting our way out of its confines.

It is an ironic symptom of modernity that careful analyses such as White's and McSwain's do not locate accurately the crucial historical moment when modernity coalesced and thus misconstrue the ways in which we are enthralled with modernity. Ironically, even when theorists construe their efforts as a departure from modernity, like the new public administrationists, they find themselves still enmeshed in its framework. Most of the public administration literature, however, contains both less irony and less historical analysis. Modernity also has important implications for the persistent legitimacy question so often addressed in the field of public administration.

Modernity, Legitimacy, and Public Administration

Although it is clear that sufficient literature exists within the field of public administration to justify at least one chapter on the historical development of public administration, only a handful of the scores of public administration textbooks published since World War II have done so (e.g., Rosenbloom, 1989; Stillman, 1987). Virtually all such textbooks conclude, however, with a chapter on future prospects of the field, echoing modernity's theme of progress.

The recently published volume (Lynn & Wildavsky, 1990) on the "state of the discipline" of public administration has an initial section titled "Professional History and Theory." Unfortunately, only one of five chapters in this section is explicitly historical in approach, and that chapter (Henry, 1990) begins its analysis in the 1930s. Two authors of chapters in this section, Dwight Waldo and John Rohr, have written extensively elsewhere on public administration history, but their entries in this section are not concerned significantly with historical analysis. One can only conclude that the "state of the discipline" includes little in the way of historical study.[4]

When public administration's historical development is mentioned, in virtually every case, Woodrow Wilson's (1887) essay "The Study of Administration" is cited.[5] Interestingly, Van Riper (1983) has recently called its salience into serious question. He notes that Wilson's essay was not cited in the central publications of political science or public administration between 1890 and World War I, and that indeed the article had little apparent influence until the 1950s.

Probably the next most cited historical figure in the development of public administration thought is German sociologist Max Weber (Cuff, 1978; also Weber, 1979). His work also had minimal impact in the field until the 1950s, remaining untranslated into English until the late 1940s. Moreover, the reading of Weber's work has been selective and often out of context.[6] In the public administration literature, the focus has been on what Weber wrote about bureaucratic organization, and especially that part of it concerned with the internal organization of bureaucracies. Weber, of course, was far less concerned with the process of rationalization as it impacted the internal workings of organizations than he was with the social implications of the process of rationalization. The former is both more consistent with modernity and far easier to treat ahistorically than the latter.

One of Weber's central themes was legitimacy, particularly legitimate authority. Clearly, as modernity was coalescing, Weber saw the increasing legitimacy of bureaucratic authority, based as it was on scientific procedure and professionalism. The issue of legitimacy has been an important one for public administration as well.

Recent discussions of legitimacy in public administration are not symptomatic of an ostensible transition to a postmodern era (Marshall & White, 1990); rather they are simply the latest versions of attempts to reconcile the tensions between democracy and administration endemic to a liberal state (Stillman, 1991). These tensions date from the American founding, but they are brought to the forefront and exacerbated by modernity and become more prominent during and after the Progressive Era. Waldo's *The Administrative State* (1948) is a thorough analysis of these tensions covering the first half of the 20th century. Later versions raise and extend the same themes (Karl, 1987; Kass & Catron, 1990; O'Toole, 1987; Wamsley, 1990).

PROFESSIONALISM AND SCIENTIFIC RIGOR IN PUBLIC ADMINISTRATION

The recent public administration literature includes prominently legitimation claims that call for increased professionalization and research-based expertise (Houston & Delevan, 1990; McCurdy & Cleary, 1984; Perry & Kraemer, 1986; Stallings & Ferris, 1988). These legitimation claims are in keeping with the themes of modernity and represent an orthodoxy in public administration that became fully visible in the Progressive Era and has continued, albeit with ebbs and flows, to the present.

The calls for increased professionalization are perhaps most prominently marked by the publication of two full symposia recently in the *Public Administration Quarterly* (Winter 1985, Spring 1986). Although professionalism is most concerned with the practice of public administration, it is also of serious concern to academics in the field for reasons spelled out clearly in historical perspective by Larson (1977):

The unification of training and research in the modern university is a particularly significant development. As graduate and professional schools emerged at the top of the educational hierarchy, the professions acquired not only an institutional basis on which to develop and standardize knowledge and technologies; they also received in university training, a most powerful legitimation for their claims to cognitive and technical superiority and to social and economic benefits (p. 136).

Of course, public administration is still poorly organized as a profession by comparison with law or medicine, for example, and is unlikely, in the American context where government has consistently been viewed as little better than a necessary evil, to achieve the degree of professionalization to which many clearly aspire.

In the orthodox view, a well-organized discipline must have a scientific knowledge base. The calls for greater scientific rigor in public administration follow this credo, which gained ascendancy during the Progressive Era. In spite of acknowledgment of other research traditions, such as the interpretive or critical (White, 1986a), this literature judges public administration research according to the "criteria that conventionally define careful systematic study in social science" (McCurdy & Cleary, 1984, p. 50). (The text cited in reference to this statement is by Kerlinger, 1986.) Later, McCurdy and Cleary (1984) assert, "If public administration is to be a mature field of study, we feel it must reach agreement on criteria of this nature" (p. 55). A 1986 article by Perry and Kraemer examines "How PAR Methodologies Measure Up Against Mainstream Social Research" (p. 216). Houston and Delevan (1990) assert, "Sound theory, however, is developed only through the testing and refinement of empirical propositions derived from theory" (p. 678). They find little evidence of such work in public administration and are troubled by this.

A recent piece by Gregory A. Daneke (1990) on knowledge and epistemology in public administration is more balanced in its treatment of other research traditions. He recognizes and accords legitimacy to the interpretive and critical research traditions, among others, while advocating an "advanced systems agenda. " It is telling, however, that the article's title—"A Science of Administration?"—echoes, except for the question mark, Luther Gulick's words of just more than a half century ago (Gulick & Urwick, 1937).

There were alternative research traditions and a variety of versions of epistemology in the Progressive Era, as there were in the 1930s, and as there have been for the last quarter century. Nonetheless, the calls for increased professionalism and increased scientific rigor echo down through the decades of public administration history.

The Implications of Modernity

Modernity has fostered technical rationality, which is part and parcel of the culture at large. The continuing impact of technical rationality on knowledge and theory development in public administration can perhaps be illuminated by a brief example from another literature (Adams & Ingersoll, 1990). Recently, much attention has been paid to the concept of culture as it applies to the study of organizations. However, culture has been utilized in the study of organizations in ways consistent, for the most part, with technical rationality (Barley, Meyer, & Gash, 1988). That is, rather than focus attention on culture as the larger context of meaning within which organizations are nested, the focus was quickly narrowed to individual organizations, as if each evolved its own largely idiosyncratic "culture" de novo. Very quickly, organizational "culture" became another technique for the manager's tool bag, and many companies and agencies set out to reshape their corporate "culture" in much the same way that, say, a strategic plan might be initiated.

What accounts for the degeneration of a rich metaphor (in this case, culture) into a passing managerial fad? How is it that we in the field appear unable to think our way out of modernity sufficiently to produce anything other than ephemeral results? Both the example of the literature on organizational culture and the persistent calls for professionalism and scientific rigor in public administration remind one of *pentimenti,* the products of a long-standing practice of artists. Because canvas and stretcher bars are expensive, it has been a common practice for centuries for artists to paint over their earlier paintings in an effort to save money. Over the years, though, an image—a *pentimento*—from the earlier painting may bleed through what has been painted on top. Likewise, over the years, public administration theorists have painted new versions of public administration theories over the old, with the traditionalists (White & McSwain, 1990), the new public administration, and the interpretive and critical versions all among them. Although each of these versions of public administration is thought of as affording an entirely new view of the field, the old images continue to bleed through. These old images—images of technique and rationality—are part and parcel of modernity, and they are not so easily covered over.

Public Administration: Past and Future

Modernity exacerbates the question of a legitimate role for public administration within the American state. The tension between a meaningful, democratic politics and an expert, specialized administration, embedded in our nation's founding and intensified greatly by the flowering of technical rationality nearly 100 years ago, remains at the forefront of any possible claim to legitimacy for public administration in the American state. An atemporal public administration has considerable difficulty even addressing this question, because in its very essence it is a historical question.

Attention to public administration's past suggests that the broad parameters of knowledge and theory development in our field were established in the Progressive Era. Recent calls for increased professionalism and more scientific and rigorous research echo claims first made nearly a century ago. Thus, although there has been considerable historical scholarship in public administration, the role of historical analysis in the field remains highly problematic. Remaining enthralled with modernity, we remain unable to locate ourselves in our present historical circumstances and thus relegate ourselves to issuing "new" calls for science and rigor on into the future.

If critical, historically based studies were in the forefront of public administration research, we could more readily consider questions crucial to the present and future configuration of public administration. For example, I have argued here that the identity question in the field of public administration has both a political dimension and an epistemological dimension, which leads to one interpretation of the Progressive Era. If one were to follow Hofstadter's account, far greater emphasis would be placed on the political dimension as the chief driver of developments in public administration (e.g., Rosenbloom, 1971). Hofstadter (1955) views the Progressive Era as an epic clash between two political cultures, one the immigrant-based machine model and the other the reform-minded "Yankee" or WASP model (1955, Introduction). Within public administration thought, however, the emphasis on method and procedure—the scientific-analytic mind-set—seems warranted. As Furner (1975) argues, objectivity (science) won out over reform (advocacy) in the development of social science.

Greater attention to our history would better enable the consideration of other questions as well. Consider the relative importance of the law in contemporary public administration institutions and practices, scarcely mentioned in this discussion. A focus on the law would turn our attention much more prominently to the founding period and the thinking of Alexander Hamilton (Green, 1990), and to 1946 when the Administrative Procedure Act was passed (Rosenbloom, 1983). Such a focus (for example, on due process in law) would certainly be compatible with the Progressive emphasis on procedure, but some shift in interpretation would be called for as well. These and other important questions, which bear directly on present conditions and future prospects, need historical analysis to complement other approaches.

A genuinely open inquiry in the field of public administration is needed. Such free and open inquiry precludes hegemonic assertions as to what constitutes knowledge (and what does not). Free and open inquiry includes not only the so-called qualitative methods, but also the interpretive (Hummel, 1990) and critical (Denhardt, 1981b; Forester, 1989) traditions. Critical, historically based studies are sorely needed to address in a meaningful way both the political and epistemological dimensions of modernity as they bear on public administration. Free and open inquiry offers no easy or sentimental guarantees to a happier future for either public administration or the American state, but continued inattention to these questions will surely condemn us to the future Max Weber (1958) saw and feared 87 years ago:

> No one knows who will live in this cage in the future, or whether at the end of this tremendous development entirely new prophets will arise, or there will be a great rebirth of old ideas and ideals, or, if neither, mechanized petrification, embellished with a sort of convulsive self-importance. For of the last stage of this cultural development, it might well be truly said: "Specialists without spirit, sensualists without heart; this nullity imagines that it has attained a level of civilization never before achieved." (p. 182)

Notes

1. Waldo's work (1948) is obviously an exception, but the reference is to the recent discussion. O'Toole's 1984 article probably qualifies as an exception, but it is rather narrowly focused on the new public administration, rather than on knowledge and theory development per se.

2. Also mentioned by some in the literature are the World War II period and the New Deal (Henry, 1990; White & McSwain, 1990); the Jackson era draws some attention as well (Crenson, 1975).

3. As the highly sophisticated statistical methodologists of today are apt to point out, turn-of-the-century statistics meant rather rudimentary calculations of means and the like.

4. There are two recent handbooks of public administration (Perry, 1990; Rabin, Hildreth, & Miller, 1989). The former includes considerable historical discussion, while the latter includes none.

5. Daniel W. Martin (1989) concludes, citing a famous remark by Peter Odegard, not only about Wilson's article, but also about most "classics" of public administration, that they are "more often cited than read" (p. 426).

6. For a thorough and grounded reading of Weber's work, see Hummel (1987b).

3

On the Growth of Knowledge
in Public Administration

JAY D. WHITE

The issue of proper research and theory development in public administration has been raised again by Howard E. McCurdy and Robert E. Cleary (1984) in their article, "Why Can't We Resolve the Research Issue in Public Administration?" They express concern for the lack of adequate research being done at the dissertation level and cite research findings suggesting that very few of the recent dissertations "meet the criteria that conventionally define careful, systematic study in the social sciences" (p. 55). These criteria include purpose, validity, testability, causality, topical importance, and cutting edge significance. By not meeting these criteria, they feel that current dissertation research is not advancing knowledge in our field.

Following their prescriptions for theory building could lead to the conclusion that case studies, histories, descriptions of administrative experiences, reports of action research projects, political theories, philosophical analyses, and social critiques will not contribute significantly to the growth of knowledge in public administration. This type of research normally does not satisfy the criteria of validity, testability, and causality. Nevertheless, this type of research has contributed significantly to our knowledge of public administration.

Although Cleary and McCurdy may recognize the historical importance of descriptions and critiques for generating ideas about public administration, they claim that a "field that promotes descriptions and critiques still needs research. . . . Someone has to publicly expose the descriptions and critiques to the standards of scientific verification before they become 'usable knowledge' " (1984, p. 554). They allow that "case studies can contribute to the verification of concepts or critiques, provided that they are consciously used to do so, especially in combination with other cases or studies" (p. 554), but they remind us about the validity problems of case studies in general.

Cleary and McCurdy advocate a mainstream social science approach: the belief, as stated by Richard J. Bernstein (1976), that "the social sciences differ in degree and not in kind from the more well established natural sciences, and that the best way to achieve scientific success is to emulate the logic and methodology of the natural sciences" (p. xiii). This is evidenced by their adherence to the criteria of validity, testability, and causality; their call for testing of ideas generated by descriptions and critiques; and their appeal to Kerlinger's *Foundations of Behavioral Research* (1986) to identify the criteria for quality research in the behavioral sciences (McCurdy & Cleary, 1984, p. 55). But serious questions have been raised about the logic of the natural sciences and their exclusive use in the study of social phenomenon (Louch, 1966; Winch, 1958). Before following Cleary's and McCurdy's advice, consideration should be given to some of the contemporary views on the growth of scientific knowledge.

This article outlines a different theory of knowledge based on recent developments in the postpositivist philosophy of science and related to administrative experience. This theory gives a legitimate place to the descriptions and critiques that have been an integral part of public administration scholarship. It allows for the type of research that Cleary and McCurdy advocate, but it entails a different understanding of what counts as knowledge.

Three Modes of Research

Postpositivist philosophers of science have identified three modes of social research—explanatory, interpretive, and critical. The natural and mainstream social sciences are examples of explanatory research. Some forms of history, anthropology, sociology, law, and literary criticism are examples of interpretive research. Psychoanalysis and the neo-Marxist critique of ideology represent critical research. The logic of these modes of research has emerged through a series of debates across scientific disciplines, philosophical traditions, and the humanities.[1] The result is a theory of knowledge and its use that is broader than that of the mainstream social sciences and better represents the types of research that have been a part of public administration for more than 80 years. Each mode of research can be briefly defined according to its purpose and logic.

EXPLANATORY RESEARCH

Explanatory research stands in the philosophical tradition of positivism, which has had a pervasive influence on the logic and methodology of the natural and social sciences.[2] Explanatory research strives to build theories that explain and predict natural and social events. Theory building requires the development of a collection of related and testable laws that state causal relationships among relevant variables. The ultimate goal of explanatory research is the control of natural and social events.

The logic of explanatory research follows the deductive-nomological and inductive-probabilistic models of explanation and prediction.[3] According to the deductive model, explanations take the following form: If P occurs, Q will occur; given that P has occurred, the conclusion that "Q will occur" follows deductively, assuming, of course, a deterministic situation. The major premise is a law-like generalization stating a causal relationship: "If P, then Q." The minor premise is a statement of condition: "Given P." The conclusion "Then Q" serves as both an explanation and a prediction. The occurrence of Q can be explained by stating that P was present, while the occurrence of Q can be predicted by knowing that P is present. Deductive explanation brings facts under law-like generalizations, while prediction involves using law-like generalizations to predict the occurrence of specific events. Maslow's theory of motivation is deductive because it moves from broad generalizations about need satisfaction to specific conclusions about behavior (Duncan, 1978, p. 49). Several policy analytic techniques such as causal modeling, linear programming, and input-output analysis assume deductive causal relationships among variables (Dunn, 1981, pp. 147, 150).

Inductive explanations employ laws of statistical probability stating that "under certain conditions which constitute the performance of a random experiment, a certain kind of outcome will occur in a specified (usually high) percentage of cases" (Fay, 1976, p. 36). As the premises are arranged, they provide inductive support for the conclusion that an event has occurred or will occur. Inductive explanations move from observations of actual events to inferences about larger populations. Most of the research in organizational behavior uses the inductive model. For example, a study of the factors that affect job satisfaction in one industry is often used to explain and predict job satisfaction in other industries (Duncan, 1978, p. 50). In policy analysis, trend extrapolations using forecasting techniques such as time series analysis are based on the inductive model (Dunn, 1981, pp. 148, 150).

Both the deductive and inductive models offer explanations and make predictions possible. The fact that predictions can be made using explanatory research implies, at least in principle, the control of natural and social events. Conditions can be altered to make something happen or to stop something from happening if the resources and technology to do so are available. This assumes order and therefore generalizability and predictability in human behavior as there is in natural events. The resources and technology are not always available either in science or administration to control events, but this does not diminish the importance of control as the goal of explanatory research.

INTERPRETIVE RESEARCH

Interpretive research enhances our understanding of the sayings and the doings of actors in social situations.[4] For example, a positivist might attempt to explain why a particular job-enrichment program is failing to provide expected results by examining established hypotheses about motivation and job design. An interpretivist would enter the situation and ask the workers what they think about the program, what it means to them, what they are doing, and why they are doing it. The goal is to discover the meaning of the program; how it fits with prior norms, values, rules, and social practices; how the program may be in conflict with their prior definitions of the social situation; and what the emerging norms, rules, values, and social practices might be. Interpretive theory seeks an enhanced understanding of social situations, not only for the researcher but also for those involved in the situation.

Interpretive research stands in the philosophical traditions of phenomenology, hermeneutics, and the analytical philosophy of language.[5] Interpretation seeks to understand the meanings that actors attach to their social situations, to their own actions, and to the actions of others. The logic of interpretation follows the hermeneutic circle in which meaning emerges in recognizing relationships and patterns among wholes and parts. This is a referential process in which something is understood by comparing it to something already known. It is a logic in which the whole defines the parts and the parts in turn define the whole. Thus the logic of interpretation is circular rather than linear as in the case of the deductive and inductive models. The basic aim of the interpretive model is to develop a more complete understanding of social relationships and to discover human possibilities. Recent studies of organizational culture demonstrate the importance of interpretive methods for properly understanding norms, values, and belief systems in organizations.[6]

CRITICAL RESEARCH

Critical research seeks to change someone's beliefs and actions in the hope of satisfying their needs and wants by bringing to awareness unconscious determinants of action or belief (Geuss, 1981, p. 61). Critical research "recognizes that a certain tension exists between our own strivings and the limitations imposed on us by social conditions, even those conditions of which we are only vaguely aware. The role of theory is to reveal these contradictions and thus permit us to pursue our own freedom" (Denhardt, 1984, p. 167). Put another way, critique points out inconsistencies between what is true and false, good and bad; it compels us to act in accordance with truth and goodness. Critical research is part of the phenomenological tradition as well as critical social theory.[7]

The logic of critical research is self-reflection: "the ability to reflect upon one's own thoughts and actions in relation to an object, a person, or a social situation" (Denhardt & White, 1982, p. 166). It is the special quality of being oriented toward something and also being aware of one's self in that orientation. This relationship is the basis for making judgments of fact and value—for recognizing that things are not what they appear to be and should be understood differently, or for recognizing that things are not as they ought to be and should be changed for the good of those involved. To say that something is true or good assumes it can be related to something that is false or bad. Critical judgments cannot be made without establishing such relationships and can only be made by having knowledge of what one thinks or feels about something. This requires the establishment of a self-reflective relationship in which one sees one's self in relation to one's object of attention.[8]

Several administrative theorists recognize the need for interpretive and critical research. Bayard Catron and Michael Harmon (1981) advocate an action theory approach to organizational change that interprets the shared meanings of organizational actors. Harmon (1981) also provides an action theory approach for public administration based in large part on the interpretive phenomenology of Alfred Schutz; Robert Denhardt (1981a) offers the most comprehensive statement of explanatory, interpretive, and critical approaches to ways of knowing, deciding, and acting in public organizations. Ralph Hummel (1977) gives a devastating critique of bureaucracy and an alternative model of social action based in interpretive phenomenology. Michael Diamond (1984) demonstrates the use of critical research in his psychoanalytic models of administrative behavior. Chris Argyris and Donald Schon (1978) are working from a critical perspective in developing an understanding of the reflexive practitioner and organizational learning. Gibson Burrell and Garth Morgan (1979) have developed an encyclopedic account of functionalist, interpretive, and critical approaches to organizational analysis. The major impetus behind these contributions has been to broaden our understanding of alternative forms of administrative action that realize enlightenment and emancipation.

The Administrative Context

Much of the philosophy of science seems distant from administrative life. For example, philosophers of science establish the existence of each mode of research by grounding them in some notion of a political theory or in some anthropological and transcendental realm of experience.[9] This involves some esoteric discourse that seems far removed from administrative concerns. Philosophers are compelled to engage at this level of discourse because of the norms of their discipline. But it is also important to see how these modes of research are central to public administration and how they can be found in the administrative experience.

CONTROL

Administrators have a great interest in control, both in a scientific and prescientific sense of the word. To control something scientifically implies the ability to explain and predict the occurrence of an event or behavior. If explanation and prediction are possible and appropriate conditions manipulable, events or behaviors can be caused or prevented from happening. This represents the full realization of explanatory research for public administrators educated in the tradition of scientific management, management science, organizational behavior, and policy analysis. The prescientific interest in control is more fundamental to administrative experience, but it still relies on prediction, although in a less formal way. People need to work together to accomplish collective goals that they alone could not achieve. As Chester Barnard (1938, pp. 46-61) and Dwight Waldo (1955, pp. 5-8) point out, it is the spirit of cooperation that is central to administration, and cooperative efforts require a certain degree of predictable behavior. Control is achieved by making assumptions (predictions) about social action. Sir Geoffrey Vickers (1973) calls these assumptions a set of "mutual and self-expectations" about how people will act toward one another in differing circumstances (pp. 112-116). These assumptions amount to subtle and tacit predictions about social action. The stability of these expectations is a more fundamental form of control.

The greatest force for ensuring predictability is the establishment of the norms, values, and rules that make up the formal and informal structure of our organizations. Vickers (1973) notes that values are abstract and explicit, while norms are concrete and tacit (pp. 171-181). In an idealized organization we expect explicitly stated values from which norms and rules are logically derived. Values are statements of preferences or goals to achieve such as fairness, justice, equity, freedom, initiative, and obedience. Because they are abstract and explicit, they can be talked about, they can be agreed or disagreed with, and they can be ranked in some hierarchy of importance. In their book *In Search of Excellence,* Peters and Waterman (1982) note the importance of a common value system in controlling the behavior of subordinates who are given relatively wider degrees of freedom of decision and action when their values coincide with those of top management. In an informal way, norms dictate what actions are appropriate and which go against the norm. Norm-following behavior is predictable as long as one knows the norms and how they regulate action. Being concrete and tacit, they are difficult to talk about in any general way, but in an idealized system they should be logically consistent with the abstract and explicit values. Rules are explicitly stated norms that formalize social interaction. The extent to which they are followed effectively ensures the predictability and control of human behavior.

The bureaucratic model of organization is the classic example of an idealized system of explicit values, consistent norms, and formally stated rules. Any one organization will be more or less idealized or bureaucratic, so rule- or norm-following behavior will be more or less predictable across organizations. For most organizations the level of bureaucratization and predictability is adequate to get the cooperative work done.

UNDERSTANDING

Understanding is so fundamental to social existence that it hardly seems necessary to call it into question and examine the process of interpretation that leads to understanding. Interpretation is more common and necessary than explanation and prediction. Explanations tell us why something happened. Predictions tell us what might happen. Interpretations tell us what is the case or "just what's going on here." Making sense of one's situation is different from answering questions about what happened in the past or what might happen in the future.

Interpretation is concerned with understanding the meaning of social action and the norms, rules, and values that regulate social action. When values are stated or rules are set down in an organization, they are normally assumed to be understood and followed. We rarely inquire in any formal way as to how these values and rules are understood or what meanings are attached to them, unless of course people consistently endorse other values or break the rules. Then we might, if we are enlightened ourselves, ask them why. If we are not particularly enlightened, we might fire them, or transfer them, or punish them, or give them new rules that we hope they will understand.

Understanding and interpretation can be better appreciated if they are more directly compared to explanation and prediction. Following the logic of mainstream social science, prediction involves observing regularities in manifest behavior. The behavior of people is observed, and from those observations patterns develop that allow generalizations about such behavior in a variety of related circumstances. Interpretive research is concerned with the meanings that people attach to the norms, rules, and values that regulate their interactions. Care is taken not to impose a prior understanding of norms, rules, and values upon others, but rather to understand their beliefs and actions from their point of view. The focus is not only on what they tell us directly about the reasons for their beliefs and actions, but also on the social practices that underlie their beliefs and action. Social practices give meaning to social actions.

Why would an administrator want to interpret social action rather than explain and predict it? Much of administrative experience is a matter of making sense of what people are doing by inquiring into the reasons, motives, and intentions for their actions rather than into the causes of their behavior. For example, someone is more likely to ask the head of a department what he or she plans to do about an impending budget reduction than predict what they will do, based on some causal generalization such as "given budget cuts, department heads with the following personality characteristics or leadership styles are more likely to selectively cut programs than to institute across-the-board reductions in force." Although the latter is a prediction on which a decision could be based, it is more likely that someone will inquire into the intentions and motives of the department head and appeal to a prior understanding of what the department head thinks or feels. Taking the interpretive route also provides the opportunity to ask for the reasons for someone's actions. Often the stated reasons will make those actions more intelligible.

CHANGES IN BELIEFS AND VALUES

Administrators are concerned with critical research because it points out inconsistencies between what is true and false and what is good and bad. The practical payoffs are changes in systems of belief and of value. Critical research is the foundation for error detection and evaluation. Administrators want their models of reality (from the most simple images carried around in their heads to more elaborate mathematical representations) to be as accurate as possible. Otherwise, administrative actions run the risk of being misdirected, inconsequential, or even disastrous. Administrators also want to know how to act properly. They want to know what ends ought to be sought and what means should be selected.

Critical research raises questions about perceptions of reality and invites the use of interpretive and explanatory research to correct those perceptions. For example, when confronted with the statement "We have a problem of motivation," we cannot evaluate the efficacy of this statement without taking a self-reflective turn, that is, seeing oneself in relationship to the statement and to other possible statements of what the problem might be. Perhaps experience will suggest that leadership rather than motivation is the problem. Factual judgments about the definition of the problem cannot be made without reflection on experience. Once the question is raised, explanatory and critical research can be used to find an answer.

Critical research is also concerned with questions of what is good and bad. It facilitates evaluation, which supplies the otherwise-missing element in mainstream attempts to grapple with the fact-value dichotomy. The logic of explanatory research focuses on descriptive statements of what was or what is and predictive statements about what might be. Critical research focuses on evaluative statements about the worth of something and prescriptive statements about what ought to be. One realization of critical research in public administration is in the area of problem structuring, which William Dunn (1981, p. 133) believes is the least understood aspect of policy analysis. A problem is a mismatch between present conditions and desired conditions. It is the role of critical research to detect the discrepancy between what is and what ought to be. The logic of self-reflection is the same as in error detection, but critical research now demands that we engage in evaluative and normative discourse about what we believe is true, what we feel is right, what we hope for, and what we ought to do to make things right.

Criticism is the most radical of the three modes of research because it calls into question our most basic assumptions and asks us to evaluate them as a basis for action. Critical research does not always satisfy the critic nor does it always change beliefs and values, but it has the potential to do so. It is most appropriately used when people are suffering under misconceptions of reality or when the normative structure of society or an organization is repressing their needs for freedom and autonomy, growth and development.

Some recent developments in the philosophy of science are related to administrative experience with control, interpretation, and critique. They highlight the importance of interpretation and criticism in the growth of explanatory knowledge. They also recognize the importance of interpretation and criticism as modes of research in their own right.

Postpositivist Philosophy of Science

In the positivist philosophy of science, the rationality of scientific knowledge was once thought to be ensured by strict adherence to the rules of inference required by the deductive and inductive models of explanation, by reference to a neutral observation language, and by the existence of universal criteria to judge one theory better than another. Recent developments in the postpositivist philosophy of science reject these positions in favor of the practical rationality of theory choice based on the logic of interpretation and criticism.

THE CRITIQUE OF EXPLANATION

Positivists such as May Brodbeck (1968) and Carl Hempel (1965) defended a theory of scientific knowledge based primarily on the deductive model of explanation. Explanation consisted of bringing facts under general laws. The rationality of scientific knowledge was thought to be ensured by proper adherence to the logical rules of inference required by the deductive model. The same can be said for inductive explanations, although the deductive model was taken to be the ideal. Thus scientific knowledge was thought to grow by bringing more and more facts under deductive or inductive laws.

Postpositivists such as Stephen Toulmin (1953) and Michael Scriven (1962) argue that the logic of actual scientific explanations bears little resemblance to the deductive and inductive models. It is not simply the case that the models are too general and abstract to properly represent the complexities of scientific explanation, but that explanations are of a logically different type. The deductive and inductive models fail to describe the logic of explanation and are not particularly useful in any other way. What then is the logic of scientific explanation? Scriven (1962) argues that scientific explanation is "a topically unified communication, the content of which imparts understanding of some scientific phenomenon"; "understanding is, roughly, organized knowledge." He also argues, as others do, that "it is possible to objectively test this understanding as you would any other form of knowledge" (p. 225).

Most positivists asserted that interpretation belongs in the context of discovery, not in the context of explanation. They treated interpretation as a psychological variable rather than a logical one. As Ernest Nagel (1961, p. 484) argues, a scientist's understanding is "pertinent to questions concerning the origin of his explanatory hypotheses but not to questions concerning their validity."[10] Thus for positivists it was proper to talk about interpretation as a psychological variable in the context of discovery, but any mention of interpretation was avoided in discussions of the logic of validation because interpretation was not considered a logical concept.

Postpositivists such as Charles Taylor (1971) and Theodore Kisiel (1972) hold that interpretation plays a significant part in the validation and verification of scientific knowledge as well as in the discovery of hypotheses. Interpretation is a logical concept represented by the hermeneutic circle. It is sometimes thought of as a vicious circle that cannot be broken out of to validate or verify interpretations according to some universal rules of rationality. A postpositivist such as Paul Feyerabend (1975) argues that no independent, universal rules for judging the truth or rationality of a scientific statement have ever existed or could ever exist. Nevertheless, rules for judging the rationality of explanatory, interpretive, and critical knowledge do exist, but they are not universal and independent of interpretation and criticism. Rather they emerge through an ongoing process of interpretation and criticism, and they can be altered and changed by further interpretation and criticism.

CRITIQUE OF THE NEUTRAL
OBSERVATION LANGUAGE

Questions of validity and verification focus on the criteria used to judge the truth of a proposition, hypothesis, or theory. One positivist criterion was the correspondence theory of truth, which says that a statement is true if it corresponds to the facts of the situation. This theory of truth has many logical and pragmatic difficulties, not the least of which is the fact that many of the "facts" of scientific research are not directly experienced, observable, or measurable. This introduces the more sophisticated notion that two languages exist: a neutral language of observation and one of theory (Feigl, 1970).

Observational languages describe or measure some phenomenon in specific and concrete ways. Theoretical languages interpret the relationship among phenomena at greater levels of generality and abstraction. The distance between the two was thought to be bridgeable by a set of correspondence set rules. If the rules are known and logically followed, then the observational language would verify the truth of the theoretical conclusions. One problem with this theory of truth was finding the proper correspondence rules. Another problem was keeping the observational language pure, that is, not allowing theory to creep into observations to contaminate the objective criterion of fact.

Several arguments were proposed as a means of moving back and forth between theoretical and observational languages, including phenomenalism, instrumentalism, and operationalism.[11] Each has its own logical and pragmatic difficulties. None adequately bridges the distance between theory and observation. Herbert Feigl (1956), a noted philosopher of science, claims that these arguments are complete failures and thus "the customary sharp distinction between theoretical and observational language is . . . called into serious question, if not entirely eliminated" (pp. 17, 19). According to Mary Hesse (1980), it is now generally accepted that "the facts themselves have to be reconstructed in the light of interpretation" and that "meanings in natural science are determined by theory; they are understood by theoretical coherence rather than by correspondence with facts" (pp. 171-172). This leaves mainstream social science in an impoverished position because it assumes the existence of both languages as well as a mixture of phenomenalist, instrumentalist, and operationalist supporting arguments.

THE PRACTICAL RATIONALITY
OF THEORY CHOICE

What is the alternative? By what criteria are we to judge the acceptability of statements, generalizations, hypotheses, theories, research programs, or paradigms? These are the leading questions in the postpositivist philosophy of science, which can only be addressed here in the most general way by mentioning Karl Popper's (1966, 1972) and Thomas S. Kuhn's (1970) theories of interpretation and criticism, and Richard J. Bernstein's (1982) argument that the postpositivists are moving toward a theory of the rationality of scientific knowledge based on dialogue and practical discourse.

Popper offered the first popular attack on the positivist philosophy of science with his theory of science as the process of making conjectures and refutations in which the objectivity of scientific statements lies in their ability to be intersubjectively tested, rather than being compared with a neutral observation language. For Popper, objectivity is a matter of criticism that usually comes in the form of further testing of a statement, hypothesis, or theory to see whether it can be falsified or refuted. The more a statement sustains criticism, the more empirical it is and the more belief can be assigned to it. Once a falsifying or refuting statement is introduced, however, it becomes a competing theory. In some situations the competing theory may be clearly superior to the refuted one, so it becomes easy to accept the competing one and then subject it to further tests. In other situations, it may be difficult to determine which theory is superior. Further testing of both statements and interpretation of the results is called for. Thus Popper has shifted the criteria for objectivity from the facts themselves to criticism and interpretation. But this also produces the problem of proper theory choice, which can only be resolved through further criticism and interpretation.

Popper's theory of interpretation also lies in the origins of conjectures (statements, generalizations, hypotheses, and theories). He believes it is necessary to take a point of view that helps in sifting through the data of experience and focusing on what is relevant and intelligible. In theory formation points of view are interpretations that become "crystallized" and then amount to explanations. The difference between an interpretation and an explanation is that explanations can be tested and thereby rejected or upheld, while an interpretation remains more or less conjectural. So interpretations become explanations if some means to test them can be found. Experimental testing is common in the natural sciences, but Popper (1966) believes that in the study of society, the best we can hope for are conjectural interpretations (pp. 444-453).

Progress in the social sciences shows that replicative experimentation is possible for explanatory research. But what about interpretive and critical research? Are we trapped in a vicious circle, unable to test our interpretations and criticisms? The answer is no. Systematic procedures are available to determine the acceptability of interpretations and criticisms. They can be found in the interpretive studies of anthropology, sociology, history, and law; in the qualitative research methodology of organizational behavior; in qualitative evaluation methods; and in policy analysis.[12]

Testing in these disciplines takes on a different meaning and may require different criteria, but the logic of interpretation and criticism is the same. For example, in the theory of literary interpretation, E. D. Hirsch (1967) adopts Popper's notion of conjecture and refutation by arguing that the task of the literary critic is to show how one interpretation of a text is better than another. This is done by giving reasons for one interpretation and by showing how this interpretation better satisfies the literary criteria of legitimacy, correspondence, generic appropriateness, and coherence. Another example closer to home is Schuman's *Policy Analysis, Education, and Everyday Life* (1982), in which he uses an interpretive methodology based in phenomenology to empirically evaluate higher education in the United States. In his study, he is explicit about his methodology and the criteria by which the evaluation should be judged. He invites his readers to share in a practical discourse about the appropriateness of his methods and criteria and ultimately the validity of his work.

Although controversial, Kuhn's major work, *The Structure of Scientific Revolutions* (1970), has left a lasting impression on scientists, philosophers of science, and historians of science (Bernstein, 1982, p. 54). His history and philosophy of science have been the subject of severe criticism, but their importance cannot be denied. His concepts of normal science, problem solving, exemplars, revolutionary science, paradigms, and paradigm shifts have structured contemporary understanding and misunderstanding of scientific inquiry. More important, Kuhn's ideas point directly to the importance of interpretation and criticism in the practical rationality of theory choice.

Kuhn rejects both the deductive model of explanation and the notion of a neutral observation language as having any direct importance in the development and growth of scientific knowledge. He paints a different picture in which scientists work within paradigms. Paradigms are more or less stable ways of seeing the world. They are shared by a community of investigators who have addressed and understood past puzzles and who are presently addressing new puzzles. The community of scientists understands the existence of these puzzles and their boundaries. Puzzle solving is the task of normal science. Paradigms guide the conduct of normal science and the type of puzzle solving that makes scientific knowledge more general and precise. Problems occur for paradigms when, in the process of puzzle solving, anomalies arise that do not fit the paradigm. Questions are raised or discoveries are made that do not fit with generally accepted scientific knowledge. At this point "extraordinary science" emerges and rival paradigms that purport to explain the anomalies are offered for consideration by the community. The problem of paradigm or theory choice now emerges. The central question becomes: By what criteria are we to choose one paradigm or theory over another?

Kuhn can be criticized for not satisfactorily answering this question. He does not resort to the deductive model or the orthodox conception of theory. Instead, he characterizes the decision situation in terms of practical rationality—communicative deliberation over reasons for the acceptance or rejection of a paradigm. From the orthodox point of view, paradigm choice appears to be a subjective and judgmental matter devoid of any formal rationality. But Kuhn (1977) argues that this is not the case. Paradigms are chosen with regard to certain traditional values such as "accuracy, consistency, scope, simplicity, and fruitfulness" that serve as criteria for choice (pp. 337-338). He notes, however, that these are not particularly good criteria because they have different meanings for different people. They also often come in conflict with one another in the process of complex argumentation and mutual persuasion that ultimately results in the acceptance of a new paradigm.

Bernstein (1982, Part II) cogently argues that Popper's and Kuhn's theories of science point to the fundamental role of practical reasoning in theory and paradigm choice. This is evident in Popper's definition of theories as interpretations and his insistence on the critique of conjectures, and in Kuhn's discussion of paradigm choice. Kuhn (1977) explicitly references the importance of interpretation for his theory of science when he says,

> What I as a physicist had to discover for myself, most historians learn by example in the course of professional training. Consciously or not, they are all practitioners of the hermeneutic method. In my case, however, the discovery of hermeneutics did more than make history seem consequential. Its most immediate and decisive effect was instead on my view of science. (p. xiii)

Bernstein goes one step further than Kuhn to argue that scientists are also practitioners of the hermeneutic method. He uncovers the common ground among philosophers such as Kuhn, Popper, Feyerabend, Gadamer, Arendt, Habermas, and Rorty to show how they all assume a dialogical model of scientific rationality involving communal interpretation and criticism. He argues that this common ground is the way to avoid the unsatisfactory alternatives of either objectivism or relativism. The rationality of explanatory, interpretive, and critical knowledge is a matter of "choice, deliberation, interpretation, judicious weighing and application of 'universal criteria,' and even rational disagreement about which criteria are relevant and most important"

(Bernstein, 1982, p. 48). The conclusion is that theory building is fundamentally a practical activity in explanatory, interpretive, and critical research.

Implications

What do these developments mean for the practice of mainstream social science? Should the explanation and prediction of natural and social events be abandoned because philosophers of science have shown that the logic and theory of science is interpretive and critical, as well as deductive and inductive? The obvious answer to this is no. Explanation and prediction are facts of scientific and administrative life. The postpositivists have argued that other philosophers have been wrong in their theory of science and that our self-understanding of the logic and practice of science has been faulty. The logic of explanation and prediction needs to be rethought. Consideration needs to be given to how interpretation and criticism enter into decisions about what constitutes valid research. The criteria for assessing research should be examined, and the place of different types of research in the growth of knowledge should be acknowledged. Recognition should be given to the fact that the rationality of research is found in the dialogical model of practical discourse over the acceptability of theories, modes of research, and the criteria by which to choose theories and modes of research. The practical rationality of the scientific enterprise moves science beyond objectivity and relativism.

Because the orthodox models of empirical theory and scientific explanation do not adequately reflect the logic of scientific inquiry, an examination of what is done under the name of science is called for. A close look at mainstream social science reveals a sort of methodism and adherence to a set of norms, rules, and values that define what it means to do explanatory research in public administration. Insofar as these norms, rules, and values are derived from the orthodox model of empirical theory and explanation, they need to be reexamined for their efficacy in light of the developing theory of science. The actual context of research should offer the criteria by which to judge its significance. Courses and textbooks on research methods deal mostly with methodism and may fail to adequately address issues in the philosophy of science. Consequently, the rationality of research becomes defined as rule-following behavior. It is a mistake only to judge the quality of research according to whether or not the researcher has followed the proper research procedures. This is a truncated notion of rationality. As Alisdair MacIntyre (1977) notes, the rationality of theory choice is not concerned with following rules but with transcending them—"in knowing how and when to put rules and principles to work and when not to" (p. 454). Practical rationality is the hallmark of a good researcher in any mode.

Interpretations and criticisms should be recognized as legitimate contributions to the growth of knowledge in public administration. This is how a significant amount of knowledge about public administration has developed. Few would assert that Waldo's *The Administrative State* (1948) has not contributed to our knowledge of public administration. But if Cleary and McCurdy's criteria of causality, testability, and validity were invoked, Waldo's efforts would be discounted. Their other criteria of purpose, topical importance, and cutting edge significance seem legitimate. But insofar as the criteria of validity, testability, and causality are derived from the orthodox models of explanation and theory, they need to be rethought in light of the developments in the philosophy of science, and they should not be imposed on all research situations.

The growth of knowledge in public administration can be satisfied by interpretive and critical research as well as explanatory research. Given the issues raised here, reflection on each mode of research is called for to discover what norms, rules, and values pertain to each. The norms and rules will constitute the method of each mode of research, while the values will indicate criteria by which to judge the truth of each type of knowledge. Given the previous critique of methodism, it may seem contradictory to ask for methods and criteria for each mode of research. This is not the case. Research in any form requires methods and criteria, but it also requires the type of practical reasoning that justifies our methods and criteria. Practical reasoning is fundamentally a matter of interpretation and criticism. It is very much a political endeavor requiring the giving of reasons why one rule should be followed rather than another, or why one criterion should be met rather than another. The growth of knowledge in public administration is based on this type of argumentation.

The importance of practical reasoning comes into clear view in the process of writing a dissertation, especially when that dissertation is an interpretive or critical one (e.g., a case study, descriptive history, philosophical analysis, or social critique). Writing a dissertation involves persuading committee members, who are presumably experts in their fields, that there is something new to say, that something will be learned from it, that the field will be seen differently, and that perhaps this will change what theorists and practitioners do in the future. If this occurs, a dissertation may meet the criteria for interpretation and criticism. The responsibility for meeting these criteria rests not only with the author, but also with the committee members. All who take part in the dissertation must be willing to enter into practical discourse that will allow these criteria to be realized and agreed to.

Finally, recognition should be given to the fact that each mode of research is based in administrative experience. Practitioners are just as much concerned with explanation, prediction, interpretation, and criticism as are theorists.

Indeed, they employ the same logic of explanatory, interpretive, and critical research both formally and informally. Perhaps theorists and practitioners are not different types of people. They share common interests but different institutional frameworks.

Summary

Has the research issue in public administration been solved? Perhaps not right away. But an indication of how the growth of knowledge in public administration needs to be reinterpreted in light of the postpositivist philosophy of science has been offered. An argument has also been made about the inherently practical nature of theory development with regard to administrators' interests in explanatory, interpretive, and critical research. The importance of practical reasoning in both science and administration has also been emphasized. These are avenues to overcome the theory-practice dichotomy. The dichotomy between fact and value has also been addressed in the context of critical research that recognizes that administrators are in the business of making value judgments. Critical research provides the logic for evaluation with the notion of critical self-reflection. Without this reconstruction, value judgments fall prey to the positivist claim that they are nonrational. Finally, by focusing on the thought and action that goes into explanatory, interpretive, and critical research, a framework can be developed for understanding what theorists and practitioners do in their different circumstances. The framework may prove fruitful for improving both research and administration when each is approached from both an interpretive and critical perspective.

Notes

1. For a discussion of the role of interpretation in several disciplines see Carter (1984), Cicourel (1973), Collingwood (1956), Geertz (1973), and Hirsch (1967). For a discussion of the critical aspects of psychoanalysis and neo-Marxism, see Habermas (1971). For a discussion of the philosophical debates across disciplines, see Bernstein (1976, 1982).

2. For a discussion of the history of positivism, see Kolakowski (1968). Bernstein (1976) outlines the positivist influence on social science in Part I of his *Reconstructing Social and Political Theory*. Fay (1976) discusses the influence of positivism on public policy analysis in Chapter 2 of *Social Theory and Political Practice*.

3. For an exposition and critique of the deductive model, see Gunnell (1975).

4. The aim and logic of interpretive social science is outlined by Fay (1976) in Chapter 4 of his *Social Theory and Political Practice*. A general discussion of the role of interpretation and understanding in the cultural and social sciences can be found in Dallmayr and McCarthy (1977), Outhwaite (1975), and Rabinow and Sullivan (1979). The most comprehensive treatment of interpretation from a hermeneutic perspective is given by Gadamer (1975).

5. For an excellent discussion of how the three traditions come together, see Howard (1982).

6. For a discussion of the hermeneutic circle, see Palmer (1969). For a discussion of the hermeneutic circle and its relationship to social science, see Deetz (1973, pp. 139-159). The role of interpretation in the study of organizational culture is addressed in Allaire and Firsirotu (1984) and Barley (1983).

7. For a discussion of the critical aspects of phenomenology, see Zaner (1970). The meaning of critique in critical theory is closely examined in Geuss (1981).

8. For a discussion of how criticism and judgment are based on self-reflection, see Hirsch (1967, 1976).

9. Fay claims that all systematic approaches to social research assume a political theory (1976, p. 15). Habermas (1971, Appendix) grounds his theory of "knowledge constitutive interests" in an anthropological and quasi-transcendental realm of experience.

10. The debate on interpretation from a positivist point of view is summarized in Theodore Abel (1948-49, pp. 211-218). The postpositivist account of the debate on interpretation is summarized in Apel (1984).

11. See Gunnell (1975, Chaps. 5, 6) for an extensive discussion of the "orthodox conception of theory" and its critique.

12. At a disciplinary level, discussions about the acceptability of interpretations and criticisms can be found in the works of Carter (1984), Cicourel (1973), Collingwood (1956), Geertz (1973), and Hirsch (1967). For a philosophical discussion, see Dallmayr and McCarthy (1977), Outhwaite (1975), and Rabinow and Sullivan (1979). For a discussion of the qualitative methods of organizational research, see Das (1983). In evaluation research, see the works of Rossi (1971) and Weiss and Rein (1970). Martin Rein discusses policy analysis as the interpretation of beliefs in his *Social Science and Public Policy* (1976, Chap. 4).

4

A Science of
Public Administration?

GREGORY A. DANEKE

In a recent article, the venerable Harlan Cleveland (1988) proclaims that "it is time to put behind us the idea that the politics and administration of human endeavors are some kind of science" (p. 681). In this, as in most such pronouncements, he is both absolutely correct and fundamentally misguided. Cleveland is completely correct that policy and administrative studies cannot be a science, especially given his characterization of science as the mechanistic world of Sir Isaac Newton (also represented by the positivist label). However, because the so-called hard sciences adhere only to select aspects of this perspective, it is somewhat a straw man. Moreover, the "ecological model," which Cleveland suggests as an alternative, is nothing if not a form of science, or at least a system. Finally, and perhaps most important, if the various applied domains of policy and administrative studies do not continue to aspire to at least rigorous modes of inquiry (both empirical and philosophical), if not science, then they will continue to be relegated to the lower levels of intellectual endeavor. Meanwhile, their less self-deprecating cousins (e.g., economics and psychology) will continue to flourish and further displace them as guides to societal enterprise.

Of course, Cleveland is not alone in questioning the scientific status of the various social sciences that culminate in the study of public policy and administration. Recent years have witnessed an unprecedented level of epistemological questioning. Many who continue to do conventional empirical research have now joined in decrying the lack of theoretical development (Campbell, 1986; Cronbach, 1982). Others embrace a variety of "critical theories" that claim to expose the social construction of the social sciences (Dallmayr, 1986; de Haven-Smith, 1988). Still others are attempting to develop "naturalistic" methodologies (Lincoln & Guba, 1985). Thus far, however, much of this foment manifests itself more in a critique of positivism or neoclassical economic theory than in a coherent, alternative paradigm. Moreover, many of these partial approaches comprise elements closely associated with those of general systems theory, though not necessarily recognized as such. This article urges rechanneling of this diffuse intellectual energy into reform of systems' basic unifying paradigm and advancing it in the direction of a comprehensive design approach capable of enhancing the processes of adaptive learning and institutional evolution. For lack of a better designation, this prospective paradigm is labeled advanced systems theory (Daneke, 1990). While building on familiar constructs found in traditional general systems theory and contemporary economics (institutional as well as neoclassical), this emerging paradigm also strives to integrate a number of unique ingredients derived from recent advances in the physical, biological, and cognitive sciences (e.g., quantum logic and chaos theory).

Science as a Speculative Art

When one begins to question the scientific status of social inquiry, it is important to note that the model of science to which most of the social sciences have aspired is itself an outmoded notion. Essentially, the textbook model of science (following an inductive path from facts to the formulation of theory, to the development of explanation, to the testing of theory, and to the eventual arrival at laws and principles that facilitate prediction and control) explains little of the progress in the physical sciences. Major advances, such as the quantum revolution in physics (Crease & Mann, 1986), rely heavily on what Whitehead (1925, 1929) called speculative philosophy, where deductive notions are used to reinvent reality. What is perhaps more important to note is that economics, by far the most ubiquitous of the social sciences, is itself a deductive process; that is, it follows Whitehead's view. As the famous Austrian economist Ludwig von Mises (1949) points out, economics never has been positivist; rather, it begins with abstractions that are a priori formulations and uses them to interpret reality.[1] In a recent article, Herman Daly (1989) suggests that much of what passes for science in economics may well be a problem of Whitehead's "fallacy of misplaced concreteness." Irrespective of this criticism, it may well be that economics has become the only social science for which a Nobel Prize is given, not only because it is more mathematical, but also because, like the "hard sciences," it is more speculative in its theory building. As Elinor Ostrom (1982) contends, the lack of paradigmatic progress stems from the "domination of the languages of data analysis over the languages of theory construction" (p. 81). William Wimsatt (1986) suggests that it is through the development of new heuristics that the social sciences will overcome their current lack of progress. Wimsatt (1986) argues that the critical issue is what to do when the complexity of the systems exceeds one's power of analysis:

This too is an old problem in social science methodology, but it does not indicate a cause for despair, since exactly the same thing has happened frequently in the natural and biological sciences. Roughly, the therapy is the same in both cases: introduce idealizations, approximations, or other devices that, perhaps artificially, reduce the complexity of the problem. (p. 294)

The relatively recent rejection of positivism by a number of scholars is producing many an interesting heuristic, yet few have produced a compelling paradigm. Furthermore, many of these conceptual innovations merely reintroduce elements from past paradigms.

The Postpositivist Shuffle

Alternatives to positivist epistemology have, of course, existed for some time. Of late, these various alternatives have achieved increasing influence in the writings of public policy and public administration. Many of these alternative approaches draw either on "phenomenology" (Husserl, 1965) or the "critical" social theories of the "Frankfurt School" (especially as extended by Jurgen Habermas, 1970). The most extensive applications of these types of approaches in public administration are Denhardt (1981b; Denhardt & White, 1982), Dunn's and Fozouni's (1976) "critical" administrative theories, Michael Harmon's (1981, 1989) "action theory," Ralph Hummel's (1987b) "experiential approach," and Alberto Guerreiro-Ramos's (1981) "substantive approach."[2] Although it is difficult to generalize, the primary value of these critical formulations is essentially that they are insightful critiques. Their focus on actual practice and the influence of communicative structures is instructive, yet their methods are often vague and highly idiosyncratic. The use of interpretive knowledge or hermeneutics often fails to explicate how qualitative impressions may be effectively integrated with traditional empiricism.

The key for careful adherents, such as Jay D. White, is that the "growth of knowledge in public administration involves recognizing availability of alternative modes of empirical inquiry in the interpretive and critical traditions." They also explain (White, 1986a, 1986b) how "interpretive reason" and "power" can be "engendered by communicative interaction." Robert Stallings (1986) suggests that the "best studies" apply empirical data to "phenomenological interpretations." Yet he also admonishes that in a three-way relationship among theory, method, and practice, method entails "techniques of elaboration" and not merely the "techniques of everyday management." In short, Stallings (1986) maintains that public administration research should be driven as much by "form" as by "content."

Similar concerns have engendered the so-called naturalistic approach. Anchored in the multifaceted "emergent paradigm" of Schwartz and Ogilvy (1979), this approach has become popular among students of educational policy and organization (Lincoln, 1985). However, this paradigm emerges more as a loose-knit confederation of analogies derived from unrelated advances in physical and biological sciences than as an integrated approach. Using advances such as quantum physics as analogy, Egon Guba (1985) describes a new qualitative research approach comprising the following axiomatic constructs (pp. 85-86):

- reality as ontological, "multiple constructed realities," studied holistically and where understanding is more likely than prediction and control
- subject-object duality, mutual interaction between the inquirer and respondent accounted for in results
- idiographic body of knowledge, collecting working hypotheses, rather than general rules about differences as well as similarities in individual cases
- mutual causality, multiple interacting factors, events, and processes; plausible inferences are drawn about underlying patterns
- axiology of values, inquiry as value-bound, in the choice of problem and choice of paradigms, and as inherent in social norms

White obviously forward-looking epistemologically, the naturalistic approach is less well developed in its methodology, preferring various "ethnographic" techniques similar to those used by cultural anthropologists and other field research disciplines. Moreover, the links between theory and method are often quite obscure, and the relationship to the physical sciences is mainly metaphorical.

At the other end of the spectrum are scholars who, while fully recognizing the validity of many of the postpositivist criticisms, strive to integrate these insights with existing quantitative methodologies. A leader in this camp is legendary methodologist Donald T. Campbell. Campbell's lifelong efforts at bridging the scientific and humanistic perspectives on social inquiry have produced numerous partial reconciliations that include "multiple operationalism" (in the place of "operational definitions"), "multitrait-multimethod matrix," and "evolutionary epistemology" (a system that describes processes within the sociology of knowledge).[3] Other scholars have extended this basic approach to multiple methods or address the problem of quantitative-qualitative interface. Examples include Harold Lindstone (1984) and William Dunn (1988). Still others, particularly many of the formally oriented political scientists, have merely attempted to expand on neoclassical economic concepts with institutional or behavioral considerations (Gillespie & Zinnes, 1982).

Another group of relatively moderate postpositivists is emerging under the banner of the design science concept, derived from the work of Herbert Simon (1981) and C. West Churchman (1971; Harris, 1981). This concept basically maintains that a science of human artifacts should be patterned more after the enterprises of architecture and engineering than after the study of physical phenomena. Despite this rather prominent point of departure, the design science concept has been reintegrated into widely varying applications. For example, Schneider and Ingram (1988) imply that design is a distinct stage in the policy process to be described taxonomically. Bobrow and Dryzek (1987), on the other hand, maintain that the design science approach is a logical extension of critical theory. Trudi Miller (1984, 1989a, 1989b), however, has done perhaps the most to establish design science as a completely unique exercise, and her work is most closely aligned with Simon and Churchman. Yet the failure of others to expand significantly on this underlying intellectual heritage leaves the design concept as a misplaced metaphor, rather than as a source of new methodologies. As Linder and Peters (1988) recognize, a design process would operate at a metalevel, analyzing the process of analysis itself,[4] yet what this "purposeful arrangement of elements" will look like remains a mystery. Currently, the notion of design finds its most extensive, yet decidedly narrow, methodological development through the work of public choice theorists who apply conventional neoclassical economics and transaction cost analysis to issues of institutional design. The purposeful element is primarily efficiency (Ostrom, Feenyr, & Picht, 1988).

Another and perhaps more isolated attempt at escaping the static-mechanistic worldview of traditional science has been the adoption of the methods and concepts of biology. Following along the lines of the sociobiology movement and the work of E. O. Wilson (1975), these schools of thought largely adhere to a simple deterministic model to explain both human biological and institutional evolution. A basic Darwinian model has been applied to organizations by a school known as "population ecology" (Aldrich, 1979) and to public policy via "biopolitics" or "biobureaucracy" (White & Losco, 1986).[5] This approach finds its most elaborate articulation in Peter Corning's (1983) "synergism hypothesis." However, this view is probably most accessible in the recent work of Herbert Kaufman (1985). This discussion will have more to say about evolutionary notions below; for now, suffice it to say that such considerations are vital to full conceptualization of social change. However, human evolution may not only be more complex, but also fundamentally at variance with biological reductionism.

A final postpositivist perspective that may rate a category of its own is the "credibility" approach, which argues that policy analysis is essentially a persuasive art. Thus it should strive for rigor but not aspire to "external validity." These suggestions are judiciously developed by Barry Bozeman

(1986). Although somewhat reminiscent of Gorgias's attempt to convince Socrates that philosophy could be reduced to rhetoric, the issue of professional presentation and issues of evidence, in the absence of appeals to science, are absolutely critical. Unfortunately, space does not permit a full discussion here; however, one of the more powerful arguments for a unified paradigm is the standardization of reasonableness. What is, perhaps, more damning of the current fragmentation of inquiry is the fact that many of the more insightful elements have already been explored and ignored in previous attempts at paradigmatic progress.

Forgotten Foundations and Fruitful Formulations

If, after having read a handful of the above postpositivists, one has an eerie feeling of déjà vu, it is well justified. Many of these themes are, of course, timeless; that is, they date back to the Greek philosophers. However, some may be familiar from a more recent era, just prior to the disciplinary diaspora of the last two decades. At least three distinct yet conceptually similar approaches have dealt with the question of how to build a more viable set of concepts for applied social inquiry: the "policy science" approach, "institutional economics," and "general systems theory."

The notion of a policy science or sciences has diverse origins but is generally thought to have found its most astute and ambitious advocate in Harold Lasswell (1951, 1956, 1961, 1962, 1971). Although his vast number of complex writings are certainly open to varied interpretations, it is clear that he at least entertained many of the conceptual developments that postpositivists are beginning to explore, including a process orientation, contextualism, and the value of qualitative research. Focusing primarily on his development of a systematic contextualism, Douglas Torgeson (1985) contends that Lasswell anticipated many of the arguments being made by those who invoke critical theory.

Lasswell's basic vision of a new transdisciplinary science of public policy has dimmed a good deal over the years. However, under the editorship of Ronald Brunner (1982), the journal *Policy Sciences* maintained an interest in a broad definition of the enterprise, especially "contextual mapping," and the equal consideration of both qualitative and quantitative approaches. Its current editor, William Asher, in a recent article (1987), suggests that it is his intention to maintain this openness to a multiplicity of approaches. He goes on to suggest that the policy science approach has always been a viable alternative to the economics approach. Viable or not, it has hardly held its own against the onslaught of neoclassical theory and method. Had policy and administrative studies followed Lasswell's trailblazing, rather than being led astray by elements of political science and economics, much of the present methodological meandering might have been avoided.

Another misplaced alternative to positivist methodology is the broad-based federation known variously as "evolutionary" or "institutional economics" (Bush, 1987). In his overview piece, Jerry Petr (1984) outlines the following elements of this unique approach to social inquiry: evolutionary awareness, process orientation, technological focus, factual base, values orientation (both instrumental and ceremonial), and support for democratic ideals.

Given these diverse interests, and its long-standing antagonism to the neoclassical paradigm, it is not surprising that policy and administrative scientists are now reinventing their own versions of institutionalism. However, a few mainstream economists (Eichner, 1985) and sociologists (Hechter, 1983) provide useful accommodations, and these may prove valuable to students of policy and organization. Already some have claimed a few of the icons of the institutionalist tradition (e.g., Commons, Schumpeter, and Veblen: see March & Olsen, 1984), but their modern theorists (Boulding, 1981; Gruchy, 1987; Samuels, 1982) have had little impact thus far on policy and administration researchers.

Moving from the merely ignored to the much maligned, one arrives at applications of general systems theory. Of course, "systems" have become almost anything to anybody. For the purpose of this discussion, sociologist Walter Buckley (1967) provides a useful characterization[6] of the general systems perspective (p. 39):

- a common vocabulary unifying the several behavioral disciplines
- a technique for treating large, complex organizations
- a synthetic approach where piecemeal analysis is not possible because of the intricate interrelationships of parts that cannot be treated out of context of the whole
- a viewpoint that gets at the heart of sociology because it sees the sociocultural system in terms of information and communication nets
- the study of relations rather than entities, with an emphasis on process and transition probabilities as the basis of a flexible structure with many degrees of freedom
- an operationally definable, objective nonanthropomorphic study of purposiveness; goal-seeking system behavior; symbolic cognitive processes; consciousness and self-awareness; and sociocultural emergence and dynamics in general

This generality of systems thinking has been the cause of many misunderstandings. For example, some still associate the systems approach with positivism. As David Wilson (1980) explains, it has always been an alternative view of science:

Though it shares the same scientific attitude, it is profoundly different from the physicalism, reductionalism, one-way causality, and "truth" of logical positivism and empiricism. By investigating organized wholes of many variables, system epistemology requires many new categories of interaction, transaction, organization, and teleology, as well as a view of knowledge as an interaction between the knower and known. It is thereby dependent on multiple biological, psychological, cultural, and linguistic factors. (p. 135)

Despite this original orientation, its association with and successful applications in engineering and operations research tended to highlight its most mechanistic and positivistic elements. Moreover, the success of these narrow, closed-systems branches, and the misapplications of their metaphors to social phenomena, caused a crude caricature of systems theory to be popularized. Robert Backoff and Barry Mitnick (1986) reviewed the major criticisms directed toward the general systems movement, including definitional integrity, holism, isomorphism, and problem solving. They concluded that modifications in systems theory over the preceding years had dealt quite effectively with these major criticisms.

Although rejected as a social research paradigm, systems theory remains a primary source of practical management technique and strategy. Much of public-sector economics and virtually all of managerial economics are anchored in systems analysis. Despite the demise of grandiose reforms such as planning, programming, budgeting, and systems, "system survivors" remain essential vehicles of constructed objectivity, purposeful performance, and the service-determined productivity of public agencies at all levels of government (Brown & Pyers, 1988; Poister & McGowan, 1984; Steiss & Daneke, 1980). Debates over rational versus incremental realities notwithstanding, it is still a powerful prescriptive decision theory. Unfortunately, as noted above, practice and theory are often distinct realms.

Toward an Advanced Perspective

The realization that most administrators and policy analysts actually use or should use some variation on the systems theme does not make a paradigmatic revolution. Yet if scholars are actually interested in the influence of institutions, the context of decisions processes, or the concepts that guide the selection of design criteria, then eventually they must confront systems thinking as a cultural artifact if as nothing else. If they are also interested in rebuilding rigorous modes of inquiry amidst the ruins of postpositivism, then systems theory is an available source of infrastructure. Moreover, if they are willing to suspend judgment until they have explored a few of the more creative systems theorists, they may find elements of superstructure as well. Once reassembled and used to integrate ongoing developments in contextualism, institutionalism, and design approaches, these elements provide the basis for a new paradigm of applied social inquiry—an advanced systems perspective. These elements, among other things, include:

- a nondeterministic model of institutional evolution (through adaptive learning) that is compatible with individual freedom and choice
- a mode of cybernetic (feedback-sensitive) inquiry that allows for observer-observation interaction, mutual causality, and evolutionary experimentation
- a system for integrating newly emerging insights regarding the dynamics of natural systems (e.g., chaos theory, quantum logic, and biological resiliency) and their interface with human ecology
- a set of design criteria derived from an enhanced understanding of selection processes that allows for a restoration of purposeful action; and
- methods that not only facilitate multiattribute decisions but also enhance the comprehension of diverse human values

An appropriate starting point for the building or rebuilding of systems perspective is perhaps to reestablish some of the basic tenets from a few of systems' profound yet less known contributors. One of the most meticulous developments of systems theory as a paradigm for applied social inquiry was a product of American sociologist Walter Buckley. Buckley not only made critical modifications in existing systems theory but also developed a set of conceptual advances of his own. Unfortunately, his book, *Sociology and Modern Systems Theory,* was not published until 1967. By then, sociologists had already become disenchanted with systems theory through Talcott Parsons's (1937) more laborious development of structural functionalism. Buckley rejected the static equilibrium approach, which provided the basis for systems theory in the early 1960s. He suggested that neither the mechanical nor the organismic elements of systems theory are useful to the study of society. He envisioned a much more dynamic process that is more akin to communications theory and is highly contextual in orientation. He also anticipated some of the advances in evolutionary theory by rejecting the Darwinian model and describing processes of social entropy and evolution through institutional adaptation.

Buckley's primary focus was the ties between goal seeking, self-awareness, and self-direction within complex organizations. Buckley firmly believed that, as social researchers began to develop these linkages, they would in turn develop new analytical tools that would replace the quantitative techniques of correlation and factor analysis. Along these lines, he developed his own concept of "mutual causality," which, for him, freed systems theory from its limited notions of equilibrium and one-way feedback. He explained (Buckley, 1967):

> Only modern systems approach promises to get at the full complexity of the interacting phenomena—to see not only the causes acting on the phenomena under study, the possible consequences of the phenomena, and the possible mutual interactions of some of these factors, but also to see the total emergent processes as a function of possible positive and/or negative feedbacks mediated by the selective decisions, or "choices," of the individuals and groups directly or indirectly involved. No less complex an approach can be expected to get at the complexity of the phenomena studied. (p. 79)

In this way, Buckley also fully anticipated many concepts that would emerge under the label of adaptive learning; however, the insights of this school have not been fully integrated within a systems paradigm. Given similar concerns, David Wilson (1980), in reviewing the approaches used by federal agencies, predicted that future hybrids would evolve out of the general systems and adaptive-learning approaches. But this long awaited adaptive systems synthesis has yet to arrive.

The nearest thing to such a synthesis comes in Edgar Dunn's (1971) attempt to develop a completely unique approach to economic development policy. So forward-looking was his paradigm of social-cultural evolution that it has been virtually ignored, especially by Dunn's fellow economists. Foreseeing nearly all the elements of the emergent paradigm described above, he manages to integrate them into an evolutionary systems framework without relying on naturalistic methodologies. Dunn also seems to anticipate many of the epistemological concerns of both the critical-hermeneutic and design science approaches. For example, he differentiates his notion of design from both the physical science and standard social science methods as follows Dunn (1971):

> Classical experimental physical science takes place at two levels: analysis and system design. At the level of system design, these relationships or laws are applied to the design of deterministic systems like machine systems. . . . The social system experimenter is not exogenous to the system. . . . He is the agent of social learning—a purposive, self-actuating, but not fully deterministic process. . . . It can be characterized as evolutionary experimentation. (pp. 240-241)

Dunn also saw implications for social inquiry emerging from the quantum revolution in physics beyond Heisenberg's Uncertainty Principle and felt that an integrative discipline was needed that could facilitate these types of multiple "portals." For example, Dunn (1971) invokes Neils Bohr's "notion of complementarity" and suggests that it "can be extended to assert the complementarity for both physiological and psychological theories in human science, both human system and social systems theories in social science, and both steady state and social learning theories in social change" (p. 267). In essence, just as wave and particle theories are incomplete unless combined, deterministic and indeterminate social explanations must be integrated. This concept could be applied to qualitative and quantitative understandings as well.

Another administrative theorist who appreciated the integrative capabilities of systems theory was the late Erich Jantsch. Jantsch (1980) used systems theory to tap into newly emerging paradigms from the physical, biological, and cognitive sciences. In particular, Jantsch found in the Nobel-awarded breakthroughs of physical chemist Ilya Prigogine empirical confirmation for his own evolutionary speculations. Prigogine's innovations are also an integral building block in the new science of chaos, which uses theoretical mathematics (e.g., fractal geometry) to locate patterns (e.g., scales or self similarities) and to explore phenomena heretofore treated as random. Alvin Toffler (1984) simplifies Prigogine and Stenger's classic *Order Out of Chaos* as follows:

> All systems contain subsystems, which are continually "fluctuating." At times, a single fluctuation or a combination of them may become so powerful, as a result of positive feedback, that it shatters the preexisting organization. At this revolutionary moment—the authors call it a "singular moment" or a "bifurcation point"— it is inherently impossible to determine in advance which direction change will take: whether the system will disintegrate into "chaos" or leap to a new, more differentiated, higher level of "order" or organization which they call a "dissipative structure." Order and organization can actually arise "spontaneously" out of disorder and chaos through a process of "self-organization." (p. xv)

Douglas Kiel (1989) maintains that work in "dissipative structures" and what he calls "nonequilibrium theory" will facilitate understanding by public administration researchers of highly "turbulent" "transformational change." However, it is well to note that European operations researchers have been applying these concepts, under the rubric of "self-organizing systems," to more general systems applications for some time (Crosby, 1987; Engelen, 1988).[7]

In addition to contributing to this self-organization movement, Jantsch had more ambitious aspirations for his theory of "meta-fluxuation." He saw in dissipative structures and associated concepts a nondualistic, non-Darwinian model of evolution and a means of restoring human volition and learning to the study of dynamic social systems. Jantsch suggests (1981) that this new "evolutionary vision" is "linked to the search for commonalties in the functioning of systems pertaining to different domains, a search most notably pursued over the past few decades by General System Theory.[8] But its focus is not so much on systems, or any structural entity, [as] on the processes through which they evolve" (p. 1).

Jantsch also applied these ideas to the potential evolution of management methodologies. Conventional systems techniques (including linear programming, econometrics, and systems dynamics) work well for continuous, equilibrium phenomena. But, he suggests, existing techniques must be integrated with the research methods of "self-organizing systems," "autopoieses" (self-reproducing systems), and "Tessellation games" (which align critical dynamics in a checkerboard pattern) in order to comprehend discontinuous phenomena such as institutional change. For Jantsch (1980), this integration requires visualizing relationships between multileveled techniques, strategies, and multileveled reality. However, as these types of advanced systems domains become more fully mapped, perhaps future public administration scholars will discover less labyrinthine paths to methodological integration.

Another obscure systems thinker, Stephen Pepper, is worth mentioning briefly, especially for those advocates of design science who have yet to explore systems theory. Pepper (1966) recognized, as did Simon, that human systems design involves processes of selection. Moreover, Pepper formulated an intricate worldview that he called "selectivism." He thought that this was superior to other systematic explanations, including "mechanism, formism, organism, and contextualism." In fact, it extends the bases of contextualism to include the dynamic evolution of human intelligence and choice. Selectivism is a nonteleological device for restoring the purposive structure of self-regulating systems, which involves the interaction of individuals and institutions. Unlike Simon's (1983) attempt to unbound rationality through systems of artificial intelligence, Pepper attempts to describe how physiological, normative, and social-cultural dispositions and entities interact to mediate among values (both individual and social), choices, and behavior. Pepper (1966, p. 552) illustrates how certain selective systems and values combine to establish "lines of legislation." These notions might be applied to currently perplexing issues of economic irrationality (e.g., altruism; Axelrod, 1987; Hardin, 1988), as well as to flesh out notions of purpose or utility inherent in design approaches.

As Louis Gawthrop (1984) suggests, these issues of purpose and values are vital to public administration, and interestingly enough, he sees general systems theory as the only viable mechanism for addressing them.[9] Although Gawthrop's own systems formulations are more teleological and less conceptually rich than some of those above, they provide a critical link between general systems theory and practical public administration. Moreover, Gawthrop (1984) contributes to systems theory by making a powerful argument for the integral character of value processing. His book logically demonstrates how "the total effectiveness of the overall system is directly related to the effective integration of management, design, and ethical components" (p. 7). More important, Gawthrop argues that the current procedures of administrative policy making and pluralistic ethics have rendered public administration prostrate in terms of improving the human condition and that a systems approach is needed to restore a new sense of purpose and to facilitate what he calls "creative ethics." It will probably take many more explorations of this type, which tie systems thinking to the crucial needs of public policy makers and managers, for the new science envisioned here to emerge fully.

Conclusions: The Agathon Agenda

If the above systems formulations are not intellectually enticing, at least they illustrate how it is possible to develop systems approaches that do not automatically lead to either deterministic evolutionary aphorisms or to control hierarchies that violate human freedom. Perhaps systems theory is so overburdened with excess ideological baggage that even an advanced systems agenda that aims at midrange conceptual integration rather than grand theory will still be dismissed out of hand. Yet, just maybe, the current discontent among the prisoners of Plato's allegorical cave is becoming so intense that they will no longer be satisfied with "measuring shadows on the wall." Obviously, Agathon (the sun, or "the light") cannot be discovered from shadows; yet, it is not some type of transcendental reality. Ideally, the Agathon agenda strives toward a reintegration of the realms of theory and practice (what Plato called "praxis"). The form versus content debate in public administration is not necessarily resolved, but rather displaced through speculative experimentation. To experiment with ideas in this fashion is what various systems concepts were originally designed to do. As Donald Campbell suggests (1988), systems theory, generally conceived, provides useful devices for looking at the problems and prospects of social experimentation.

Certainly systems thinking has many flaws, which are too numerous to reiterate here. To have several enumerated in detail, one should refer to the articulate critiques of David Berlinski (1976) and Frederick Thayer (1972). It is noteworthy, however, that Berlinski and others have tended to focus on systems theory's most mathematical and mechanistic manifestations. The advanced systems paradigm, which has yet to fully emerge, would not necessarily be rooted in the same metaphors (for example, organismic or mechanical). Moreover, given the lessons learned and the reintroduction of contextual-selective and adaptive-learning concepts,[10] an advanced systems approach has many advantages over other approaches that are growing out of the current methodological miasma. These advantages include:

1. removing disciplinary blinders and facilitating integrative conceptual development, without relying solely on narrow neoclassical economic aphorisms
2. recognition of the limits of logical positivism without completely relying on relativistic notions or critical or phenomenological theories
3. reconciling the role of individual choice and freedom with the institutional, ceremonial, and technological, as well as other influences of larger systems
4. appreciating an evolutionary character of human, as well as natural systems, without relying on the narrow deterministic models of sociobiology or other neo-Darwinian constructs
5. encouraging the maintenance of rigorous methodologies while allowing for increased equality and integration between quantitative and qualitative indices

Scientific enterprises of both the traditional and modern variety tend to advance by both incorporating the elements of existing theories and explaining new phenomena. Advanced systems would allow applied policy and administrative studies to do all that they are currently doing, maintaining and conceptually enhancing many applied economics and systems analytics. Yet advanced systems would also extend concepts and techniques to embrace insights arising from paradigmatic revolutions in the other sciences. For example, advanced systems could incorporate the following types of emerging insights:

- resiliency, coevolution, and other alternatives to Darwinian concepts from the new biology and ecology
- observer-observation interaction, mutual causality, potentia, complementarity, and other ingredients of quantum logic from modern physics
- dissipative structures, order through fluctuation, and chaos theory from physical chemistry and theoretical mathematics
- theories of creativity, cognition, and intuition from computer science and cognitive psychology

By more fully applying these diverse conceptual domains, a new generation of practical tools and strategies could be developed, ones that operationalize the notion of public administration as a catalyst for constructive social change. In this fashion perhaps, techniques that occupy the soft underbelly of analysis, such as those that make up the strategic-planning process, could be placed on an equal footing with various economic or operations research methods (e.g., cost-benefit assessments). Gradually, these latter representations of independent rationality would become secondary to new decision aids that accommodate diverse societal objectives. These, along with improved criteria for purposeful design, would more readily facilitate Cleveland's (1988) ecological ethics, sense of human dignity, and participative due process than would abandonment of the search for systematic modes of inquiry.[11] In other words, to the extent that policy and administrative studies remain anchored in the aspirations of applied social science, advanced systems promises perspectives that are no less scientific but perhaps a good deal more social.

Notes

1. Note especially his elaborate introduction (von Mises, 1949, pp. 1-71). Also note Caldwell (1982).

2. Phenomenology, generally interpreted, is also well developed in the policy studies areas; see Dallmayr (1986), de Haven-Smith (1988), and Forester (1983). For excellent philosophical overviews, also note Bernstein (1976) and Thompson (1981).

3. An excellent collection of Campbell's papers, exhibiting his vast array of epistemological contributions, is found in Overman (1988).

4. A similar point is made through a series of unanswered questions in Shangraw and Crow (1989).

5. For a critical assessment of this approach, see Caldwell (1980).

6. For a more elaborate definition, see Churchman (1968); also note Miller (1978).

7. For other applications in realms ranging from anthropology to transportation planning, see Shieve and Allen (1982). For a proposed application in the policy sciences, see Daneke (1984, 1990).

8. A more accessible version of this evolutionary vision is found in Adams (1988).

9. Also note Vickers (1970) and Steiss and Daneke (1980).

10. For a glimpse of this conceptual realm, see Michael (1973); also, for an excellent overview of recent developments in the concepts of organizational learning, see Ventriss and Luke (1988).

11. For a discussion of how such societal values could be integrated through improvements in the logic of metasystems, see Gawthrop (1984) and Steiss and Daneke (1980).

5

An Examination of the Debate Over Research in Public Administration

RICHARD C. BOX

B eginning with an article by McCurdy and Cleary in the January-February 1984 issue of the *Public Administration Review,* several authors joined an ongoing debate in PAR about the quality of research methodology in the literature of public administration. The debate included articles by White (1986a, 1986b), Perry and Kraemer (1986), Stallings (1986), and Stallings and Ferris (1988) and recent contributions by Houston and Delevan (1990), Hummel (1991), and Cleary (1992). In addition, there was an author's exchange between McCurdy and Thayer in 1984. Authors in this series have used discussion, argument, and data drawn from dissertation abstracts, PAR articles, and articles in other journals in an effort to determine whether scholars in public administration produce work that compares favorably with that in other fields.

In the title of their article, McCurdy and Cleary asked the question, "Why Can't We Resolve the Research Issue in Public Administration?" They used four criteria to evaluate public administration dissertation abstracts from 1981 as an indicator of research in the field and found that it was lacking in methodological rigor. McCurdy and Cleary were not sanguine about the condition of public administration research and concluded that the standards that guide public administration research should be questioned (McCurdy & Cleary, 1984, pp. 53-54).

This concern with the quality of public administration research was reflected in a PAR series of articles by Perry and Kraemer (1986), White (1986b), Stallings and Ferris (1988), and Houston and Delevan (1990). These authors examined dissertations and journal articles in assessing research quality. Although they acknowledged the value of "alternative" methodologies that are not part of "mainstream" social science research (such as case studies, interpretive research, and critical theory), as a whole they found public administration research to be lacking in the rigor characteristic of mainstream research. In addition to this methodological deficiency, it was found that public administration research focuses on discussion of problems or issues relating to professional practice rather than on developing or testing theoretical propositions.

The series discussion has not been entirely negative regarding the quality of public administration research. Thayer disagreed strongly with what he saw as McCurdy and Cleary's (1984) attempt to lock public administration research into a narrowly positivist quantitative "straightjacket" (p. 552). White (1986a) made a case for the usefulness and conceptual validity of non-positivist research such as that based on interpretive or critical theory. Perry and Kraemer (1986) called for refinement of case study methodologies in recognition of the widespread use of case studies in public administration (p. 224).

Cleary's 1992 article found that public administration research has improved in the interval since his initial work. Using dissertation abstracts from 1990, Cleary found that, compared with 1981, a larger proportion of research projects had an identifiable research purpose and dealt with cause-effect relationships. However, he also found a decrease from 1981 to 1990 in the proportion of dissertations dealing with "important topics" in the field, such as the distinctive character of public administration and the nature of the politics-administration interface (Cleary, 1992, p. 57). In addition, this comparison of dissertation abstracts was based on two isolated years so that a trend is difficult to establish.

The argument presented here is that the PAR series has produced an unduly pessimistic view of research in the field and that this view is the result of inappropriate assumptions about what is acceptable as research in public administration. The discussion below looks at the methods used by the series' authors in comparing public administration research to that in other fields, examines series assumptions about the value of various types of methodologies and writing styles, and attempts to evaluate the question of whether public administration researchers are addressing the important issues in the field. The purpose of the article is to present a broader and more hopeful view of research in public administration, one based on a desire both to correct shortcomings and to emphasize the strengths of work being done in a dynamic and growing field of knowledge.

Comparing Public Administration With Other Fields

Beginning with McCurdy and Cleary, the PAR series' authors have evaluated research in public administration against "mainstream" social science research techniques. McCurdy and Cleary (1984) used dissertations in public administration as the data for their analysis, finding that "[f]ew of these doctoral projects meet the criteria that conventionally define careful, systematic study in the social sciences" (p. 50). As an example of a source for determining "careful, systematic study," McCurdy and Cleary (1984) cite Kerlinger's text *Foundations of Behavioral Research* (1986), which contains chapters on topics such as variance and covariance, probability, analysis of variance, multiple regression, factor analysis, and so on—in short, a guide to positivist statistical research (p. 50). Stallings (1986) suggests that the disciplines characterized as mainstream include economics, political science, sociology, and psychology—disciplines that are not practice-oriented, but rather are "primarily interested in knowledge for the sake of knowledge" (p. 238).

Three difficulties emerge from this choice of mainstream social science disciplines as a comparative universe for evaluating the quality of public administration research. First, the assumption that traditional positivist methods are the appropriate standard for comparison may not be accurate. Sprinkled throughout the series are comments acknowledging the validity and usefulness of case studies, interpretive methodologies, critical theory, and so on, but there is a clear bias toward quantitative analysis as being the primary means by which knowledge in the field may be legitimately accumulated. This point of view may be valid, or such an interpretation may be excessively narrow, producing a view of public administration research that is unnecessarily pessimistic and judgmental.

Second, though the series' authors find public administration research to be deficient in relation to that of the mainstream disciplines, this assertion is based on personal perceptions rather than empirically demonstrated differences. The universe of academic work surveyed in the series is limited to dissertations and journals within the field of public administration. Although public administration research is found to be "applied, atheoretical, and noncumulative" (Houston & Delevan, 1990, p. 674), at no point is the status of research in the so-called mainstream disciplines determined using the same measures used to examine work in public administration. Thus the premise that public administration research is inferior to the so-called mainstream disciplines is assumed but not established. Third, no attempt is made in the PAR series to compare public administration research with that in other practice-oriented disciplines such as law, planning, architecture, business administration, education, and so on. It may be reasonably argued that these or other practice-oriented disciplines are more suitable for comparison to public administration in relation to their substantive content, linkage between academicians and practitioners, and ways of acquiring and using knowledge. If this is true, the series has formed conclusions about public administration research based on a faulty selection of comparative fields of study.

Given these three difficulties with the assumptions inherent in the PAR series, it may be that series' authors have accurately measured the use of specific research techniques in the field but have failed to establish a sound basis of comparison on which to base the kind of value judgments that appear in the series. Thus the assumption that the problems and issues of public administration would be best understood through application of research techniques used by mainstream social science may produce unnecessarily negative appraisals of work in public administration.

It could be that the needs of public administration scholars and practitioners would be better met by studying the ways of knowing used by applied disciplines in which a strong theory-practice link is essential and a variety of methodologies are accepted as valid ways to perceive reality. It may also be that even mainstream social science disciplines display a significant range of techniques for knowledge accumulation and that the series focus on one aspect of the mainstream research picture yields a distorted view of research in these fields generally.

The Style of Scientific Writing in Public Administration

It would be helpful at this point to discuss the style of writing found in public administration journals. The PAR series has found public administration research to be methodologically weak because of its lack of quantitative rigor. In addition, series authors criticize public administration research for concentrating on "research that is in its early conceptual phase, identifying concepts and issues for future research," rather than testing existing theories (Houston & Delevan, 1990, p. 678).

In this view, work that expresses, debates, or formulates concepts is seen as preliminary to the real work of scientific research, the quantitative analysis of relationships between specified variables. In the article that began the PAR series, McCurdy and Cleary found that public administration dissertations that did not address an important issue in the field were more likely to meet McCurdy and Cleary's (1984) definition of "validity" in the methodological sense than those that did deal with an important issue. They concluded from this that, "[b]y virtue of their nature, the major issues may be precisely those issues that cannot be resolved with any sort of certainty" (p. 53).

In the book *The Conduct of Inquiry* (1964), Kaplan identified different cognitive styles in scientific writing. The styles range from the literary (concerned with particular persons or sets of events, such as biographies) to formal mathematical models. In between are some styles of scientific writing that rely entirely on conceptualization and speculation, some that use a mixture of empirical observations and conceptual propositions, and some that are focused primarily on the use of mathematics to formulate and test ideas. In advocating that public administration research should be based on complex quantitative techniques, PAR series authors expressed a wish to rely on such techniques as the focus of the conceptual enterprise, a situation in which, in Kaplan's words, "[s]tatistical data do not serve . . . only as a body of evidence; they are processed so as to generate new hypotheses, and even new patterns of conceptualization" (p. 260).

Although this quantitative style serves well in certain research settings, it is not the only style recognized by Kaplan as valid scientific writing. Conceptual writing or that which mixes concepts and empirical observations, though not necessarily in a complex quantitative format, was also seen as valid. The PAR series debate over methodologies assumes that "mainstream" methodologies are those that rely heavily on statistical manipulation; those that do not rely on such techniques must therefore be outside the mainstream and are called "alternative." But the types of research identified as alternative, such as critical or interpretive theory, are not so much alternative research methodologies as alternative theoretical approaches in contrast to positivism. By equating scientific research with statistical methodologies, PAR series authors have attempted to narrow the range of acceptable research techniques to an extent that excludes not only critical and interpretive theory or methodologies like case studies, but also the forms of conceptualization, debate, discussion, and proof that are the stuff of traditional writing in the social sciences.

Sociologist C. Wright Mills (1959) called this extreme positivist position "abstracted empiricism," a school of thought built around statistical methodology instead of ideas. The reason for the narrowness of this model of research, according to Mills, is its insistence on equating the scientific method with a specific type of methodology drawn from the natural sciences. As Mills (1959) put it, "[t]he Scientific Method that is projected here did not grow out of, and is not a generalization of, what are generally and correctly taken to be the classic lines of social science work. It has been largely drawn, with expedient modifications, from one philosophy of natural science" (p. 57).

Adherence to this philosophy produces confusion about appropriate methodologies, the validity of findings, and the definition of empirical research. Referring to the effects of the abstracted empiricist view of science as a "sort of methodological inhibition" (1959, p. 57), Mills raised these questions as follows:

Those in the grip of the methodological inhibition often refuse to say anything about modern society unless it has been through the fine little mill of The

Statistical Ritual. It is usual to say that what they produce is true even if unimportant. I do not agree with this; more and more I wonder how true it is. I wonder how much exactitude, or even pseudo-precision, is here confused with "truth"; and how much abstracted empiricism is taken as the only "empirical" manner of work. (pp. 71-72)

PAR and other public administration journals contain research written in the style Mills called abstracted empiricism, but they also contain work that illustrates the styles of scientific writing Kaplan described as primarily conceptual or conceptual mixed with empirical observations for proof or illustration. Most journal issues contain articles that present, analyze, explore, argue, and critique ideas, problems, and issues important to public administrators and those who theorize about the field of public administration without resorting to complex statistical methodologies. Some of this work discusses issues of central concern to the field, like the articles found in the January-February 1987 issue of PAR. This issue was dedicated to assessing the relationship of the "American Constitution and the Administrative State" on the centennial anniversary of what Waldo (1980) has referred to as "self-aware" public administration as dated from Woodrow Wilson's 1887 essay "The Study of Administration." This issue is a landmark for those interested in questions of development of the American administrative state. It is also an important reference point for teachers and students in public administration; its value to academicians and practitioners in understanding the relationship of public administration to the broader societal context is considerable.

In addition to articles written in these conceptual or mixed styles that discuss issues in the field, many others have had the objective of making contributions to the advancement of theory. Some of this work is "conceptual" in the sense used by the series' authors; that is, it formulates rather than tests theoretical propositions. But not all such work is solely conceptual, and it is possible that the conceptual pieces were working on McCurdy and Cleary's "major issues," which are of such size and complexity that they are not suitable for evaluation using quantitatively testable propositions.

The questions addressed by authors working in these styles may eventually be ripe for the type of research advocated by some of the series' authors; there may come a time in which complex quantitative treatment of large-scale sample data or use of an experimental design would help to clarify or validate ideas set forth in "alternative" methodological formats. Although such research may serve to clarify some of these questions, with others it may create uncertainty as successive efforts at specification of variables, definition of terms, drawing of a suitable universe for sampling, disagreement over adequacy of data and interpretation of results, and so on, cause confusion rather than progress toward discovering some objective truth on which all may agree. It may be that reality consists of a complex mixture of perception, measurable phenomena, interpretation, and assessment of the pragmatic usefulness of theory for practice instead of solely the ability to measure phenomena quantitatively.

The PAR series itself is illustrative of the points made above. Articles in the series are presented in more than one style, but none uses complex statistical techniques. Instead, some use logical argumentation and some use argumentation supported with examples or descriptive statistics. Does this lack of quantitative rigor mean that the series adds little to knowledge of this important issue in public administration? Is the series thus noncumulative, nonvalidatable, incapable of advancing theory, inferior to mainstream literature? Whether or not a reader of this series agrees with its conclusions, surely the answers to these questions are negative, indicating there may be something questionable about the conclusions reached by series authors who are critical of public administration research.

The Usefulness of Research

The question of the usefulness of theory for practice is of particular significance in a field such as public administration where an important test of the value of theory is its ability to help in both understanding and shaping real-world action. In a recent response to the claims of research inadequacy raised by PAR series authors, Hummel (1991) has suggested that managers in the public service know what kind of information is both valid and useful to them in daily practice. Although they make use of scientific research, such knowledge is too narrow and limited to be used exclusively as a guide to action. As Hummel (1991) said of the decision-making process of managers, "this means not only puzzle solving that requires hearing from many sources—technical, scientific, rationalist, interpersonal, psychological, political, ideological, cultural, etcetera—but the art of feeling one's way with all one knows across a great divide to open up the potential of an unknowable future" (p. 39).

This pragmatic approach to the use of knowledge is in conflict with the distinction drawn by Stallings (1986, pp. 236-237) between the knowledge of the practitioner (knowledge of the substantive content of a field, or "acquaintance with" it) and the knowledge of the academician (knowledge of the abstract and theoretical form of the field, or "knowledge about" it). Stalling's point was that practitioner-based knowledge cannot be validated because firsthand experience is idiosyncratic. Hummel believes that such firsthand experience is the basis of administrative action and behavior, and as such is the proper sphere of research in the field.

Houston and Delevan (1990) argued that research that meets standards of methodological rigor is that which uses "experimental, quasi-experimental, or correlational designs (with appropriate statistical tools)." They gave the impression that these statistical tools ought to be relatively complex multivariate techniques and that use of such techniques is synonymous with competent empirical research (pp. 677-678).

Further, Houston and Delevan suggested that the lack of such rigor in the literature of public administration may explain the disaffection of practitioners for academic writing. Using their narrow definition of empirical work that primarily included complex statistical techniques, Houston and Delevan speculated that the lack of empirical research explains the "gap that exists between theory and practice," accounting for the "often muttered phrase: 'That's fine in theory but it doesn't work that way in practice' " (1990, p. 678).

We may be struck by the use of such an intuitive representation of reality in an article devoted to furthering quantitative rigor. But if it can be accepted that practitioners often do feel that the writing of academicians is removed from the needs of daily practice and is therefore of little use to them, the next step is to ask why this is so. Is it because practitioners crave research containing findings embedded in multiple-regression equations, factor analyses, or similar techniques? This author has spent a number of years as a practitioner and teaches practitioners; he has seen little evidence of such desires among those who do administration. On the contrary, practitioners are more likely to regard such research as too abstract to be of any real value and lacking in substantive connections to actual problems they face.

Theory is often found to be unrelated to practice. If so, it is because it is written in language that serves as a code of communication for academicians. This code is not easily accessible to nonacademicians; often there is little attempt to connect theory to practice through use of examples, case studies, and so on, or the use of complex statistics confuses and alienates all but the technician before the punchline is reached. This does not necessarily mean that Hummel's position need be adopted without question. Stallings argues that the daily realities of practice cannot alone drive theory building because the type of knowledge required for one is different from that needed for the other, and this makes sense. But it is also true that public administration is an applied field. Public administration research will be of little value to the field to the extent that it becomes divorced from the reality of practice, its language makes it inaccessible to practitioners, or it becomes the province of a few insiders who handle "data sets" instead of studying real people as they do real work. It could even be argued that at some point it will not be a reflection of reality so that its "truth value" may come into question along with its pragmatic usefulness.

Issues of Central Concern
to Public Administration

Some PAR series authors find that, along with a lack of methodological rigor, public administration research suffers from an inability to identify central issues of importance to the field. Thus Stallings and Ferris (1988) said that "[n]ew directions for public administration research will come from asking fundamental questions about the nature of the public sector and its relationship to the wider society of which it is a part" (p. 585).

Perry and Kraemer (1986) put forward two areas of study as being particularly important in public administration: "The study of characteristics that distinguish public administration from other administration" and the "political-administrative system interface." The latter category includes responsiveness to the political system, legitimacy of the administrative system, legislative oversight of agencies, representativeness of administrative agencies, and civil service reform (p. 221). Cleary (1992) also cited these two broad concerns as central to the field (p. 56).

In identifying the relationship of politics and administration (not the long-discredited dichotomy, but what Denhardt [1990] referred to as "the continuing tension between political and organizational concerns" [p. 53]) as central to the study of public administration, Perry and Kraemer were in concert with several other writers who have spent time considering this issue. For example, Waldo (1980) found that "[n]o problem is more central to public administration, the existential, real-world enterprise, and to Public Administration, the self-aware enterprise of study and education, than the relationship of politics and administration" (p. 65).

Has public administration research indeed been giving attention to these concerns? To find out, the author examined PAR articles over the five-year period from 1985 to 1989. The intent was not to create yet another survey of the literature resulting in judgments about the adequacy of public administration research, but simply to discover what subjects seemed to be of central concern to PAR authors. Rather than identify subjects dealt with in all articles during the period, a screening technique was used that divided the articles into three groups as follows:

1. articles that build, extend, or modify a theory, model, or hypothesis
2. articles that discuss or illustrate broad issues, trends, or ideas in public administration or governing

3. articles that discuss, illustrate, or survey problems or questions of professional practice

Only those articles falling in the first two groups were analyzed and coded for the subjects they dealt with. Although articles about problems of professional practice are clearly of value to readers of PAR, they do not help with the present goal of discovering the extent to which public administration theorists are concentrating on core issues.

There were 230 articles in the survey. Special issues, symposia, author's exchanges, and book reviews were excluded. It was found that 37 articles (16%) fell into the theory category, 40 articles (17%) fell into the issues category, and 153 articles (67%) were placed in the practice category (see Table 5.1). These findings are roughly in accord with those of Perry and Kraemer (1986), who found that 80% of the PAR research in their survey was problem-oriented rather than theory-oriented (p. 217).

Within the theory category, 8 of the 37 articles were directly related to the issue of politics and administration (see Table 5.2). They included articles on such topics as the relationship of city managers and city councils, models of the role of the administrator, models of city manager plan abandonments, and so on. There were 4 theory articles about the relationship between the public and private sectors, with specific focus on items such as public choice, public goods, and privatization. The public-private topical area is similar in content to the core area definitions of Perry and Kraemer's distinction between public and other administration and Stallings and Ferris's concept of the relationship of the public sector to the wider society of which it is a part.

In the category of issue-related articles, the topical area receiving the most attention (11 articles) was broadly labeled the field of "public administration." It included articles about important people in the field, questions of the proper role of government, the significance of Woodrow Wilson, and so on. This topical area, like the public-private relationship, is related to the core field question of the relationship of the public and private sectors and public and private administration (though there is considerable variation within this topic area; some of the articles discussing personalities in the field are only peripherally related to core field questions).

The politics-administration relationship was the primary focus of five of the issue category articles, including pieces on public virtue, bureaucracy and professionalism (there were also two other articles that focused specifically on bureaucracy as a topic area), federal career and political administrators, and so forth. There were six articles in the issues category coded for the topic of the public-private relationship.

A wide range of topics were recorded in this survey of theory- and issue-related subjects covered in PAR; there were 16 different topical areas in the

TABLE 5.1 Categorization of PAR Articles, 1985-1989

ARTICLES PLACED IN THE THEORY CATEGORY			
Author(s)	*Volume*	*First Page*	*Topical Coding*
J. Svara	45	221	politics/administration
B. Romzek	45	282	motivation
H. Jenkins-Smith, D. Weimer	45	485	policy
S. Yeager, J. Rabin, T. Vocino	45	570	motivation
G. Guess	45	576	regulation
R. Pfund	45	593	decision making
W. Browne	45	620	politics/administration
A. Etzioni	46	8	decision making
J. Conant	46	48	reorganization
J. Perry, T. Babitsky	46	57	public/private
R. Rodgers	46	67	conflict resolution
P. Ingraham, C. Ban	46	152	politics/administration
S. Maynard-Moody, D. Stull, J. Mitchell	46	301	reorganization
B. Wechsler, R. Backoff	46	321	strategic management
J. Ferris, E. Graddy	46	332	public/private
J. Montgomery	46	407	bureaucracy
J. Regens, R. Rycroft	46	423	regulation
G. Henry, S. Harms	47	153	politics/administration
C. Miller	47	239	politics/administration
C. Newell, D. Ammons	47	246	politics/administration
T. Cooper	47	320	ethics
D. Berman, L. Martin	48	637	local government
K. Mueller	48	719	organizational death
P. Arnold	48	726	reorganization
D. Fiorino	48	764	conflict resolution
W. West	48	773	regulation
J. Chapman	48	800	planning
G. Protasel	48	807	politics/administration
J. Conant	48	892	reorganization
G. Gilbert, A. Hyde	48	962	motivation
L. Champney	48	988	public/private
A. Fleischmann	49	337	planning
D. Kirchheimer	49	353	finance
M. Stephenson, G. Pops	49	463	conflict resolution
D. Hodges, R. Durant	49	474	politics/administration
W. Lyons, D. Lowery	49	533	public/private
L. Kiel	49	544	nonequilibrium theory
ARTICLES PLACED IN THE ISSUES CATEGORY			
Author(s)	*Volume*	*First Page*	*Topical Coding*
H. Cleveland	45	185	information
B. Brown, R. Stillman	45	459	public administration
D. Pugh	45	475	public administration
H. Frederickson, D. Hart	45	547	politics/administration

(Continued)

TABLE 5.1 Continued

ARTICLES PLACED IN THE ISSUES CATEGORY			
Author(s)	*Volume*	*First Page*	*Topical Coding*
D. Thompson	45	555	ethics
M. Dimock	46	3	creativity
J. White	46	15	public admininistration research
C. Goodsell	46	105	public administration
C. Beard, W. Beard	46	107	bureaucracy
L. O'Toole	46	113	public administration
C. Levine	46	195	public administration
J. Perry, K. Kraemer	46	215	public administration research
J. White	46	227	public admininistration research
R. Stallings	46	235	public administration research
T. Kolderie	46	285	public/private
J. Rehfuss	46	454	bureaucracy
H. Sapolsky, J. Aisenberg, J. Morone	47	135	innovation
L. Fisher	47	213	supreme court
F. Sherwood	47	221	public administration
J. Fesler	47	291	presidential organization
D. Martin	47	297	comparative admininistration
W. Richardson, L. Nigro	47	367	politics/administration
P. Ingraham	47	425	politics/administration
T. Mitchell, W. Scott	47	445	public administration
R. Moe	47	453	public/private
H. Sullivan	47	461	public/private
R. Kearney, C. Sinha	48	571	politics/administration
R. Stallings, J. Ferris	48	580	public admin. research
E. Staats	48	601	public administration
J. Aberbach, B. Rockman	48	606	politics/administration
L. Gottschalk, R. Uliana, R. Gilbert	48	613	leadership
D. Martin	48	631	public administration
H. Cleveland	48	681	science
A. Wildavsky	48	753	public administration
D. Morgan, R. England	48	979	public/private
D. Pugh	49	1	public administration
K. Kraemer, J. Perry	49	9	public administration research
D. O'Brien	49	411	federalism
T. Miller	49	511	public/private
L. White	49	522	public/private

TABLE 5.2 Theory Versus Issues Articles

Theory Articles		*Issues Articles*	
politics/administration	8	field of public administration	11
public/private	4	public administration research	6
reorganization	4	public/private	6
conflict resolution	3	politics/administration	5
motivation	3	bureaucracy	2
regulation	3	comparative administration	1
decision making	2	creativity	1
planning	2	ethics	1
bureaucracy	1	federalism	1
ethics	1	information	1
finance	1	innovation	1
local government	1	leadership	1
nonequilibrium theory	1	presidential organization	1
organizational death	1	science	1
policy	1	supreme court	1
strategic management	1		
Total	37	Total	40

Notes on Topical Coding

1. "Politics/administration" includes articles that focus on the relationship between elected and appointed officials, such as discussions of administrative roles, time or task allocations between officials, reform efforts, and so on.
2. "Public/private" involves the relationship of public administration to the broader society, including discussions of public goods, privatization, traditional administrative theory versus public choice, and so forth.
3. "Field of public administration" identifies articles that discuss the field generally, prominent personalities in public administration, public perceptions of administrators, professionalism and public service, and so on.
4. "Public administration research" includes articles evaluating the quality of research in the field of public administration.

theory category (out of 37 articles) and 15 (of 40 articles) in the issues category. Some of the other theory-related topics included administrative reorganization, decision making, policy, and conflict resolution. Some of the other issue-related topics included comparative administration, federalism, leadership, and the Supreme Court. It may be that some articles coded for the politics-administration relationship, the public-private relationship, or the field of public administration could also have been coded for other subject areas. However, it appeared that these topical areas, which are related to the core issues of public administration, could accurately be identified as the primary focus of the articles thus designated.

Although the proportion of articles devoted to core issues in this survey of PAR research may not seem very large, it appears that authors who publish in PAR are not ignoring the questions that the series' authors and others identify as central to the field. In addition, if symposium articles left out of the sample such as those in the January-February 1987 administrative centennial issue (or the March-April 1989 issue on the Minnowbrook II conference) were counted, the number of articles addressing issues of importance to the field would be substantially larger.

Conclusion

The PAR series appears to have identified some areas of needed improvement in public administration research. To the extent that dissertations in the field are not linked to theory and journal articles fail to address basic questions that confront public administration, change is essential. However, if the discussion in this article is accurate, the PAR series assessment of research in public administration is excessively gloomy, and this gloomy view has developed for reasons that fall into three broad categories.

First, some of the series' authors have compared public administration research to research in other fields without actually studying the work done in those fields. Instead, they have drawn an idealized picture of the character of so-called mainstream research methodology and found public administration work to be inferior to an assumed rather than demonstrated standard. This problem is compounded by the assumption that the mainstream fields, fields that are not practice-related in the same way as is public administration, are the appropriate comparison universe for public administration. As a result of these assumptions, it is difficult to determine from the series articles exactly how public administration really compares with other fields, and whether the fields discussed in the series are actually useful for the comparisons being made.

Second, much of the PAR series work is based on the assumption that public administration research should conform to the standards and techniques of a particular variety of empirical research, one that dramatically narrows the ways in which knowledge may be acquired, understood, and communicated. This assumption is based on a value judgment that automatically narrows the thrust of the series to one of advocating for a particular view of knowledge in public administration. What is lost is the potential for an objective assessment of the current status and needs of researchers and practitioners in the field. This is not a matter of the need to perform research that adds to knowledge in the field; everyone would accept such a goal as imperative. It is a matter of how knowledge is gained and how flexible and creative public administration researchers will be in exploring questions in the field.

Third, the fear expressed by some PAR series authors that public administration researchers are not addressing the central problems of the field may not be accurate. The survey of PAR articles reported here indicates that attention is being given to these topics, though it is an open question whether the amount of attention is sufficient and whether the quality of the work is adequate to the task. In addition, the results might be much different if the survey were extended to other journals. On the broadest level, the question of whether the problems identified by series and other authors as central to the field are the right ones deserves additional thought.

In summary, research in public administration is in need of constructive change resulting from healthy debate over the nature of the problems to be addressed, appropriate methodologies, the linkage of theory and practice, and ways in which public administration research can be usefully compared to that of other fields. But pessimism about the field based on a narrow view of the nature of knowledge and research methodologies is premature and to some extent inaccurate. Hopefully, future work in this area will broaden the debate and allow a more comprehensive look at the quality and usefulness of public administration research.

PART 2

Assessments of Published Research

Research published in scholarly journals enjoys a special status throughout the academic world. Manuscripts (except for special cases such as
editorials or invited pieces) are published in these journals only after
undergoing a process of blind review by several referees, who themselves are typically published experts in the relevant discipline or sub-
discipline. Thus research published in the premier journals of a field
should represent the "best and brightest" work in that field. How might
one assess the quality of published research in an applied field such
as public administration? One of the ways chosen by authors of chapters
in Part 2 is a comparison of the methods used with those of mainstream
social science research. These authors are convinced that more rigorous and sustained use of scientific methodologies would lead to an
improved body of research in public administration.

After reviewing research methodology in the pages of the *Public
Administration Review* from 1975 to 1984, James L. Perry and Kenneth
L. Kraemer conclude in Chapter 6 that recent public administration
research is basically applied, is noncumulative, and lacks adequate
institutional support. In addition, much of the research involves problem delineation or variable identification, suggesting that public administration research is at an immature stage of development compared
to other social sciences. They recommend a more intense focus on

core issues in the field, obtaining more institutional support for research, and several specific methodological improvements.

In Chapter 7, Robert A. Stallings and James M. Ferris extend the work of Perry and Kraemer by examining research in the *Public Administration Review* from 1940 through 1984. They also found that much of the research is at the early stage of conceptualizing problems and discussing areas for inquiry, and that little of the research involves an analysis of causal relationships or theory testing. One might expect conceptual research to be high in the early years of a field's development, which it was, but Stallings and Ferris note that, even in the 1980s, conceptualizations remain the most frequently reported form of research, constituting 70% of PAR articles. They also speculate that one of the reasons why more mainstream social science research does not appear in the pages of the leading journal in the field is because researchers choose to send their work to other journals.

David J. Houston and Sybil M. Delevan address that speculation in Chapter 8. They examine the nature of empirical research in six public administration-related journals by focusing on the purpose of published research, as well as the research designs and statistical techniques that are employed. Their findings were consistent with previous studies. Public administration journals disseminate academically oriented research that largely is underfunded, conceptual, nonempirical, and engages in little theory testing. What little empirical research is published varies with respect to empirical rigor. Their study suggests that a cumulative knowledge base is not being developed by public administration scholars, at least not based on social scientific principles.

6

Research Methodology in the
Public Administration Review,
1975-1984

JAMES L. PERRY

KENNETH L. KRAEMER

Public administration was in an early stage of development when Luther Gulick (1937, pp. 191-195) called for a "science of administration." Gulick's exhortation became a source of heated and continuing controversy that centers around positivist versus alternative views of appropriate research methodology.[1] This article examines the last 10 years of *Public Administration Review* methodology and suggests directions for its future development.

Two general methods are used in this study: historical and statistical. Past and current assessments of research methodology in public administration are reviewed in order to set the context for this analysis. Also, published research in PAR from 1975 to 1984 is analyzed statistically to provide a baseline for evaluation of the state of research methodology. In the final portion of the article we generate some recommendations for future directions within the field.

Clarifying Definitions

At the outset we need to clarify some definitional ambiguities. What, precisely, do we mean by research methodology? Do quantitative methods delimit the scope of this subject matter? Do we include activities both academic and practical? Answering these questions requires some judgment, but the literature on social inquiry offers useful guidelines.

In search of a working understanding of methodology, we rely on Kaplan's (1964) discussion of this concept in *The Conduct of Inquiry.* He distinguishes several senses of methodology: (a) techniques, the specific procedures used in a given science, (b) honorifics, a ritual invocation attesting to concern with meeting standards of scientific acceptability, and (c) epistemology, involving the most basic philosophical questions about the pursuit of truth. It is the first of these senses that has the greatest bearing on this inquiry.

In addition, our primary concern is methodology used in academic research, that is, in the conscious effort to advance knowledge about public administration. Methodologies for administrative research, such as program evaluation, client surveys, and productivity measurement, are focused on generating knowledge about the problems of particular organizations or programs and are excluded from the scope of this study because of their essentially instrumental orientation. They are oriented to the practice of administration than to the study of administration.

As the foregoing suggests, methodology and research are closely linked. Methodology exists to guide the conduct of research; methodology is reflected in research. As a practical matter, therefore, our assessment of public administration methodology is also necessarily an assessment of public administration research.

Recent Critiques of Public Administration Research

Recent discussions of public administration research methodology have been characterized by two predominant streams. The first is concerned with the degree to which research is adding to a verifiable knowledge base that we can use to improve public administration as an applied science. The second stream is concerned with methodology issues, that is, the type of research questions that we can pierce with our methodologies, and whether our methodologies produce usable knowledge.

Several recent works have looked at different bodies of research in public administration from the standpoint of their contributions to knowledge. Garson and Overman (1983) reviewed public management research, as a subset of public administration research, for the years 1981-1982. They concluded that the research was fragmented, noncumulative, and underfunded. McCurdy and Cleary (1984) analyzed abstracts from public administration doctoral dissertations published in the *Dissertation Abstracts International* for 1981. They found that the vast majority of dissertations neither dealt with significant issues nor were conducted in such a way as to produce findings in which one could have much confidence. They concluded that the lack of methodological progress, as evidenced by the low quality of dissertations, is the result of inadequate standards among leading public administration programs as well as the nature of the field itself. Jay D. White's (1986b) recent replication of McCurdy and Cleary's analysis found that dissertation research is not published and therefore not communicated beyond the dissertation committee. He concluded that whatever the reasons that explain the lack of publication (for example, poor quality, lack of interest in publishing the dissertation), dissertation research does not appear to be a major source of knowledge in the field.

The second stream of discussions is concerned with the methodology issue and has been joined by a number of public administration theorists, most notably Catron and Harmon (1981), Denhardt (1984), Hummel (1977), and White (1986a). White (1986a) argues that most critiques of public administration research have been grounded in models of research predicated on positivism, indicative of the natural and mainstream social sciences. He argues, however, that public administration research has not been viewed in light of two other modes of research—the interpretive and critical modes. He suggests that growth of public administration knowledge be interpreted in light of all three modes of research.

This article is able to shed light on this second question only indirectly. Its primary purpose is to assess how PAR methodologies measure up against mainstream social science research. Whereas Garson and Overman looked at contract and grant research and McCurdy, Cleary, and White looked at dissertation research, we look at another subset of research in the field—PAR articles.

Research Methodologies in Use

Research articles published in PAR from 1975 to 1984 are the population for this analysis. Symposia articles, Professional Stream essays, review essays, and special issues were excluded from the domain of analysis. Included are 289 articles. Each was coded on 12 variables, about half reflecting purely descriptive information and the others requiring some interpretation of the contents of the article. These variables are discussed briefly below, and the appendix presents the complete coding scheme.

ANALYTIC CATEGORIES

Seven variables provided primarily descriptive information, some of it purely for identification purposes, about each of the cases: year of publication, volume, issue number, author(s), author's organization, general subject area, sources of research support. Four other categories were used to record information about the methodology used in the study.

Research stage is a taxonomic variable derived from earlier work by Rogers and Agarwala-Rogers (1976). It represents the stage of social science research, reflecting the purpose for which the study was conducted. These

TABLE 6.1 Classification of Research Stages

Research Stage	Research Purpose
1. Problem delineation	To define what we are looking for and the extent to which it constitutes a social problem
2. Variable identification	To identify variables that might be linked to the problem and to describe possible relationships among these variables
3. Determination of relationships among the variables	To determine the clusters of relevant variables required for prediction and to analyze their patterns of relationships
4. Establishment of causality among the variables	To determine which factors are critical in promoting or inhibiting the problem
5. Manipulation of causal variables for policy formation purposes	To determine the correspondence between a theoretical problem solution and the manipulatable factors
6. Evaluation of alternative policies and programs	To assess the expected, as well as the unanticipated, consequences of various programs and policies before and after they are applied on a large scale and to determine the effectiveness of such programs in overall problem solution

research stages and purposes are summarized in Table 6.1. *Research methodology* was adapted from an earlier taxonomy by Caldwell (1968). The categories of this taxonomic variable reflect general methods of inquiry used in the social sciences. *Methods of empirical analysis* was based on Gordon et al. (1974), Rogers and Agarwala-Rogers (1976), and Vogel and Wetherbe (1984). This variable applied only to studies that used empirical observation. The categories of this variable range from case study to controlled field experiments. Each category of the taxonomy represents increasing internal validity (Campbell & Stanley, 1963). *Focus* is a dichotomous variable that distinguishes whether the study was oriented toward theory building or problem resolution.

RESULTS

Descriptive Characteristics of Research

Figures 6.1 through 6.5 present bar charts for research by subject area, source of research support, stage, methodology, and methods of analysis. The distribution of research by topic, as shown in Figure 6.1, confirms the broad distribution of research in the field. No topical area accounts for more than 20% of research, but six areas represent more than 10% each: adminis-

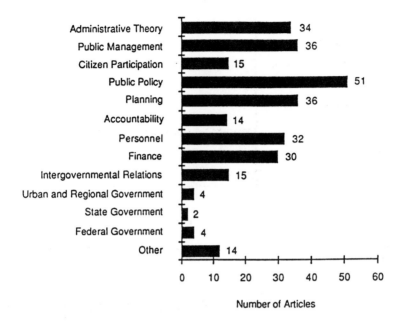

Figure 6.1. Distribution of 1975-1984 PAR Articles by Subject Matter

trative theory, public management, public policy, planning, personnel, and finance. Though the data are not shown in the figures, 80% of research was problem-oriented rather than theory-oriented.

The low levels of research support are apparent from Figure 6.2. Eighty percent of the articles failed to identify sources of institutional support. The most important category of sponsorship was "other," which consisted primarily of research funds provided to faculty by their universities. The National Science Foundation supported the largest amount of published research, but it was identified in only about 5% of the articles.

Most articles reported research at an early stage of development, as reflected in Figure 6.3. Seventy percent of the articles dealt with either problem delineation or variable identification. Although more than 20% of the articles focused on the relationships among variables, only about 5% of the research was conducted at the three most advanced stages.

Figure 6.4 indicates that the general research methodologies are essentially restricted to logical argumentation, legal briefs, or empirical analysis. Methodologies often associated with interpretive or critical theory—that is, historical or descriptive approaches (White, 1986b, pp. 5-7)—were infrequently represented. Mathematical models or comprehensive literature reviews were

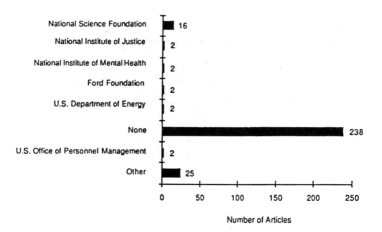

Figure 6.2. Sources of Research Support Reported in 1975-1984 PAR Articles

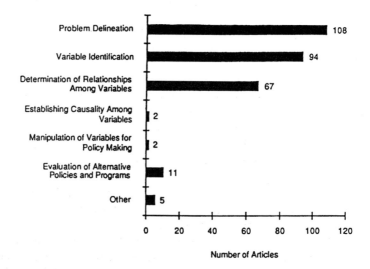

Figure 6.3. Distribution of 1975-1984 PAR Articles by Research Stage

employed in less than 3% of the articles. Somewhat surprising is the relatively large proportion (52%) of empirical research. Figure 6.5 indicates, however, that a large share of this empirical research was of the case study variety (37%) and that much of the rest was cross-sectional (52%). Very little empirical research involved field experiments, structural equations, or longitudinal studies.

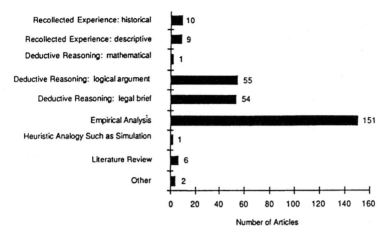

Figure 6.4. Distribution of 1975-1984 PAR Articles by General Research Approach

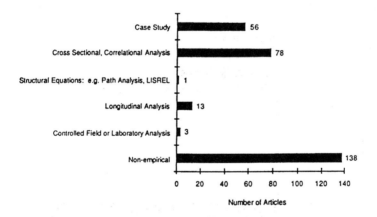

Figure 6.5. Distribution of 1975-1984 PAR Articles by Methods of Empirical Analysis

Changes in Research Methodology Over Time

As a means for identifying changes in public administration research methodology, the data were categorized into two five-year periods: 1975-1979 and 1980-1984. The broad distribution of research by topic during these two periods did not change appreciably, but shifts occurred in the importance of research topics (Table 6.2). Administrative theory, citizen participation, planning, and personnel all declined in significance as a proportion of total research. Finance, intergovernmental relations, and public policy increased significantly as focal areas for research.

TABLE 6.2 Comparison Between 1975-1979 and 1980-1984 Distributions of
Articles by Subject Area

Subject Matter	Number of Articles		
	1975-1979	*1980-1984*	*Total*
Administrative theory	18	16	34
Public management	13	23	36
Citizen participation	9	6	15
Public policy making	9	42	51
Planning	20	16	36
Accountability	4	10	14
Personnel	15	17	32
Finance	6	24	30
Intergovernmental relations	4	11	15
Urban and regional government	1	3	4
State government	1	1	2
Federal government	4	0	4
Other	8	6	14
Total Number of Articles	112	175	287

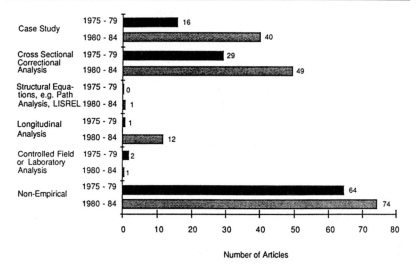

Figure 6.6. Comparison Between 1975-1979 and 1980-1984 Distribution of PAR
Articles by Methods of Empirical Analysis

Few differences for the two periods were found for research sponsorship
or research stage. In contrast, general methodologies changed significantly,
with much greater emphasis on empirical analysis from 1980 to 1984. The
increase is accounted for almost entirely, however, by expansion in use of
case studies (Figure 6.6).

Discussion

A question raised by this analysis of *Public Administration Review* articles is the extent to which this evaluation of the state of research methodology is generalizable to the field as a whole. Other public administration, political science, and management journals that deal with public administration research have not been included in the database. However, given that PAR is a publication of the major professional society whose goal is to advance the art and science of public administration, it is reasonable to assume that strengths and weaknesses of the field are reflected in it.

We think it is useful to note the factors that led us to choose PAR research articles for this analysis. First, PAR has been recognized as the major public administration journal among political scientists as well as public administration scholars (Giles & Wright, 1985). Second, PAR research articles are peer-reviewed. This process ensures that articles meet broad professional standards. Third, program prestige ratings are highly correlated with publications by faculty in PAR. In their study of reputation and productivity of public administration programs, Morgan, Meier, Kearney, Hays, and Birch (1981) found that the coefficient of determination between reputation and publication in PAR was around .65. This statistic testifies to the prestige of PAR among academics in the field.

Although some might argue for a more inclusive sample, we believe that a purely random sample would produce similar results. As evidence, we cite the substantive correspondence between the original analysis of doctoral dissertations by McCurdy and Cleary and the reanalysis, based on a broader sample, by White. Moreover, we explicitly excluded political science journals such as the *American Political Science Review* and the *Political Science Quarterly* precisely because they are mainstream political science journals and not mainstream public administration journals. Finally, we believe that adding data from other public administration journals, such as the *American Review of Public Administration* (formerly the *Midwest Review of Public Administration*) and the *Public Administration Quarterly* (formerly the *Southern Review of Public Administration*), would not appreciably alter (and may worsen) the picture drawn from PAR data.

Admittedly, PAR is not a mirror image of public administration research. It has a dual set of objectives aimed simultaneously at communicating with practitioners and advancing the science of the field; and this dual set of objectives obviously has implications for the content of PAR articles and the representation of research methodologies published in the journal. Beyond serving these professional goals of the Society, editorial policy during this period may have had some effect on the content; for example, editorial policy might have been aimed at achieving some kind of balance between academic and practitioner articles. Therefore, generalizations from this research must be made with appropriate caution.

With these cautionary and explanatory notes in mind, we believe three evaluative statements can be drawn from the foregoing findings about public administration research. First, public administration research is primarily "applied" rather than "basic." Nearly three fourths of the articles dealt with either problem delineation or variable identification; less than one fourth dealt with theoretical relationships among variables. Moreover, the research lacks detachment from immediate and instrumental concerns. Most of the articles reporting on empirical research were of either the case study or cross-sectional survey variety; few articles involved field experiments, structural equations, or longitudinal studies. Finally, the underlying purposes of doing research tend to be problem-oriented, which limits development and testing of empirical theory. Eighty percent of the articles in PAR were problem- rather than theory-oriented. Problem-oriented research tends to reduce the chances that the conditions for sound theory will be met (Kronenberg, 1971).

Second, public administration research has not been cumulative. Both the methodology and the stage reflected in public administration literature indicate that research is not cumulative. Figure 6.4 shows that only 2% of the articles are literature reviews of empirical research. Moreover, our personal reading indicates that much of the literature provided only citation reference to previous research and did not seriously engage the linkages between the current article and prior or contemporary research.

Further, relatively few public administration scholars pursue research actively or pursue research issues to advanced stages of development. There are more than 200 public administration programs in the United States, yet 51% of the authors affiliated with academic institutions were from only 22 universities, and 20% were from 6 universities. Few authors in the sample are consistently represented, that is, five or more articles in 10 years. These findings are in line with White's findings that few public administration dissertations are published. Only 17% of the 142 dissertation authors in 1981 published refereed articles based on these dissertations (White, 1986b, p. 13). It appears, therefore, that research is not a high value for individual faculty, doctoral students, or public administration programs.

Third, public administration research lacks adequate institutional support (university and extramural funding, organized research institutes, collabora- tive groups, external rewards). The primary indicator of support for research was financial. Eighty percent of the articles failed to identify sources of financial or other institutional support. We believe this omission is not the result of poor reporting, journal policy, or author ingratitude. Rather it is an indicator of the low level of such support. To compare the level of support for public administration research with another professional field, we analyzed reported support for articles published in the Academy of Management's two publications, the *Review* and *Journal,* for calendar year 1984. From a total of 105 articles, 40% acknowledged some type of support, 22% reported receiving extramural support, and another 18% received assistance from their universities. This is twice the proportion of articles in PAR.

Thus, given the assessments above, we find ourselves in basic agreement with Fritz Mosher (1956), who, more than 30 years ago in a review of research methodology in public administration, wrote:

> The field has not channeled its research efforts; its scope of interest seems unlimited; it has not developed a rigorous methodology; it has been pretty blase about definitions; it has not agreed on any paradigms or theorems or theoretical systems; it has not settled on any stylized jargon or symbols; with a very few experimental exceptions, the field has not been modeled or mathematized into an "adminimetrics."

STEPS TO ADVANCE RESEARCH METHODOLOGY

In order to advance the status of research methodology in public administration, we believe the following changes are necessary.

1. Focus on Core Issues in Public Administration

As noted above, public administration is a remarkably diffuse field encompassing contributions from many disciplines. It is also a relatively "small" field, in terms of scholars pursuing its study, when compared with similar fields such as business administration. Public administration, therefore, may need to focus the scope of its scholarship if progress is to be made in understanding phenomena within its general domain. Two core issues could provide this focus:

> *The study of characteristics that distinguish public administration from other administration.* This could be attacked as both an issue of political philosophy and an empirical issue. An approach based on political philosophy would concentrate, as suggested by Woodrow Wilson, on those "public purposes" that define public administration.
>
> *Political-administrative system interface.* This second anchor we propose for a redefined public administration core is the study of phenomena at the interface of the political-administrative system. Among the issues that would be the object of research given this definition of legitimate concerns are (a) responsiveness or nonresponsiveness to the political system, (b) legitimacy of the administrative system in carrying out its politically mandated functions, (c) legislative oversight of administrative agencies, (d)

representativeness of administrative agencies, and (e) administrative reform (e.g., civil service reform for increasing the responsiveness of administrators to both the executive and the public).

Criteria of research significance. As a complement to focusing public administration research on core issues, more attention needs to be given to doing cutting-edge research. Both of the analyses of abstracts of doctoral dissertations in public administration arrived at the same conclusions: Most dissertations did not reflect good judgments about timely and important research. Although the dialogue about criteria for defining and evaluating the significance of a research topic to the field has not advanced to the stage of producing agreement about such criteria, the development and application of standards about research significance would be a major stride in public administration research methodology.

2. Institutionalize Research

It is apparent that public administration research is very much a product of norms and incentives institutionalized within the field. Substantial advancements in research methodology can occur if new norms and incentives are legitimated. These changes would need to include:

Upgrading the importance of research in faculty roles. At the micro level, considerable progress can be made by better developing the capacity and incentives for public administration faculty to do high caliber research. For existing faculty, vehicles such as the Interuniversity Consortium on Political and Social Research summer program could be used to upgrade faculty research skills. Faculty incentives can be influenced by institutionalizing research as a promotion and merit criterion. The faculty tenure and promotion policies of individual universities could be significantly reinforced by the National Association of Schools of Public Affairs and Administration's (NASPAA's) adoption of standards that defined research as a faculty responsibility and required that PA faculty be substantially engaged in teaching, service, and research prior to accreditation. A recent study by Joseph Uveges (1985) indicated that NASPAA standards have had a modest impact on MPA curricula and program autonomy. Thus, some evidence indicates that the leverage of NASPAA standards might contribute to institutionalizing research.

Increasing the importance of Ph.D. programs in schools of public administration. A change related to upgrading faculty research roles involves increased emphasis on research-oriented Ph.D. programs. After reviewing abstracts for 142 doctoral dissertations written in 1981, McCurdy and Cleary

(1984) concluded that weaknesses in public administration research methodology were partly a function of inadequacies in doctoral-level research training.

Developing research unit/public administration program ties. An expanded emphasis on the value of research would be greatly facilitated by stronger ties between formal research units and public administration programs. Universities of public administration units should give serious consideration to funding research units at high levels relative to the instructional programs, for example, one half the program resources. This objective would be advanced by seeking to upgrade the role of governmental research bureaus so that they respond to local needs but in the context of general research interests within the field.

Increasing funding for public administration research. Without financial resources, adequate research about public administration cannot occur. This is an issue that needs to be resolved collectively by the profession and leading public administrators. The National Academy for Public Administration might initiate a dialogue with Congress about the needs for and benefits from research on public administration. Given the scale of the modern administrative state and its centrality in society, Congress might consider creation of a national institute along the lines of the National Institutes of Health. Within the current fiscal climate such proposals would appear to be inopportune, but the scale of problems of modern public administration could easily justify a moderate amount of earmarked funds likely to repay the initial investment in a few short years.

3. Specific Methodological Improvements

In addition to changing incentives and norms, specific improvements are needed in research methods used by public administration scholars.

More extensive use of meta-analysis. One of the most important of these changes involves steps to make research more cumulative. Kronenberg's (1971) earlier call for a public administration proposition inventory was one means for dealing with this problem, but it has not been implemented in the 15 years since it was suggested, probably because it was dependent on a large-scale, collaborative effort. An alternative means for making research cumulative is wider use of meta-analysis. *Meta-analysis* refers to the set of methods used for cumulating knowledge across studies (Hunter, Schmidt, & Jackson, 1982). These methods include literature reviews, counting statistically significant findings, and averaging results across studies. Also, the empirical analysis indicated that literature reviews were reported relatively infrequently in PAR, and few studies advanced to mature stages of social science research. Both of these findings suggest the need for more attention to meta-analysis. An ancillary benefit of greater use of meta-analysis is that it can also be valuable for integrating results across different academic fields, which is a particularly important objective for an interdisciplinary enterprise such as public administration.

Case study methodology. Case studies have been stereotyped as a "method of last resort," "exploratory," and an "attractive nuisance" (Miles, 1979; Yin, 1981a). Given these critical views about case study methodology, it might be appropriate to call for a significant reduction in the use of case studies in public administration research. Instead, we believe case studies will continue to be a popular method given the subject matter of the field and, furthermore, that a call for abandonment of case studies fails to consider a revisionist view that has developed in the past decade (Yin, 1981b; Yin & Heald, 1975). Although major improvements still need to be made in case study research, recent refinements in the conduct of case studies have increased their validity (McClintock, Brannon, & Maynard-Moody, 1979; Yin & Heald, 1975). Considering their widespread use in the field, public administration scholars might undertake further refinements in the case study methods as a means for enhancing public administration research and generally contributing to development of social science methods.

Qualitative methodologies. Another specific area for improvement is the use of qualitative methodologies within public administration. A grasp of qualitative methodologies is becoming increasingly important as "interpretation" and "rhetoric" regain prominence and respectability in the social sciences (Winkler, 1985). The empirical analysis confirmed public administration's already strong preference for qualitative research, albeit a diminishing one, but it also questioned the adequacy of the researcher's grasp of the tools and craft associated with qualitative methodology. There has been a small explosion of materials in recent years about qualitative research (Van Maanen, 1979; Glaser & Strauss, 1967), and public administration scholars need to become both more proficient practitioners of this craft and contributors to the advancement of these methods.

Advanced quantitative methodologies. The call for better qualitative methodology is not a slap at its opposite number—more appropriately its complement—quantitative methodology. Although the empirical analysis indicated a significant increase in the amount of quantitative research in public administration, the techniques used were primarily confined to simple correlation and linear regression analysis. This represents an advance in the field's application of quantitative techniques, but public administration still lags behind other social sciences in the application of advanced statistical techniques. Thus public administration scholars need to make more substantial use of causal analysis, structural equation models, and longitudinal statistical methods and to develop working competence with new statistical methodologies sooner after they become available to social scientists than they do currently.

Two examples of advanced statistical techniques that would significantly enhance opportunities to investigate research questions characteristic of the field are Box-Jenkins time series models and covariance structural modeling. Box-Jenkins is a technique for modeling changes in a time series of data to test the effects of specified interventions. Although it has not yet been widely applied, it has already been used to study such issues as the policy implications of economic change and the effects of the CSRA merit pay intervention on organizational performance (Catalano, Dooley, & Jackson, 1985; Pearce, Stevenson, & Perry, 1985).

Covariance structural modeling, commonly known as LISREL (Joreskog & Sorbom, 1981), is a causal data-analysis technique that is much more powerful than path analysis, which became popular in the 1960s. LISREL permits simultaneous estimation of the relationship between observed measures of latent independent and dependent variables. LISREL has begun to appear with increasing frequency in sociology and management journals for research problems involving social and individual behavior.

Some attention needs to be given not only to specific techniques that might be integrated into the field but also to how those techniques are acquired by students and scholars. An earlier study of empirical research in public administration and political science found a high degree of methodological stability over time. Scholars kept using familiar, traditional approaches rather than learning new methods (Gazell, 1973). Thus the field needs to develop support systems—for example, research workshops and doctoral consortia at professional conferences—to facilitate learning. Such support systems are equally applicable and necessary for public administration scholars interested in positive, interpretive, or critical research modes to develop and stay abreast of appropriate research methodologies. Quite clearly such steps are only a partial answer. However, they are necessary not only for moving the field to the forefront, but also for improving average research craft in public administration.

Conclusion

Even if all the suggestions outlined above could be implemented instantly, it would take several years before their consequences would be noticeable. However, although some of our suggestions require collective or institutional action, many can be implemented by individual scholars in the routine practice of their craft. For example, individual scholars can stay with research issues over the long term, improve the methodologies associated with case studies, and increase the application of more advanced statistical methodologies appropriate to the problems of public administration. The acceptance of these suggestions by the public administration community could serve to advance both the science and the art of public administration.

Note

1. See, for example, the classic debate between Dahl (1947) and Simon (1947). Waldo (1984) and others (Biller, 1982; Blankenship, 1967; Honey, 1957) have continuously engaged research in public administration. Most recently, See McCurdy and Cleary (1984) and White (1986b).

Appendix:
Codebook for Analysis of PAR Articles, 1975-1984

Variable 1: Year (1975-1984)

Variable 2: Volume (35-44)

Variable 3: Number (1-6)

Variable 4: Title

Variable 5: Author(s)

Variable 6: Institutional affiliation(s)

Variable 7: Topic
    1. administrative theory/bureaucracy/organizational theory
    2. managerial roles/public management
    3. citizen participation/representation
    4. public policy making/policy analysis/policy evaluation
    5. planning/administrative systems
    6. accountability/responsiveness/public interest values
    7. personnel
    8. other
    9. budgeting/finance
    10. intergovernmental relations
    11. urban and regional government
    12. state government

13. federal government

Variable 8: Source of Research Support

1. National Science Foundation
2. Office of Naval Research
3. National Institute of Justice
4. National Institute of Mental Health
5. Ford Foundation
6. U.S. Department of Energy
7. none indicated
8. other
9. U.S. Office of Personnel Management

Variable 9: Research Stage/Purpose

1. problem delineation
2. variable identification
3. determination of relationships among variables
4. establishing causality among variables
5. manipulation of variables for policy making
6. evaluation of alternative policies and programs
8. other

Variable 10: Research Methodology

1. recollected experience: anthropology
2. recollected experience: historical
3. recollected experience: descriptive
4. deductive reasoning: mathematical
5. deductive reasoning: logical argument
6. deductive reasoning: legal brief
7. empirical analysis (inductive inference)
8. other
9. heuristic analogy such as simulation
10. literature review

Variable 11: Method of Empirical Analysis

1. case study
2. cross-sectional, correlational analysis
3. structural equations: e.g., path analysis, LISREL
4. longitudinal analysis
5. controlled field or laboratory analysis
6. not applicable
8. other

Variable 12: Focus

1. theory building or mostly theoretical
2. problem resolution or mostly practical

| 7 | Public Administration Research: Work in PAR, 1940-1984 |

ROBERT A. STALLINGS

JAMES M. FERRIS

The current state of research in the field of public administration has been much debated in recent years. Some writers have discussed research methods employed by doctoral students in the course of their dissertations (McCurdy & Cleary, 1984; Stallings, 1986; White, 1986b), while others have commented on appropriate research strategies for the field as a whole, including its university-based faculty (White, 1986a).[1] Using empirical evidence, Perry and Kraemer (1986) presented an initial examination of the methods of research actually used in the field during the period 1975-1984 as evidenced by articles published in the *Public Administration Review.*

This article extends the work of Perry and Kraemer. Like those authors, we analyze actual data on characteristics of reported research rather than merely stating our likes and dislikes. We investigate changes in the types of research designs and methods used in the study of public administration over time as reflected in PAR. The purpose of our study is to identify trends in research during the past 45 years as reflected in this journal. Whereas Perry and Kraemer made comparisons between the periods 1975-1979 and 1980-1984, we analyze data for five-year intervals from the inception of PAR in 1940 through 1984. Thus we empirically examine for the first time some trends in the research base of the field and are able to speculate about what these trends may indicate regarding the future of public administration research.

Methods and Data

In designing a study to examine the types of methods used in research in the field of public administration over a 45-year span, we have chosen to focus on the *Public Administration Review.* This is the most feasible data source for the historical perspective we seek. Research in any academic field is conventionally reported in two types of publications: (a) books or monographs and (b) professional journals. As a source of data about the nature of research, books and monographs in particular present serious problems. Who decides which books and monographs make up the field? How does one draw boundaries around the field? Who was the intended audience of the book?[2] Because of the difficulty of answering these questions satisfactorily as well as the enormous task of coding what would unquestionably be a lengthy list of titles, studies of research within a given field focus instead on the professional journals. But which journals? The conventional preference is for refereed journals that are of general interest to the field as a whole and therefore contain a cross-section of research. This usually means the selection of those journals that are official publications of the principal organizations in the field. Hence in examining research in the social sciences, for example, journals such as the *American Political Science Review,* the *American Economic Review, and the American Sociological Review* have been used.[3]

The *Public Administration Review* bears the same relationship to research in the field of public administration as do these other journals in their respective disciplines. Other journals are less satisfactory for a number of reasons. Interdisciplinary journals such as *Administrative Science Quarterly* focus on generic management questions that transcend the boundaries of the public sector. Journals such as *Public Personnel Management* are by design meant to be of interest to only a subset of those in the field. Still others such as *Administration and Society* are relatively new (it is only 15 years old) and thus do not represent a sufficient source of data on the field over time.[4] Hence the most satisfactory data source is the PAR. In addition to being the official journal of the main professional organization, it is most representative of research of general interest to the field over a long time period.

An examination of the table of contents of PAR reveals a variety of headings under which published works are organized. We suspected, as did Perry and Kraemer, that the greatest probability of finding research was in those refereed pieces published under the heading "articles." To verify that exclusion of symposia, special-issue articles, and Professional Stream articles did not create an underestimate of research approaches and methods, we examined symposia and Professional Stream pieces separately. A simple random (i.e., equal-probability) sample of 80 symposia pieces published in the PAR during the period 1965-1984 was compared with regular articles. For both types of research approaches (Table 7.1) and types of research designs (Table 7.2), symposia pieces differed little from regular articles. We also examined all 200 pieces published under the heading "From the Professional Stream" since September 1966. We found that these professional stream pieces were even less reflective of research than were those published under the heading

"Symposia." Prior to 1976 the large majority consisted of short opinion pieces, many of which had originally been given as speeches. After 1976, a new editor (Louis Gawthrop) changed the format, and professional stream pieces became longer, more reflective, and more closely linked to the literature. This section title was discontinued in 1986. Throughout, the tendency was for professional stream pieces to focus on the nature of public service. By concentrating on articles, therefore, we are not likely to overlook major categories of research published under the heading of "Symposia" or "Professional Stream."

Thus following Perry and Kraemer we examine refereed works published under the "Articles" section of the PAR. These articles represent research in the field of public administration to a greater extent than pieces published in other segments of this journal. We exclude from analysis not only symposia and professional stream articles but also book reviews, review essays, and all special issues. The result is a universe of approximately 1,200 articles for the period 1940-1984. Because Perry and Kraemer (1986) had already coded all 289 articles appearing in the decade 1975-1984 in terms of research methods employed, we incorporated their previously published data in our analysis. For the period 1940-1974, a simple random (i.e., equal probability) sample of 176 research articles was selected using systematic or kth case sample (Babbie, 1973, pp. 92-93). The title, abstract, acknowledgements, section headings, and any tables or figures were examined initially. Each article was coded with references to three sets of variables: (a) research approach and research methods, (b) topic area within the field of public administration, and (c) author characteristics. If the article could not be coded on each of these variables from an initial screening, then the entire text of that article was read.[5]

In the case of research approach and methods, we have chosen a slightly different coding scheme from that employed by Perry and Kraemer. Because many of the variables used by them lacked categories that were mutually exclusive, we do not replicate their coding scheme in a straightforward manner.[6] We rearrange the categories of the variables they called "research stage" into three new binary variables as follows. Articles whose principal purpose was to delineate a problem or to identify a crucial variable for future research are assigned a score of 1, while all articles whose aim or purpose was something other than these are assigned a score of 0. This variable, CONCEPTUAL, represents the proportion of articles for each time period whose purpose was to conceptualize a researchable problem. Similarly, articles describing research whose principal purpose was either to describe bivariate relationships among pairs of variables or to demonstrate multivariate causal relationships among variables are scored 1 with all other articles scored 0. This variable is named RELATION. A third binary variable, EVALUATE, is constructed by assigning the score 1 to articles whose

TABLE 7.1 Comparison of Research Approaches in Articles in the *Public Administration Review*, 1965-1984[*]

Interval	Conceptual		Relation		Evaluate	
	Article	Symposium	Article	Symposium	Article	Symposium
1965-74	74.7 (56)	25.0 (11)	4.0 (3)	9.1 (4)	8.0 (6)	13.6 (6)
1975-84	69.9 (202)	29.5 (13)	24.6 (71)	11.4 (5)	3.8 (11)	15.9 (7)

[*]Values in the columns are the percentage of articles in the category for that time interval; values in parentheses are the total number of articles of this type per time interval.

TABLE 7.2 Comparison of Research Designs in Articles and Symposia in the *Public Administration Review*, 1965-1984[*]

Interval	Case Study		Multivariate	
	Article	Symposium	Article	Symposium
1965-69	10.0 (3)	9.1 (1)	10.0 (3)	0.0 (0)
1970-74	2.2 (1)	0.0 (0)	2.2 (1)	0.0 (0)
1975-79	14.3 (16)	18.4 (7)	25.9 (29)	0.0 (0)
1980-84	22.9 (40)	16.7 (1)	28.6 (50)	0.0 (0)

[*]Values in the columns are the percentage of articles in the category for that time interval; values in parentheses are the total number of articles of this type per time interval.

purpose was to analyze a specific policy or program and a score 0 to all other articles.

In addition to these variables describing the purpose of the research, we create two new binary variables that indicate contrasting styles of research. The variable CASE STUDY takes a value of 1 for articles presenting typically qualitative data (Taylor & Bogdan, 1984) from a single case study (the kind of research labeled interpretive by White, 1986a),[7] and a value of 0 for articles with all other types of research designs. The variable MULTIVARI-ATE distinguishes between articles in which the results of multivariate statistical analysis were reported; the former are scored 1, while all other articles are scored 0.

Two additional sets of variables capture topics that are often used to delineate the field of public administration, the policy-management dichotomy, and level of government (i.e., local, state, federal). For this purpose, we adopt a multiple coding strategy. Up to three subject areas can be selected for each article, thereby creating a multiple-response variable for research topic. For example, a single article that examined the administration of state personnel departments could be categorized under three headings: administrative theory, personnel, and state-level. The use of multiple rather than single codes prevents forcing of an arbitrary selection of the one "best" subject area into which an article fits. This is a departure from the technique of Perry and Kraemer, who assigned each article to only one subject category.

Based on this set of identifiers, we then categorize the articles by the extent to which the research had a management or a policy focus and by the extent to which the research focused on a specific level of government. We create two binary variables, MANAGE and POLICY, to represent whether or not the research had such a focus based on any of the three multiple-response variables. Following categories created by Perry and Kraemer (1986, Figure 1, p. 217), the management variable is created by assigning a score of 1 to articles dealing with the topics of administrative theory, planning, or personnel and assigning a score of 0 to all other articles. The policy variable is scored 1 for articles dealing with citizen participation, accountability, or public policy with all other topics scored 0. Likewise, we are interested in whether any trend in research attention is discernible across the three levels of government and thus create three binary variables, LOCAL, STATE, and FEDERAL. In all three cases, articles are scored 1 if they deal with research on that level of government, 0 if they do not.

Finally, we are interested in changes over the past five decades in the *contributors* of research to the field. We examine two variables that describe whether the research reported in the article had been formally supported by a grant of any sort (FUNDING, scored 1 if yes, otherwise 0) and whether the

TABLE 7.3 Research Approaches in Articles in the *Public Administration Review,*
1940-1984*

Interval	CONCEPTUAL	RELATION	EVALUATE
1940-44	31.6 (6)	0.0 (0)	63.2 (12)
1945-54	55.0 (22)	32.5 (13)	10.0 (4)
1955-64	85.7 (36)	11.9 (5)	2.4 (1)
1965-74	74.7 (56)	4.0 (3)	8.0 (6)
1975-84	69.9 (202)	24.6 (71)	3.8 (11)
χ^2	22.91	26.34	94.66
df	4	4	4
p	0.000	0.000	0.000
Cramer's V	0.22	0.24	0.45

*Values in the columns are the percentage of articles in the category for that time interval; values in parentheses are the total number of articles of this type per time interval.

senior author[8] held an academic appointment at the time the article was published (ACADEMIC, similarly scored 1 if so, 0 otherwise).

Tables 7.3 and 7.4 contain percentages of articles by time periods, with raw frequencies in parentheses, for research approach and research design, respectively. Both a test of significance and a measure of association are presented for each bivariate relationship. The test of significance indicates whether differences in the frequencies of various types of articles over time are statistically significant (i.e., not randomly distributed). The measure of association describes the extent to which trends in research vary as a function of time. Tables 7.3 and 7.4 contain the same information for the policy-management dichotomy and level of government, respectively. Table 7.5 contains the same information for researcher characteristics. For those variables where Perry and Kraemer presented frequencies for the two five-year periods (i.e., 1975-79 and 1980-84), we group the data into five-year intervals, resulting in a total of nine data points since 1940. For all other variables, we group the data into 10-year intervals, resulting in five data points, including the 1975-84 data in Perry and Kraemer.

Findings

Patterns of research approach and research design are depicted in Table 7.3. Articles that identify or conceptualize a problem (for example, for later research) increased from the inception of the PAR to a peak in the decade 1955-64. They have since declined in frequency but not to the level of the 1940s. Even in the 1980s, conceptualizations remain the most frequently

TABLE 7.4 Research Designs in Articles in the *Public Administration Review,* 1940-1984[*]

Interval	CASE STUDY	MULTIVARIATE
1940-44	31.6 (6)	0.0 (0)
1945-49	100.0 (21)	0.0 (0)
1950-54	5.3 (1)	0.0 (0)
1955-59	0.0 (0)	9.1 (2)
1960-64	0.0 (0)	0.0 (0)
1965-69	10.0 (3)	10.3 (3)
1970-74	2.2 (1)	2.2 (1)
1975-79	14.3 (16)	25.9 (29)
1980-84	22.9 (40)	28.6 (50)
χ^2	116.75	44.66
df	8	8
p	0.000	0.000
Cramer's V	0.50	0.31

[*]Values in the columns are the percentage of articles in the category for that time interval; values in parentheses are the total number of articles of this type per time interval.

TABLE 7.5 Policy Management Topics in Articles in the *Public Administration Review,* 1940-1984[*]

Interval	MANAGE[**]	POLICY[**]
1940-44	79.0 (15)	47.4 (9)
1945-49	76.2 (16)	33.3 (7)
1950-54	89.5 (17)	57.9 (11)
1955-59	95.4 (21)	31.8 (7)
1960-64	85.0 (17)	35.0 (7)
1965-69	70.0 (21)	63.3 (19)
1970-74	62.2 (28)	62.2 (28)
1975-79	58.9 (66)[***]	19.6 (22)[***]
1980-84	41.4 (72)[***]	33.1 (58)[***]
χ^2	55.41	41.88
df	8	8
p	0.000	0.000
Cramer's V	0.35	0.30

[*]Values in the columns are the percentage of articles in the category for that time interval; values in parentheses are the total number of articles of this type per time interval.
[**]Because of the aggregating of multiple response variables, the columns in this table may sum to more than 100%.
[***]These figures are based on Perry and Kraemer's single-code approach.

reported form of research, making up 70% of articles in the PAR, as Perry and Kraemer noted. Research emphasis seems to have shifted back and forth between conceptual efforts (CONCEPT) and policy and program evaluation (EVALUATE). During periods in which the latter were declining, the former increased in frequency. The peak period of evaluation-centered research was 1940-1944.

Trends in more conventional social science-type studies—that is, those exploring bivariate and multivariate relationships between variables (RELA-TION)—constitute a mixed pattern. Perhaps stimulated by the same forces that affected the social sciences after World War II wherein quantitative and statistical techniques grew in popularity, these types of studies reached their highest point in the mid-1950s. Even then, such studies amounted to only one third of the research articles published. After a prolonged decline from 1955 through 1979, this form of article has shown a strong resurgence in the early 1980s.

Somewhat ironically in light of recent statements by White (1986a), Thayer, and others, public administration research using a case study approach (CASE STUDY) has only been prominent in articles appearing in PAR in one brief period. The exception is the period 1945-1949 when all research articles reported results based on case study designs (Table 7.4). The long-term trend since 1956 has been a slow increase in this type of research, less than a 1% increase per year on the average. There has been a slightly more rapid increase in such research since 1975, a pattern similar to but lagging behind the renewed popularity of qualitative research in other fields such as sociology. Still, research employing case study designs makes up less than one fourth of research published in the PAR in the period 1980-1984. Multivariate an-alyses (MULTIVARIATE) have increased at only a slightly higher rate during these same periods. The frequency of multivariate analyses, often seen as the rival of case studies, has been stable for the past 10 years. It currently represents only about one fourth of all studies published in PAR, far less than in most of the traditional social science disciplines from which public administration draws.

Trends in the substantive topics to which research in public administration has been addressed over the years are presented in Tables 7.5 and 7.6. It is clear from the data that the proportion of articles in PAR on management topics (MANAGE) has declined in recent years. Such research increased steadily to a peak in 1955-1959 when 95% of all research articles published in PAR dealt with this topic. Management topics have persistently and steadily declined since then. In the 1980s less than half of all research articles addressed management-related topics. The pattern of research articles on policy (POL-ICY) fluctuates between decades of high interest (e.g., 60% of all articles in the mid-1960s) and alternating decades of relatively low interest (for example,

TABLE 7.6 Level of Government Emphasized in Articles in *Public Administration Review*, 1940-1984[*]

Interval	LOCAL	STATE	FEDERAL
1940-44	5.3 (1)	5.3 (1)	42.1 (8)
1945-49	0.0 (0)	4.8 (1)	47.6 (10)
1950-54	5.3 (1)	21.1 (4)	57.9 (11)
1955-59	9.1 (2)	22.7 (4)	50.0 (11)
1960-64	20.0 (4)	5.0 (1)	25.0 (5)
1965-69	23.2 (7)	16.7 (5)	30.0 (9)
1970-74	22.2 (10)	2.2 (1)	35.6 (16)
1975-79	**	**	**
1980-84	**	**	**
χ^2	11.41	12.45	7.50
df	6	6	6
p	0.08	0.05	0.28
Cramer's V	0.20	0.27	0.21

[*]Values in the columns are the percentage of articles in the category for that time interval; values in parentheses are the total number of articles of this type per time interval.
[**]Because of the type of coding technique used by Perry and Kraemer, these values are too small to report.

one third of articles during 1955-1965). The pattern of research articles on policy topics is cyclical rather than linear.

In terms of the levels of government with which research published in PAR has dealt over the years, local government (LOCAL) appears never to have been a major research focus during the period examined. However, the increased interest in the early 1960s seems to have remained constant for more than a decade, although at a modest level (always less than one fourth of the published articles). The heyday of research on state-level topics (STATE) was clearly the decade of the 1950s. The major focus of research in PAR over the entire 45-year period has been at the federal level (FEDERAL). Although the peak levels of interest observed in the 1950s have never been repeated, interest slowly returned in the early 1970s. A further indication of the constant level of interest in federal government topics, differences in the frequencies of articles published over time are not statistically significant for this variable ($p = 0.28$).

Finally, in Table 7.7 we note some trends regarding the characteristics of those who contribute research articles in PAR. First, many recent writers (e.g., Perry and Kraemer) have commented on the lack of financial support for research in this field. Our data clearly show that lack of research funding (FUNDING) is not a new problem. The "peak" (if one could call it that) was the 11% of published articles in the early 1970s that acknowledged some

TABLE 7.7 Researcher Characteristics of Articles in the *Public Administration Review,* 1940-1984[*]

Interval	FUNDING	ACADEMIC
1940-44	0.0 (0)	15.8 (3)
1945-49	0.0 (0)	42.0 (9)
1950-54	5.3 (1)	47.4 (9)
1955-59	9.1 (2)	54.6 (12)
1960-64	5.0 (1)	50.0 (10)
1965-69	6.7 (2)	63.3 (19)
1970-74	11.1 (5)	64.4 (29)
1975-79	—	N.A.
1980-84	20.0 (51)[**]	N.A.
χ^2	4.88	15.26
df	6	6
p	0.56	0.02
Cramer's V	0.17	0.29

[*]Values in the columns are the percentage of articles in the category for that time interval; values in parentheses are the total number of articles of this type per time interval.
[**]For the 10-year period 1975-84 as reported in Perry and Kraemer.
N.A.: Not applicable.

form of research support. The slight fluctuations over time are not statistically significant ($p = 0.56$). Second, there has been both a steady and statistically significant increase in research papers authored by university faculty (ACADEMIC). Before the mid-1950s, less than half of the research articles appearing in PAR were by university-based senior authors. By the early 1970s, nearly two thirds of all papers were credited to senior authors on university faculties.

Discussion and Implications

The recent history of research in public administration, as demonstrated by articles published in PAR, differs little from the state of affairs nearly a half century ago. Research is still dominated by efforts to conceptualize researchable problems, delineate possible areas of inquiry, and describe objects for study. Little causal analysis or theory testing has taken place over the years, and causal analyses, while significantly more frequent now than in previous decades, constitute only a small proportion of current research.[9] Many social scientists contend that qualitative research methods represent one avenue for advancing research from a descriptive and conceptual initial stage of development toward more advanced stages where causal structures can be specified and tested (Glaser & Strauss, 1967; Lofland, 1971). One of the most common forms of such qualitative research involves the use of case study designs. Interestingly, research using the case study approach has been even less frequently reported in the PAR over the years than has that using multivariate statistical methods. It remains to be seen whether the recent resurgence of both types of research is part of a random pattern or the beginning of new research directions in the field.

We now return to the question of the *Public Administration Review* as an outlet for published research in this field. Undoubtedly there is more research that can be labeled "public administration" than that appearing in PAR. However, as the official refereed journal of the professional association, it is the single best indicator of the state of research in the field over time. Moreover, its contents are a good indication of the value placed on research by professionals and of the role of research in the field.

Given this premise, why would article-length research reports on general public administration topics be underrepresented in the PAR? There are at least three possible answers to this question. One might be that authors of research articles submit their work elsewhere. They may feel, for example, that readers of other journals are more interested in and better able to utilize their findings than are the readers of PAR. A second possibility is that the editorial process may not facilitate the publication of more research articles over the years. For example, Dwight Waldo (1966, p. 237), editor of PAR from 1966 to 1977, expressed a preference for articles reviewing research reports rather than articles reporting on individual research projects. A third explanation might be that the relatively smaller number of research articles appearing in the PAR over the years is indicative of the amount of methodologically sound research produced in the field. In other words, the peer-review process, rather than disfavoring research articles, in fact may have performed its gatekeeping function by only recommending publication of the more solid pieces of research submitted.

The issue of funding for public administration research may be seen from a different vantage point in light of these data. The meager level of current research support noted recently by Perry and Kraemer has been a pattern persisting virtually unchanged since 1940. In light of our data on the lack of movement from problem delineation to theory testing or causal modeling, we raise two questions. Does the lack of research support suggest that proposals for research on topics uniquely related to public administration do not successfully compete for funding from federal agencies and private foundations? If this is the case, it would indicate that proposed public administration research is not held in very high regard by those who review proposals for these organizations. Alternatively, could it be that the lack of support for research in the field simply means that researchers do not undertake research tasks such as data collection and data analysis and therefore do not require research funding? Perhaps researchers are content to continue the description and conceptualization that has characterized research in this field for nearly half a century. This interpretation would mean that the current state of research funding in the field is really self-imposed.[10]

Finally, while research reflected in articles published in PAR has increasingly been housed within universities, as judged by the affiliations of senior authors, such a setting for research seems not to have produced major changes in the *type* of research conducted. This is especially noteworthy in view of other research on the professions. Everett Cherrington Hughes (1960), one of the most widely respected students of the professions, identified the emergence of research as a major indicator of the transformation of an occupation into a profession. He observed that, over time, researchers become differentiated from practitioners. They move into academic positions in the professional schools of universities and pursue careers markedly different from practitioners. The nature of their research changes; it becomes more like that of the social science disciplines in its orientation (Hughes, 1960, pp. 56-57). Such a pattern, however, does not seem to characterize the field of public administration.[11] Its research orientation does not differ noticeably between periods of practitioner dominance and those in which academicians have dominated. Indeed, this debate about the nature of research in the field has been going on for more than half a century (Dahl, 1947; Simon, 1947).

Speculating on the Future of Public Administration Research

It is persistence rather than change that characterizes the nature of research articles published in PAR over the past half century. We are inclined to speculate that the reason for this is that public administration has clung self-consciously to its emphasis on practice. Its initial evolution from political science focused heavily on the distinction between practice and scholarship as a justification for the need for a separate field (Caiden, 1984). Tension still persists today between the scholarly interests of political scientists and the practitioner-focused interests of public administrationists where both faculties are housed within the same university department.

If the field of public administration is clinging to its practitioner focus as a justification for its existence within higher education, then such self-consciousness may be self-defeating in the long run. For a variety of reasons discussed in more detail elsewhere, a research agenda for the field is not likely to emerge from the world of everyday practice in the public sector (Stallings, 1986). Furthermore, deferring responsibility for research to other disciplines is risky. It cannot be assumed that they (e.g., sociology or economics) will show any sustained interest in questions relevant to the core concerns of public administration. The emergence of a research agenda for the field will only result from a broader focus than the more limited emphasis on management problems, analyses of policy choices, and evaluation of specific programs. New directions for public administration research will come from asking fundamental questions about the nature of the public sector and its relationship to the wider society of which it is a part.

Ironically, our data show that the majority of research articles published in PAR since 1940 have attempted to define research problems or to conceptualize topics for research. Why has this research not gotten underway? Perhaps we have been dealing with the wrong problems. Perhaps we have been asking the right questions in ways that are not amenable to empirical investigation. Perhaps we have no interest in finding the answers to our questions. Or perhaps we think we already know the answers. Whatever the explanation, two things are clear: (a) we have produced a long list of questions to pursue, and (b) there are numerous research methods available with which to pursue them. What the field of public administration needs is a strategy for coupling important questions with the techniques for answering them.

Notes

1. Another series of papers examines the relationship between faculty research and the prestige of graduate programs in public administration and public affairs. See, for example, Morgan, Meier, Kearney, Hays, and Birch (1981), Morgan and Meier (1982), and Ferris and Stallings (1988).

2. There are lists of books and monographs in the field of public administration. For example, see McCurdy (1986). He uses 81 other listings to determine the most frequently used books and monographs in the field. It is not, however, a random sample of book-length research in the field, but it is a subset of those works that are most influential. Moreover, such a list does not resolve questions involved in identifying a workable source list from which a sample of published research may be drawn. For a discussion of the relationship between universe, sampling frame, and probability sample, see Babbie (1973), especially pages 76-82 and 88-91. It is true, however, that McCurdy's list may be used to look at other research questions. For example, it could be used for examining research approaches and designs used in the subset of works that have been most influential.

3. It is also typically the case that more than one journal from the field or discipline is used. In studies of sociology, for example, the three leading general-interest journals (i.e., *American Sociological Review, American Journal of Sociology,* and *Social Forces*) are used. However, in the field of public administration, only the *Public Administration Review* meets the criteria we set.

4. Another study might usefully examine the evolution of new journals in the field of public administration over time. The creation of new journals around specific subfields may reflect developments and changes of research interests or other dynamics in the field.

5. We thank Judy Erikson, Thomas Mbelu, Eliawony Meena, Masefinela Mphuthins, Daisy de Asper Valdes, Isahak Yeop, and especially Paul David Marsh for their assistance with the coding and preparation of these data.

6. Codes for discrete variables such as those identifying types of research methods must meet two criteria: (a) their categories must be *exhaustive* (i.e., categories must exist for all known variables of the phenomenon), and (b) the categories must be *mutually exclusive* (i.e., there must be one and only one category into which the phenomenon being coded can properly be placed). See Kidder (1981, p. 302). It is the failure to meet this second criterion that constitutes a major weakness in the Perry-Kraemer study. In fairness, the problem lies not so much with Perry and Kraemer themselves but in the work of others whose coding schemes they borrowed. See their reference to Caldwell (1968), Gordon et al. (1974), Rogers and Agarwala-Rogers (1976), and Vogel and Wetherbe (1984). We have recoded some of their data and revised their coding scheme to eliminate other weaknesses and to make more readily understandable the data that we analyzed.

7. This style of research is distinct from that which we have previously characterized as conceptual. It follows in the tradition of naturalistic inquiry evolving out of Max Weber's method of *verstehen*. The general aim of this approach is to reconstruct a *Weltanschaung* from the point of view of actors in an unfolding social setting. For a discussion, see Weber (1949). Of course, as Berger correctly points out, the act of interpretation in this vein does not distinguish qualitative from quantitative research; see Berger and Kellner (1981, pp. 17-55).

8. Affiliation of only the senior author is coded to avoid creating exhaustive and mutually exclusive sets of categories for various combinations of joint authorship that would result in numerous distinctions with very small cell frequencies. The selection of senior authors follows the academic convention of listing as first author the individual who bears the greater (or greatest) responsibility for both the substance and presentation of materials in an article.

9. Although multivariate statistical analyses are only one way of performing causal tests, other causal techniques such as experimental and quasi-experimental designs have been used so infrequently in public administration research that we had too few cases to include in this analysis.

10. Undoubtedly, other hypotheses could be advanced. An interesting topic for investigation would be the comparative analysis of funding patterns across different professional fields and social science disciplines.

11. Comparative data on research published in official journals of other fields such as social work, education, and library science would provide a better sense of the extent to which our findings regarding research in public administration are unique. In other words, trends in published research over time may look "offline" when judged against research published in refereed journals in traditional social science disciplines but at the same time look quite similar to publication patterns in other professional fields. Comparative research on publication patterns across different fields is a worthwhile topic for future research.

8

Public Administration Research: An Assessment of Journal Publications

DAVID J. HOUSTON

SYBIL M. DELEVAN

This article examines the nature of empirical research in six public administration-related journals by focusing on the purpose of published research, as well as the research designs and statistical techniques that are employed. Consistent with previous studies, it is reported that public administration journals disseminate academically oriented research that largely is underfunded, conceptual, and nonempirical and engages in little theory testing. Furthermore, what little empirical research that is published varies with respect to empirical rigor. This study suggests that a cumulative knowledge base is not being developed by public administration scholars, at least not based on social scientific principles.

Since before Luther Gulick (1937) first expressed the need for a "science of administration," the nature of research in public administration has been a major topic of debate (Blankenship, 1967; Dahl, 1947; Honey, 1957; Simon, 1947; Waldo, 1984). A central focus of this debate has been the empirical rigor of published research. For example, methodological critiques offered more than 20 years ago by Frederick Mosher (1956) and Lynton Caldwell (1968) argued that public administration had not channeled its research efforts, lacked a rigorous research methodology, and was far from the creation of an environment in which empirical theories could be developed and tested. Consequently, the field has not systematically produced a cumulative and meaningful body of knowledge.

More recently, methodological critiques based on analyses of published research articles in the *Public Administration Review* have been offered by Perry and Kraemer (1986) and by Stallings and Ferris (1988). These authors have concluded that public administration research has not utilized sophisticated research methods, hence the field is characterized by research that is applied, atheoretical, and noncumulative. However, the question that these studies raise is whether PAR is representative of research conducted throughout the field and a sound source for gauging the nature of public administration research in general.

The purpose of this study is to examine the generalizability of these recent critiques. For this reason, this study examines the nature of empirical research in six public administration-related journals other than PAR. The focus is on the purposes of journal publications, their research designs, and the statistical methods they employ.

Empirical Critiques of
Public Administration Research

Debate concerning the nature of public administration research has developed two emphases (Perry & Kraemer, 1986). The first emphasis challenges the basic social scientific assumptions that many scholars bring to the research process and focuses on what constitutes valid research. This issue is normative, because it examines the methodologies that scholars should be using. Addressing this emphasis, White (1986a) identifies three categories of research: explanatory, critical, and interpretive. Many argue that the last two modes have been ignored in empirical studies of public administration research, but that they are legitimate alternatives to the positivistic social scientific tradition (Catron & Harmon, 1981; Denhardt, 1984; Hummel, 1977; White, 1986a).

The second emphasis in this ongoing debate is concerned with the research that scholars are doing, as well as their current contributions to the development of a theoretically sound and useful body of knowledge. Scholars examining this empirical question accept the social scientific tradition as relevant to the study of public administration. The thrust of these critiques is an assessment of the empirical rigor of public administration research as required by the social scientific approach. Although both emphases are important in this ongoing debate, the present study focuses on the latter aspect.

Recent critiques of published research have called into question the empirical rigor and development of public administration literature (Dunn, 1984; Garson & Overman, 1983; Hedge & Mok, 1987). Even doctoral dissertations are characterized as applied, atheoretical, and lacking in empirical rigor, and thus they have little impact on knowledge in the field (McCurdy & Cleary, 1984; White, 1986b). In general, the conclusion drawn is that research in the field engages in little theory testing and therefore does not contribute to the development of a coherent body of knowledge.

More challenging critiques of public administration research have been offered by studies that have examined the nature of published research in the field's premier journal, PAR. In one such study Perry and Kraemer (1986) found that most of the articles in their sample were at the initial stages of research, that is, identifying problems and variables for future studies. Few projects went beyond this conceptual purpose to engage in empirical theory testing. As a consequence, these published articles do not systematically use social scientific methodologies or their alternatives, and they are underfunded. The result is a body of literature that is primarily applied and noncumulative and that limits the development and testing of empirical theory.

An extension of the Perry and Kraemer study was carried out by Stallings and Ferris (1988), who examined the methodological trends of research published in PAR throughout the journal's history (1940-1984). In their study a similar conclusion was reached: Most research published in PAR is conceptual and not directed toward the development of empirical theory or the testing of causality. In addition, these articles infrequently used the more sophisticated multivariate analyses commonly found in other social scientific journals.

In light of the challenge for research that these critiques offer, an important issue of the generalizability of these results must be addressed. These studies assume that PAR articles are representative of all research published in public administration. Certainly, if one journal is to be the focus of such a study, then PAR is the single best source as it arguably is the premier journal in the field.

It can, however, be argued that research published in PAR is not representative of all public administration research. For example, because PAR is sponsored by the principal professional organization, the American Society for Public Administration (ASPA), it enjoys a wide circulation among academicians and practitioners. It thus must communicate research to individuals with a wide variety of interests and methodological competencies, encouraging the publication of broad articles that can be read by a general audience.

Empirically sophisticated pieces on narrow topics may therefore be sent to other journals where highly specialized articles may have a better chance of acceptance. For these reasons, research published in PAR actually may be less methodologically narrow in application than that published in other journals, thereby underrepresenting empirically sophisticated and cutting-edge research projects. Accordingly, the purpose of this article is to extend previous research on this topic by providing an analysis of research articles published in sources other than PAR.

Data

The data for this project were gathered from a content analysis of published research in six public administration-related academic journals. The journals selected for this analysis include *Administration & Society* (A&S),

Public Administration Quarterly (PAQ), *International Journal of Public Administration* (IJPA), *Public Budgeting and Finance* (PBF), *Review of Public Personnel Administration* (ROPPA), and *Policy Studies Review* (PSR). Three of these journals—A&S, PAQ, and IJPA—were selected to represent general public administration journals other than PAR.[1] The remaining journals were selected as being representative of specialized publications in three prominent areas of the field, that is, budgeting, personnel, and public policy.[2] This sample makes it possible to compare the nature of research in general journals to that published in more specialized ones.

For each journal included, a systematic sample was drawn from all articles and symposium pieces published during the five-year period 1984-1988.[3] A sample of approximately 6 or 7 articles per year was picked from each journal.[4] Thus the total sample is composed of 218 articles from the 6 journals previously identified.

Each article selected was coded according to two general sets of characteristics. The first set addresses general article and author characteristics, such as the number of authors, university affiliation, and academic rank of the principal author,[5] as well as funding support for the research.

The second set of characteristics pertains to the major purpose of the research and the empirical methodology employed. Borrowing from the coding scheme developed by Stallings and Ferris (1988), each article was coded according to its purpose as falling into one of the following three categories: to identify or conceptualize a researchable issue (CONCEPTUAL), to examine relationships among variables (RELATION), or to analyze a particular policy or program (EVALUATE). A second variable was created to represent the type of research design employed in the study and contains the following categories: nonempirical, preexperimental, case study, correlational (nonexperimental), quasi-experimental, and experimental.[6] Additional variables were created to represent the statistical techniques, type of data, and unit of analysis employed in the project.

Findings

This analysis seeks to address several questions regarding the nature of public administration research. The most basic question is straightforward: Who publishes in public administration journals? Descriptive information relevant to this question is provided in Tables 8.1, 8.2, and 8.3. As these tables indicate, public administration research tends to be single-authored and dominated by established academicians (i.e., associate and full professors). Only PBF does not follow this trend because a large portion of its

TABLE 8.1 Number of Authors

	Journals					
Number of Authors	A&S	IJPA	PAQ	PSR	PBF	ROPPA
1	24 (80)	24 (62)	21 (60)	29 (57)	23 (64)	18 (67)
2	4 (13)	9 (23)	9 (26)	17 (33)	13 (36)	7 (26)
3	2 (7)	5 (13)	5 (14)	3 (6)	0 (0)	2 (7)
4	0 (0)	1 (3)	0 (0)	2 (4)	0 (0)	0 (0)
Total	30 (100)	39 (101)	35 (100)	51 (100)	36 (100)	27 (100)

$\chi^2 = 17.670$
$df = 15$
$p = 0.280$
Cramer's V = 0.164

NOTE: Cell entries are frequencies, and numbers in parentheses are column percentages. Percentage totals may not sum to 100 because of rounding.

TABLE 8.2 Principal Author Affiliation

	Journals					
Principal Author Affiliation	A&S	IJPA	PAQ	PSR	PBF	ROPPA
University	30 (100)	38 (97)	30 (86)	47 (94)	22 (61)	26 (96)
Nonuniversity	0 (0)	1 (3)	5 (14)	3 (6)	14 (39)	1 (4)
Total	30 (100)	39 (100)	35 (100)	50 (100)	36 (100)	27 (100)

$\chi^2 = 38.092$
$df = 5$
$p = 0.000$
Cramer's V = 0.419

NOTE: Cell entries are frequencies, and numbers in parentheses are column percentages.

articles are authored by nonacademicians, suggesting that it is a common outlet for research by practitioners.

Beyond these basic descriptive characteristics the level of financial support for public administration studies is an important reputational indicator of the field's research. Thus the second question examined in this study is, What is the frequency of funding for public administration research? As the pattern exhibited in Table 8.4 suggests, the articles in the present sample are largely unfunded. However, this funding pattern varies across journals, as A&S and PSR articles are funded at higher rates than articles in the other four journals, a pattern that is statistically significant ($p = 0.014$).

TABLE 8.3 Academic Rank of Principal Author

Principal Author's Rank	Journals					
	A&S	*IJPA*	*PAQ*	*PSR*	*PBF*	*ROPPA*
Instructor/student	1 (3)	1 (11)	2 (7)	2 (5)	0 (0)	2 (8)
Assistant professor	7 (24)	3 (33)	5 (17)	5 (12)	6 (27)	7 (29)
Associate professor	13 (45)	1 (11)	8 (28)	19 (45)	7 (32)	10 (42)
Professor	8 (28)	4 (44)	14 (48)	16 (38)	9 (41)	5 (21)
Total	29 (100)	9 (100)	29 (100)	42 (100)	22 (100)	24 (100)

$\chi^2 = 13.828$
$df = 15$
$p = 0.539$
Cramer's V = 0.172

NOTE: Cell entries are frequencies, and numbers in parentheses are column percentages. Percentage totals may not sum to 100 because of rounding.

TABLE 8.4 Research Support

Reported Funding	Journals					
	A&S	*IJPA*	*PAQ*	*PSR*	*PBF*	*ROPPA*
Yes	9 (30)	2 (5)	4 (11)	10 (20)	3 (8)	1 (4)
No	21 (70)	37 (95)	31 (89)	41 (80)	33 (92)	26 (96)
Total	30 (100)	39 (100)	35 (100)	51 (100)	36 (100)	27 (100)

$\chi^2 = 14.304$
$df = 5$
$p = 0.014$
Cramer's V = 0.256

NOTE: Cell entries are frequencies, and numbers in parentheses are column percentages.

Table 8.5 compares this funding pattern for the sample of public administration articles examined to that reported by research articles in the principal journals of four related social science disciplines: generic management (*Administrative Science Quarterly*, or ASQ), political science (*American Political Science Review*, or APSR), sociology (*American Sociological Review*, or ASR), and economics (*American Economic Review*, or AER). The data for these four journals represent reported sources of funding for the universe of articles published during the period 1984-1988.[7]

Table 8.5 indicates that public administration research is funded at a much lower rate than that of the other disciplines, a finding that is statistically

TABLE 8.5 Source of Funding Across Social Science Journals

	Journals				
Source of Funding	P.A. Journals	ASQ	APSR	ASR	AER
None	189 (87)	59 (53)	122 (51)	116 (38)	198 (51)
University	14 (6)	13 (12)	16 (7)	35 (12)	19 (5)
External	14 (6)	22 (20)	86 (36)	117 (39)	130 (34)
University and external	1 (1)	18 (16)	36 (6)	35 (12)	38 (10)
Total	218 (100)	112 (101)	239 (100)	303 (101)	385 (100)

$\chi^2 = 152.908$
$df = 12$
$p < 0.001$
Cramer's V = 0.206

NOTE: Cell entries are frequencies, and numbers in parentheses are column percentages. Percentage totals may not sum to 100 because of rounding.

significant ($p < 0.001$). Whereas only 13.3% of the public administration articles in this sample reported financial support, at least 47% of those articles published in these other social science journals acknowledge funding. Furthermore, external funding sources are used heavily by scholars in these other disciplines but largely are untapped sources for public administration scholars. This finding suggests that the funding picture for public administration research is even worse than previous studies have concluded (Perry & Kraemer, 1986; Stallings & Ferris, 1988).

The third question relevant to this study of public administration literature is, What is the major purpose of the published research? The data in Table 8.6 address this question by reporting the purpose of the research articles published in each journal. As was found in previous studies, public administration literature is dominated by articles intended primarily to develop conceptual issues for future research (CONCEPTUAL). Less frequent are empirical efforts to examine relationships among variables and thus to test empirical theories (RELATION). Even less frequent is the evaluation of public policy (EVALUATE).

However, this pattern is not consistent across the journals sampled in this study, indicating statistically significant differences ($p = 0.001$) in the focus among these public administration journals. Among the general journals, IJPA publishes more research directed toward theory testing than either A&S or PAQ. A more obvious difference exists among the three specialized journals, because ROPPA is a frequent publisher of empirical research, while PBF and PSR largely publish conceptual papers.

TABLE 8.6 Purpose of Article

	Journals					
Purpose	*A&S*	*IJPA*	*PAQ*	*PSR*	*PBF*	*ROPPA*
Conceptual	22 (73)	21 (54)	23 (68)	37 (74)	25 (76)	8 (30)
Relation	8 (27)	14 (36)	8 (24)	8 (16)	5 (15)	18 (67)
Evaluate	0 (0)	4 (10)	3 (9)	5 (10)	3 (9)	1 (4)
Total	30 (100)	39 (100)	34 (101)	50 (100)	33 (100)	27 (101)

$\chi^2 = 30.955$
$df = 10$
$p = 0.001$
Cramer's V = 0.270

NOTE: Cell entries are frequencies, and numbers in parentheses are column percentage. Percentage totals may not sum to 100 because of rounding.

The trends in public administration research identified thus far support the findings of previous studies; that is, public administration research typically is directed by academicians of senior rank, with little financial support, for the purpose of identifying and delineating problems and concepts for future research. However, it would be premature to conclude at this point that public administration scholars do not engage in rigorous empirical research. To address the issue of the quality of the field's empirical research, it is first necessary to examine the rigor and sophistication of the empirical research that is conducted.

This leads to a fourth question: What methodologies are employed by empirical studies in public administration literature? This question is addressed by examining the research designs, statistical techniques, type of data, and unit of analysis used in these published articles. Because of the small number of articles classified as testing relationships empirically ($n = 61$), these articles (RELATION) are treated together in one category and are not disaggregated by journal.

The most basic issue related to the nature of empirical research addresses the research designs that are employed in these studies. It is generally accepted among social scientists that studies testing theoretical propositions should utilize experimental, quasi-experimental, or correlational designs (with appropriate statistical tools).[8] The data reported in Table 8.7 indicate that correlational designs are the most commonly used and that these studies make little use of the more sophisticated quasi-experimental and experimental designs.

An examination of the statistical tools employed in these articles is presented in Table 8.8. Statistical techniques serve three main functions in the conduct

TABLE 8.7 Research Designs Used in RELATION Articles

Research Design	Frequency
Preexperimental	2 (3)
Case study	4 (7)
Correlational	51 (84)
Quasi-experimental	1 (2)
Experimental	3 (5)
Total	61 (101)

NOTE: The numbers in parentheses are percentages. Percentage total does not sum to 100 because of rounding.

TABLE 8.8 Statistical Techniques Used in RELATION Articles (N = 61)

Statistic	Frequency
Univariate	37 (61)
Bivariate correlation	20 (33)
Crosstabs	22 (36)
Chi-square	4 (7)
ANOVA	3 (5)
Bivariate regression	1 (2)
MANOVA	1 (2)
Multivariate regression	25 (41)
Path analysis	3 (5)
Factor analysis	5 (8)
Nonlinear regression	1 (2)
Other	3 (5)

NOTE: The numbers in parentheses are percentages. Multiple techniques were employed by researchers in many projects, accounting for the percentage total.

of social scientific research: description, inference, and control (Blalock, 1979, pp. 4-7). The frequent use of univariate statistics (e.g., frequency distribution, mean, standard deviation) indicates that description is a common function served by statistics in public administration research.

The second use of statistics is to make inferences about a population based on the observed behavior of a sample (Blalock, 1979, pp. 4-7). The degree to which statistics serve this function is represented here by the use of statistical hypothesis testing as reported in Table 8.9. Of the 61 RELATION articles in this analysis, 42 (68.9%) reported the use of statistical hypothesis testing, indicating that statistical tools are commonly used to make inferences from a sample to a population.

The third function of statistics, to control for plausible rival hypotheses, is important in public administration research given the frequent use of

TABLE 8.9 Statistical Hypothesis Testing in RELATION Articles

Article Reports Hypothesis Testing	Frequency
Yes	42 (69)
No	19 (31)
Total	61 (100)

NOTE: The numbers in parentheses are percentages.

TABLE 8.10 Level of Statistical Techniques Used in RELATION Articles

Level of Statistical Technique	Frequency
None	1 (2)
Univariate	7 (11)
Bivariate	17 (28)
Multivariate	36 (59)
Total	61 (100)

NOTE: The numbers in parentheses are percentages.

correlational designs (Nachmias & Nachmias, 1987, pp. 133-136). With the absence of random assignment and control groups that characterize experimental designs, correlational designs must rely on multivariate statistics to serve this control function. As previously identified in Table 8.8, multiple regression was the most common multivariate technique used within the sample in this study.

The data reported in Table 8.10 take this examination one step further, because this frequency distribution represents the highest level of statistics reported in an article. An article classified as univariate reported only univariate statistics, whereas one classified as bivariate used bivariate but not multivariate techniques. This table indicates that a fair number of articles examined in this study use multivariate techniques ($n = 36$ or 60%). Twenty-four articles (40%) report only bivariate or univariate techniques and thus do not use statistics to serve the function of control. This finding is somewhat troublesome given the frequency with which correlational research designs are used in this sample of articles.

Lastly, Tables 8.11 and 8.12 provide a description of the type of data used in empirical public administration research. As would be expected with the common use of correlational designs, most articles in the sample use cross-sectional data, with few longitudinal studies undertaken. In addition, most of this research used the individual as the primary unit of analysis.

TABLE 8.11 Type of Data Used in RELATION Articles

Type of Data	Frequency
No data set used	1 (2)
Cross-sectional	45 (74)
Longitudinal	5 (8)
Cross-sectional and longitudinal	10 (16)
Total	61 (100)

NOTE: The numbers in parentheses are percentages.

TABLE 8.12 Primary Unit of Analysis for RELATION Articles

Primary Unit of Analysis	Frequency
Individual	33 (54)
Group/organization	9 (15)
City/county	6 (10)
State	9 (15)
Nation	1 (2)
Other	3 (5)
Total	61 (101)

NOTE: The numbers in parentheses are percentages. Percentage total does not sum to 100 because of rounding.

Discussion

In general, the findings of this study support the argument that public administration research is engaged in little theory testing. Published articles tend to represent research that is in its early conceptual phase, identifying concepts and issues for future research. Sound theory, however, is developed only through the testing and refining of empirical propositions derived from theory. Perhaps the persistent lack of empirical research explains the gap that exists between theory and practice, accounting for the often muttered phrase, "That's fine in theory, but it doesn't work that way in practice."

The type of empirical research conducted suggests that what little theory testing is done is rather basic in nature. This is the case as the projects examined in this study almost exclusively rely on correlational designs, which do not permit the study of behavior over time or the strategic control of external factors influencing the relationships under study. In addition, a number of empirical articles in this sample report only univariate and bivariate statistics, suggesting that the causal arguments drawn from these projects are weak, because plausible rival hypotheses often cannot be dismissed. Even the infrequent use of more advanced causal modeling or nonlinear statistical techniques indicates that only simple linear theories are being tested by public administration scholars.

Several reasons can be offered to explain the findings reported here. First, this analysis could be criticized for too narrowly defining research that engages in theory testing. The social scientific perspective on which this analysis is based may bias this study in a way that ignores the use of alternative methodologies (e.g., critical theory or interpretive theory). However, previous research has found little to suggest that these alternative methodological frameworks are being employed (White, 1986b). It is also important to note that only five articles were identified in this sample that explicitly used an alternative methodology.[9] This further suggests that alternatives to the social scientific approach are not systematically used in public administration literature.

Several additional reasons can be offered to explain the current state of public administration research. In part, the historical character of the field with its focus on practice may well contribute to a lack of theoretical research. The field traditionally has been viewed as a training ground for the public service and has focused on the importance of practice as separate from academic inquiry (Caiden, 1984). This has led public administration programs to adopt multiple missions that require not only academic research of public administration faculty but also professional service (Perry & Kraemer, 1986). In this respect public administration has "clung self-consciously" to an emphasis on practice, thereby hindering its intellectual development (Stallings & Ferris, 1988).

Also, a perceived antiquantitative bias exists among some public administration scholars, further reducing the use of these techniques in published literature (McCurdy & Cleary, 1984). In part because of the partial separation between public administration and political science, scholars in public administration have resisted use of techniques that are associated with the behavioral revolution in general and political science in particular. This has resulted in the expressed need that public administration must develop its own qualitative methods.

A more methodological explanation relates to the availability of data that can be used empirically to test theories. Few data sets are collected to facilitate numerous or long-term studies of administrative phenomena. One indicator of this lack of available data is the Inter-University Consortium for Political and Social Research (ICPSR) *Guide to Resources and Services, 1988-1989,* which devotes only 6 out of 568 pages to describing data sets under the topical heading "Organizational Behavior."[10] Available data are either at the individual level or aggregated to the city, state, or national level. This is most likely the result of the difficulty of collecting data in an organization and across organizations (Dunn, 1984). Because many theories developed in public administration address the behavior of individuals or groups in organizations, a mismatch exists between the unit of analysis and the theory being tested. Thus scholars are left to collect their own data for each study and, subsequently, are discouraged in the undertaking of empirical research.

More fundamentally, the current state of research may be an indication that the field lacks a broad theoretical framework or paradigm to guide and inspire scholars. Vincent Ostrom (1974) argued that American public administration is in a state of crisis that is "invoked by the insufficiency of the paradigms inherent in . . . traditional theory," and he directed attention to the need for an alternative paradigm to solve this "intellectual crisis" (pp. 16-17). More recently, Howard E. McCurdy (1986) wrote of the public administration literature as possessing "no unifying theory . . . to help guide the investigator" (p. iii). Public administration scholars, therefore, may not possess the basic theoretical frameworks for guiding the systematic identification of significant research questions, much less the selection of appropriate hypotheses and research tools to answer the questions put forth. This situation has contributed to a lack of theory building, as well as the noncumulative nature of the research that characterizes public administration literature.

To address these problematic issues, several things can be done. First, public administration scholars must seek to agree on the acceptable criteria and research tools for determining valid research. This would entail the acceptance and development of both quantitative and qualitative methodologies as complementary, rather than contradictory tools. Second, more effort must be focused on the collection of data to support the testing of theories on organizational or administrative behavior. Third, the role of doctoral programs in the preparation of future scholars must be settled to ensure more systematic preparation of students in the theories and methods relevant to scholarship in the field. Lastly, more debate must take place assessing the "crisis of identity" that Ostrom identified, leading to the development of general theoretical frameworks to guide research in a manner that existing theories cannot.

Conclusion

Several general conclusions can be drawn from this analysis that are consistent with the findings of Perry and Kraemer (1986) and Stallings and Ferris (1988). First, public administration journals generally represent a source for the dissemination of academically oriented research. Second, public administration research generally receives an even lower level of financial support than has been previously determined. Third, this published research generally focuses on the conceptual development of issues for future research and is nonempirical.

The conclusion that can be drawn from this last finding is that public administration is engaged in little empirical theory testing and building. This situation is troublesome. For any discipline to mature it must have at its base a solid research foundation. Moreover, this study suggests that such a cumulative knowledge base is not being developed, at least not based on social scientific principles.

The latter point is not meant to imply that no empirical research devoted to the testing of theory is being conducted. A small amount of such theory testing is undertaken and often possesses methodological rigor. The problem is that these studies are the exception and not the rule. The maturing of public administration as a discipline requires a change, because the field must engage in more empirical theory development than currently is the case.

Additional questions can be raised regarding the nature of public administration research; these, however, are beyond the scope of this analysis. A more focused study of the use of qualitative techniques would help overcome the limitations of recent studies that have largely focused on quantitative research as relevant to theory building. Furthermore, an underlying assumption of this present study is that research on public administration is conducted by public administration scholars and is published in public administration journals. Additional studies could focus on research conducted by scholars who are not in public administration programs or who publish in journals that are not traditional public administration journals. Addressing these and other related questions will offer a more complete picture of the nature of public administration research. Such an understanding will lead to the identification of factors that influence the nature of public administration research and ultimately overcome some problems that plague scholars in the field.

Notes

1. The goal of this selection was to identify journals that were representative of the entire field and not to select journals that maximized a qualitative criteria such as prestige or impact. Such assessments of journal quality are difficult to make because variations are likely to occur across individuals, years, and operationalizations of quality. For example, see Colson (1990) and Vocino and Elliott (1982, 1984). For this reason, journals in this category were selected based on two criteria: (a) publication of articles on a broad range of topics in the field, and (b) being well established (i.e., continued publication for the past 10 years).

2. The specialized journals were chosen to represent established publications in each subfield. For this reason, PBF and ROPPA were selected because they are the sponsored journals of the budgeting and personnel sections of ASPA. PSR was randomly chosen from among three journals (PSR, *Policy Studies Journal,* and *Journal of Policy Analysis and Management*), which are the

journals sponsored by the two leading policy organizations, Policy Studies Organization and Association for Public Policy Analysis and Management.

3. Editorials, speeches, introductions to symposia, and book reviews were omitted from this analysis because their primary purpose generally is not the contribution of original research to literature.

4. A sample frame equal to four articles, or a sampling ratio of 1 to 4, was used for each year. Because the number of articles per year varies among the journals, the sample size also varies for each journal.

5. For coauthored articles, the first author listed is considered the principal author. Data not reported here indicate that first authors are representative of all authors for these articles in terms of university affiliation and academic rank.

6. Although the case study is considered a type of preexperimental design (Campbell & Stanley, 1963), here it will be coded separately because of its assumed common use throughout public administration literature.

7. Published articles and research notes are included in this analysis.

8. These categories of research designs are distinguishable by their internal validity. The higher a design's internal validity, the more confident one can be about the causal arguments that are made on the basis of a study's findings. Of these three categories, experimental designs are the most internally valid and correlational designs are the least internally valid.

9. An article was determined as having used an alternative methodology if the author identified in the text that she or he was doing so or if several references were cited that dealt with an alternative methodology.

10. The ICPSR is a major source of data sets addressing social phenomena. Although data sets listed under other headings in this guide may be relevant to public administration, the small number of data sets under the heading "Organizational Behavior" gives a rough indication of the number of data sets created for the primary purpose of studying organizational phenomena.

PART 3

Assessments of Doctoral Research and Education

Doctoral education in the most fundamental sense is the means by which an academic discipline or field reproduces itself. The quality of doctoral education—and the quality and techniques of research approaches learned—determines to a considerable degree the future progress of the field. It follows that the discussion of research within public administration would turn to doctoral education and research, and this is the focus of Part 3. Indeed, the recently renewed and heightened debate on research in public administration was fueled in part by the publication of an article titled "Why Can't We Resolve the Research Issue in Public Administration?" (McCurdy & Cleary, 1984). McCurdy and Cleary examined doctoral dissertation research and found that "[f]ew of these doctoral projects meet the criteria that conventionally define careful systematic study, in the social sciences" (1984, p. 50). Moreover, according to their analysis, most of the dissertation research did not address an issue of importance to the field. Cleary's more recent examination of doctoral research in Chapter 10 captures the essence of the work he did with McCurdy 10 years ago.

   In Chapter 9, Jay D. White replicates the work of McCurdy and Cleary to see if public administration dissertation research was as bad as they said it was. He finds that it was. Roughly half of the dissertations did not conform to the standards of mainstream social science research. He also finds that close to half of the dissertations did not pretend to be in the mainstream. They appeared to be a mix of theoretical arguments, histories, and descriptions of some administrative or policy event. More important, he could not tell if the nonmainstream research was guided by some alternative methodological or philosophical framework, which it should be but probably was not. On the assumption that dissertation research might lead to publications in scholarly journals, White also tracked the publications of a sample of dissertation authors only to discover that very few of them have published anything since receiving their terminal degree. He concludes that dissertation research does not seem to be a major source of knowledge in the field.

Robert E. Cleary claims in Chapter 10 that the quality of doctoral dissertation research in public administration has improved over the past decade. Applying the methods and criteria he and McCurdy (1984) used earlier on dissertations completed in 1981 to dissertations completed in 1990, Cleary finds the most recent group to be "in total and on the average, superior research projects." One area where there has been little improvement is in the selection of topics, and he argues that attention should now be given to the subject matter addressed in dissertations.

Robert A. Stallings, a sociologist by education, lends an "outsider's" perspective on doctoral research in Chapter 11. He argues that research problems in the field should be determined by the analytic form of public-sector activity rather than by the substantive content of specific events. The recognition that firsthand experience in the world of practice results only in an "acquaintance with" type of knowledge, according to Stallings, is prerequisite to achieving a more constructive relationship among theory, research, and practice. The methods of research rather than the techniques of management provide the analytical skills necessary for theoretically significant inquiry.

9

Dissertations and Publications in Public Administration

JAY D. WHITE

Surveys of more than 300 dissertation abstracts raise serious questions about the quality of dissertation research in public administration. The primary issues center on the proper scope and methods for dissertation research. The question of scope necessarily entails drawing a boundary around what is in and outside the domain of legitimate research topics. The question of method raises issues about what constitutes valid knowledge in public administration and how such knowledge grows. At present, neither scope nor method is well defined.

These questions are addressed here in three ways. First, recent dissertation research is examined to show the types of dissertations being done and to assess their quality. Second, the results of an analysis of the influence of dissertation research on journal publications is presented to demonstrate how little of this research is publicly communicated. Third, metatheoretical issues involved in writing a dissertation are discussed, focusing on improvement of research and the growth of knowledge in public administration.

The ideas presented here should contribute to an ongoing dialogue about the proper nature of research in public administration. Such dialogue is the essence of scientific rationality, which is presupposed by all research efforts that claim to contribute to our stock of knowledge.

Howard E. McCurdy and Robert E. Cleary (1984) examined 142 dissertation abstracts published in the 1981 edition of *Dissertation Abstracts International* (DAI). Using the criteria of purpose, validity, theory testing and causal relationships, central importance of topic, and leading edge importance of topic, they concluded that "[f]ew of those doctoral projects meet the criteria that conventionally define careful, systematic study in the social sciences" (1984, p. 50). They were in search of mainstream social science research, and they found little of high quality. My casual reading of more than 400 abstracts dating from 1979 to 1984 suggests the same pattern. A more formal examination of their data base and an additional 163 abstracts published in the 1980 edition of DAI leads me to agree with their general conclusion.[1]

In examining McCurdy and Cleary's sample year, I discovered some different results and some conflicts of interpretation. For example, 37% of the 1981 sample dissertations satisfied my test of validity, where McCurdy and Cleary report only 21% as meeting their test of validity. Similarly, by my reading 83% were of central importance, while they reported only 45% of the dissertations as addressing topics or subjects of direct importance to the field. We were closer on the other criteria. Obviously I was looking for something different in assessing validity, and I cast a wider net around topics of importance. The methodological comment at the end of this chapter gives a detailed account of how we differed on each criterion and also addresses some of the issues of using abstracts as a basis for information about dissertations.

The following criteria were used to examine 305 abstracts published in 1980 and 1981 (see Table 9.1).[2]

1. Purpose: Could the purpose of the dissertation be inferred from its title or from statements in the abstract?

2. Validity: Could validity be inferred from statements about research design, sampling techniques, sample size, experimental or quasi-experimental methods, or statistical controls?

3. Theory Testing: Could theory testing be inferred from statements about testing existing theories or developing theoretical frameworks from literature reviews or field research?

4. Hypothesis Testing: Was there any mention of hypotheses, hypothesis testing, or even model development and testing?

5. Causality: Was there any discussion of causal relationships or of any key words (e.g., correlations, independent and dependent variables, multivariate analysis, etc.) that might suggest a search for causal relationships?

These criteria differ from McCurdy and Cleary's, but they are still consistent with the conduct of mainstream social research.

Although my criteria are perhaps more generous than McCurdy and Cleary's, the results of the analysis are not more encouraging. Ninety percent of the abstracts suggested a clear research purpose. Only 29% satisfied the criterion of validity. Only 39% suggested that an established theory was tested. Only 38% seemed to involve some form of hypothesis testing. Finally, only 30% suggested a concern for causality.

If these criteria have validity, they can be used as a measure of the scientific quality of dissertation research. Unfortunately, the results are alarming from this perspective. Data in Table 9.2 indicate that in all only 16% satisfied all

TABLE 9.1 Percentage of Dissertations Satisfying the Criteria

	Year		
Criteria	1981	1980	Total
Purpose	86% (122)	93% (151)	90% (273)
Validity	37% (53)	21% (35)	29% (88)
Theory testing	29% (41)	48% (79)	39% (120)
Hypothesis testing	42% (60)	34% (56)	38% (116)
Causality	34% (48)	26% (42)	30% (90)
N	142	163	305

TABLE 9.2 Percentage of Dissertations Satisfying the Criteria

	Year		
Number of Criteria	1981	1980	Total
Five	15% (21)	17% (27)	16% (49)
Four	19% (27)	9% (15)	14% (42)
Three	7% (10)	6% (10)	7% (20)
Two	12% (17)	25% (41)	19% (58)
One	35% (49)	36% (59)	35% (108)
None	13% (18)	7% (11)	10% (29)
N	142	163	305

five criteria, 14% satisfied four criteria, 7% satisfied three criteria, 19% satisfied two of the criteria, 35% satisfied only one criterion, and 10% satisfied none of the criteria. Thus it would seem that only 37% of the dissertations satisfied three or more of the criteria and that 63% satisfied three or fewer criteria.

More than half of the dissertations failed to meet more than two criteria. This can be explained in part by the presence of 20 theoretical dissertations, 116 histories or descriptions of some political or administrative event, and reports on the development of 7 mathematical models. Thus 143 (or 47%) of the authors did not set out to do mainstream social science research.

Of the nonmainstream research projects, eight abstracts mentioned participant observation as a research method and several involved field research, but only one mentioned a specific alternative methodological framework (ethnomethodology) as a guide to research. A handful were reports of action research projects that follow a more or less established procedure for organizational change. None of these abstracts mentioned a specific philosophical framework such as phenomenology, hermeneutics, critical theory, or analytical philosophy as a methodological grounding. Nonmainstream dissertations have a legitimate place in public administration but not without an anchor in an alternative philosophical framework or method. A few of these nonmainstream dissertations were clearly in the realm of political theory where scholarship is defined in terms of logical analysis and persuasive argument. Given that much of our knowledge in public administration is a matter of political theory, it was surprising to find so few dissertations of this nature.

Seventy-one dissertations fall into the broad category of a policy or program evaluation. Forty of these projects were case studies. In general, these dissertations tried to assess the effect of a specific policy initiative or program change, either within a single organization or political jurisdiction or across organizations or political jurisdictions. Fourteen (39%) of these policy evaluations satisfied three or more criteria, suggesting some sophistication in their methodology and that some confidence could be assigned to their conclusions. The others were descriptions, histories, or conceptual analyses, perhaps rich in interpretive insights but lacking confidence that their conclusions could be generalized to other situations.

Eighty-three (27%) of the doctoral research projects were what McCurdy and Cleary call "practitioner" dissertations. They addressed specific management issues in a single agency or simply drew data from a single agency. An example of this type of dissertation might be a report on a state agency's experience with zero base budgeting (ZBB). In a few cases one could reasonably guess that the author was employed by the agency and was a significant actor in whatever process or set of events was reported in the dissertation. Agency experience can be a rich source of information about public administration, but serious questions can be raised about how knowledge from these dissertations is shared with the rest of the field.

The occurrence of a practitioner dissertation degree could not be predicted by whether the candidate received a Ph.D. or a DPA degree. The latter is sometimes thought of as a practitioner's degree, but several of the Ph.D. dissertations were of the practitioner type, while several of the DPA dissertations were more academic in nature.

The National Association of Schools of Public Affairs and Administration (NASPAA) offers a *Matrix of Professional Competencies* as a guide for the development of professional master's degree programs in public affairs and administration. If this matrix is taken as defining the scope of the field, then 10% (17) of the dissertations were clearly outside public administration. Some of these studies fall within the domain of general political science or some other field or discipline. An example would be a study of voting behavior within a political jurisdiction. Other studies were simply made in a public organization with no specific link to public administration issues. An example might be a study of job satisfaction in a welfare agency where the agency seemed to represent only a convenience sample.

Dissertations were written in departments of political science, public administration, management, and business and in independent schools or colleges of public affairs or administration. Some of the research reflected the author's institutional home. For example, a few of the dissertations written in political science departments focused on more traditional political science issues such as voting behavior or the politics of the budgetary process. Some of the dissertations written in schools or colleges of public affairs focused on broad policy initiatives or were policy or program evaluations. This gives the impression that the institutional location of public administration education has some influence on the topics chosen for research.

The overall pattern of doctoral research is consistent with the fact that public administration research can focus on a variety of topics, typically the domain of other fields or disciplines. For example, there were dissertations on burnout, administrative law, budgeting, presidential power, voting behavior, education, comparative administration, role conflict and ambiguity, affirmative action, collective bargaining, operations research, terrorism, science policy, health policy, organizational change and development, professionalism, information management, water resource projects, bureaucracy, and so on. Many of the dissertations could just as easily be listed under DAI's field headings of political science, sociology, business administration, management, educational administration, social work, and urban and regional planning. Obviously, public administration is a field comprising many topics, and dissertation research responds to this.

McCurdy and Cleary seem to be correct in their assessment of dissertation research in public administration. Roughly half of the research does not conform to the standards of mainstream social science and therefore does not have the potential to contribute to the growth of knowledge in public administration, at least as knowledge is defined from the mainstream perspective. Close to half of the dissertations do not pretend to be mainstream. Unfortunately, it is not clear what they pretend to be beyond a few theoretical dissertations and many histories or descriptions of some administrative or policy event. Elsewhere (White, 1986a), I have criticized the notion that mainstream social science is the only way to contribute knowledge to the field and have argued for interpretive and critical approaches to knowledge acquisition and use. The histories and descriptions as well as the theoretical dissertations may have the potential to be interpretive and critical modes of research, but this cannot be determined from reading the abstracts because they make no explicit reference to alternative methodologies or philosophical frameworks.

Two interrelated questions emerge from this analysis of dissertation research:

1. Should all dissertation research conform to the standards of mainstream social science?
2. Are there topics of importance to the field of public administration that need to be addressed from an alternative methodological framework?

An affirmative answer to the first question means that mainstream methodology and technique will drive the research process. This may be putting the cart before the horse if the second question is answered affirmatively. If mainstream research methods are given priority, then some important topics may not be addressed. If the topics are given priority, then questions of method and technique must be adapted to the specific situation. Some of those topics may not call for a mainstream approach but may deserve examination anyway. However, this does not absolve the researcher from the responsibility of seeking out a legitimate alternative approach.

Analysis of Influence

To see what influence dissertation research has on the growth of knowledge in public administration, an analysis was conducted to discover what dissertation research is published, how many successful doctoral candidates have subsequently published, and whether or not their publications have been related to their dissertations. Unfortunately, the major findings are that few dissertations from the sample gave rise to articles, and few of the authors have published in scholarly journals. Assuming that these samples are representative across several years, then it seems that requiring someone to write a dissertation is no guarantee that knowledge in the field will increase.

The names of the dissertation authors from the 1980 and 1981 DAI data bases were traced electronically through the *Social Science Citation Index* (SSCI) from 1978 to 1985.[3] These years were chosen to remain consistent with the prior research and on the assumption that plenty of time should be given to an author to transform dissertation research into published material. Comparisons were made between the title of the author's dissertation and the titles of the author's publications to see if any connection could be made. A wide net was cast on the assumption that the dissertation research minimally sparked a research question or idea that was developed after the dissertation.

Data in Table 9.3 shows that only 25% of the 305 dissertation authors have published at least one item in a journal listed in SSCI.[4] Little difference exists between the years. Twenty-seven percent of the 1980 dissertation authors have published at least one item. Twenty-two percent of the 1981 authors have pub-

TABLE 9.3 Dissertations and Publications

Item	1981	1980	Total
Dissertations	142	163	305
Published authors	31 (22%)	44 (27%)	75 (25%)
Total publications	83	128	211
Publications related to dissertation topic	38 (46%)	67 (52%)	105 (50%)
Publications outside PA	7 (8%)	13 (10%)	20 (9%)

TABLE 9.4 Comparison of Types of Publications (%)

	1981	1980	Total
Refereed articles	59% (49)	65% (83)	63% (132)
Book reviews	35% (29)	29% (37)	31% (66)
Symposium articles	2% (2)	<1% (1)	1% (3)
Research notes	4% (3)	5% (7)	5% (10)
Total publications	100% (83)	100% (128)	100% (211)

lished at least one item. There were 211 publications in all. This figure excludes four nonrefereed articles in trade magazines and four foreign publications.

Of the total publications, 50% were in the same general topic area as the dissertation research. Thus only half of the publications were directly related to the dissertation research. In addition, 9% of the publications were not in the field of public administration. This brings the total dissertation contribution to the field down to 191 publications.

A look at the patterns of publication after writing the dissertation is alarming. Only 2% (4) of the 1980 dissertation authors and 4% (6) of the 1981 dissertation authors have published four or more items. In all, only 3% of the 305 dissertation authors demonstrate a sustained commitment to scholarly research and publication. Without information about other fields or disciplines, the significance of these data is difficult to determine, but it does not seem to be a strong contribution given the amount of time and energy that went into producing 305 dissertations.

Among the 211 publications, there were 132 refereed articles, 3 symposium articles, 66 book reviews, and 10 research notes or comments (see Table 9.4). At first glance, 211 publications does not seem to be a weak publication record. A closer look at each type of publication is in order.

The 132 articles were contributed by 65 authors. This means that only 21% of the 305 dissertation authors have published a refereed article. Of the

132 articles, 46% (61) were coauthored. Only 70 of the 132 articles were in the same subject area as the author's dissertation. Thus it would seem that only 53% of the articles have the potential to contain knowledge or information that was developed in writing the dissertation.

Perhaps the most surprising finding here was that 12 people are responsible for 52, or almost 40%, of the journal articles; one person contributed eight articles, one person contributed seven articles, one person contributed five articles, seven people each contributed four articles, and four people each contributed three articles. These 12 major contributors of journal articles represent only 4% of the total 305 dissertation authors. One wonders if those dissertation authors who published fewer than three refereed journal articles are looking forward to tenure and will get it. This is probably unlikely at an institution that stresses research.

An examination of the other published items reveals a similar pattern. Of the 66 book reviews, only 21 (56%) were in the same topic area as the author's dissertation, and 9 of the book reviews (14%) were not related to public administration. Only 5 of the 10 research notes were related to a dissertation topic, and another research note was not related to public administration. None of the three symposium articles (of which one was coauthored) were related to the author's dissertation. It is clear that a few individuals (23% of the published authors and 5% of all dissertation authors) were selected to do book reviews on the basis of their dissertation research. Of these seven book review authors, five have published journal articles. A book review is an indirect outlet for the knowledge acquired by an author during dissertation research. Again very little of the knowledge acquired by the 305 dissertation authors has found its way into publication, even by this indirect route.

A look at where this material appeared is interesting. The *Public Administration Review* published 22 articles and 5 book reviews. One person contributed 4 articles, and another person contributed 2 articles. Thus two people are responsible for 27% of the articles in the leading journal in the field. The *American Political Science Review* published 1 article and 22 book reviews. The *Policy Studies Journal* published 3 articles, 3 book reviews, and one research note. *Public Personnel Management* published 6 articles, 3 book reviews, and 3 symposium articles. The *Academy of Management Review* published 1 article and 2 book reviews. The *Bureaucrat* and *State Government* each published five articles. Two articles appeared in *Administration & Society*. There was a smattering of publications in related journals of interest such as *Administrative Science Quarterly,* the *Journal of Politics,* and *Urban Affairs Quarterly.* There were also a few publications appearing in journals more removed from public administration such as *Exceptional Children, Gerontologist, Medical Care, Mental Retardation, Current Anthro-*

pology, Judicature, Growth and Change, Studies in Comparative Communism, and *Pest Control.*

On the basis of this analysis, it seems fair to conclude that most research from the 305 dissertations was not communicated beyond a small group of people, namely, the dissertation committee. There are several possible reasons for this: (1) The topic was of little importance to anyone but the author and maybe one or two members of the dissertation committee; (2) the research was of such low quality that it did not get published; (3) although possibly of high quality, the research might not have been suitable for general publication (as in the case of an agency-specific program evaluation); (4) the research may have been outside the mainstream of social science and had difficulty being accepted; (5) outlets for public administration research may be too limited; (6) the author may have been "burned out" from writing the dissertation and may never write again or may take more time to get back to writing; or (7) the author had no interest in publishing (perhaps because the author did not pursue an academic career). Whatever the reason, dissertation research does not seem to be a major source of knowledge in the field.

Metatheoretical Issues

The choice of a topic and the selection of research methods are the two central questions that must be satisfactorily answered by the author and the dissertation committee. However, no independent and universal criteria can be used to answer these questions. Instead, issues about the legitimacy of a topic and appropriate research methods must be resolved by all parties to the dissertation through reasoned argumentation influenced by possibly differing beliefs and values. This argument comes from the postpositivist philosophy of science that traditionally addresses such metatheoretical issues.

Philosophers of science once believed that the truth of a scientific hypothesis, generalization, or theory could be ascertained by strict adherence to the rules of inductive and deductive explanation or by correspondence to an objective "thing" language devoid of any theoretical interpretation. Some influential contemporary philosophers of science (Bernstein, 1982) have rejected these guarantors of truth and rationality because they fail to resolve issues of incommensurability among theories, research programs, and paradigms.

The history of science has shown that when two theories are in contention for the explanation of the same phenomenon or when one theory does not logically contain the other, the choice of one theory over another is made not by appeal to universal and independent criteria of truth and rationality but rather by appeal to a more or less stable set of values such as "accuracy, consistency, scope, simplicity, and fruitfulness" (Kuhn, 1977, pp. 321-322).[5] This does not mean, however, that theory choice is merely a matter of personal preference and is therefore irrational or nonrational. Such decisions entail communication, deliberation, argumentation, and judgment. They are a matter of practical discourse where reasons are offered for choosing one theory over another.

Decisions about legitimate topics and appropriate methods for dissertation research are of the same logical type as decisions about accepting or rejecting a theory, research program, or paradigm. Given any group of committee members, there exists a potential for incommensurable positions regarding topics of dissertation research and how the research should proceed. There is also the potential to work through legitimate differences to support high quality research.

The members of the dissertation committees must decide if a proposed topic falls within the scope of public administration and the methods appropriate for its study. Each party to the decision will be influenced by his or her beliefs about the terrain of public administration and by his or her standards for research. For any proposed topic or method, more or less good or bad reasons can be given to support or reject it. The task is to examine those reasons, to persuade others to accept or reject them, and to open one's self to persuasion from others. Critical decisions about any dissertation will be made at this level of discourse. Decisions should be reached with as much discussion as possible, free of any form of coercion or domination.

An advantage of this practical discourse model for defining the scope and method of research is its recognition of the dynamic nature of the field. Fifteen years ago a doctoral student would have had a hard time finding a committee to support his or her interest in privatization. Today this is a legitimate topic. Fifteen years from now it might not be. Political winds and economic conditions could shift privatization away from central concern.

Some guiding questions create an arena for discourse and commitment: What is the purpose of the research? Is the topic relevant to public administration? Must it be of central importance? Should it be of cutting-edge significance? What methods are appropriate to study the topic? Should a topic be rejected because of technical difficulties in using mainstream social science techniques? Can alternative, and equally legitimate, approaches be identified?

Perhaps a more fundamental question is whether the dissertation experience will prepare the student to become a consistent contributor to knowledge in the field. The expectation that dissertation research will immediately find its way into publication may be unrealistic, but if scholarly achievement is a standard for terminal degree holders, then the dissertation experience should at least prepare academicians for research and publication.

Implications

Doctoral research in public administration is not going to escape its institutional heritage or its broad topical focus. Dissertations will continue to be written in a variety of institutional settings, on a variety of topics that may also belong to other fields or disciplines, but a clear linkage to public-sector concerns should be maintained. Policy and program evaluations will continue to be written because of public administration's central concern for the relationship between theory and practice. Such dissertations are a rich source of "usable knowledge" and should be nurtured with methodological rigor. Practitioner dissertations will also continue to be written. There is a place for these dissertations and a place for doctoral level practitioner education, but such research and such education is not an excuse for poor scholarship.

Research in public administration can draw on alternative methodologies and philosophical frameworks accepted in other fields or disciplines. If a doctoral student wants to study the organizational culture of a municipal police department, he or she might legitimately adopt the semiotic approach of cultural anthropology, which is fundamentally interpretive. If a student wants to effect change in an organization, he or she might adopt a psycho-analytic approach that follows the logic of critical social science. Dissertation committees should be sensitive to the multiplicity of possible topics and the availability of appropriate methods employed in other disciplines. This may mean inviting experts from other fields or disciplines to join the dissertation committees.

Attention should be paid to the low influence of dissertation research on publications. If fewer doctoral graduates will be entering academia, then those who do should be nurtured in the role as future contributors to knowledge in the field. If dissertation research is of such low quality that it will not find its way into print, then action must be taken to improve research skills. If a disproportionate amount of applied research is being conducted, then more emphasis on basic research is called for (and maybe with a de-emphasis on applied research). If good but not mainstream research is failing to get published, then the definition of what constitutes appropriate research needs to be discussed. If there are too few outlets for research, then more should be started.

The issues surrounding the quality of dissertation research need to be publicized. It is uncertain how many public administration educators are aware of the poor quality of much of the research and of how little of it contributes to knowledge in the field. Then specific issues need to be addressed. At the forefront are concerns about practitioner dissertations, the lack of basic research, and the imbalance between mainstream and nonmainstream research. Initially, these issues will not disappear by merely discussing them,

but communicating a concern for them to the wider body of public administration educators may get them thinking about where they stand with regard
to the issues. It may even get them to change the way they advise students,
sign off on proposals, and ultimately approve the research.

NASPAA is one avenue for providing more information about dissertation
research. For example, it might establish a clearinghouse for dissertation
abstracts by requiring all member institutions to submit abstracts and then
make them available to member institutions. DAI does not include all
relevant public administration dissertation abstracts under the field heading
of "Public Administration." Relevant dissertations are listed under other
field headings, but it is unreasonable to expect any one person to dig them
out. Beyond correcting this problem, disseminating the abstracts would help
interested researchers keep abreast of the field.

NASPAA might also provide information about the discipline itself. For
example, it might compile statistics, much as the American Political Science
Association does, on the number of doctoral graduates, whether they are
employed as practitioners or academicians, successful academic placements,
recent position changes, number of articles published in relevant journals
each year, and so on. This would provide valuable information about changes
in the field.

NASPAA's Special Task Force on the Status of Research in Public Administration is aware of the quality of dissertation research and the publication
patterns of terminal degree holders. It may want to consider further research
on research in public administration. It is relatively easy to sample the
journals in the field through on-line bibliographic retrieval services to find
out what programs and institutions are contributing knowledge to the field.
It is also easy to sample recent journal articles to see if the same pattern of
research is to be found in published material. Much of the published material
in the field may be similar to the types of dissertations that are completed.
A firmer knowledge base about research in general is called for. Such knowledge
may change expectations about future dissertation research and publications.

Members of the task force could also design a model course for doctoral
research that would take into account not only mainstream social science
practices but also alternative approaches. This would not be a methods
course in the narrow sense of the word but one that would explore the
philosophical principles underlying a variety of approaches to social research, as well as advanced qualitative and quantitative techniques. Such a
course might also focus on identifying questions of central importance and
appropriate ways of answering them.

I have attempted to assess the nature and quality of dissertation research
in public administration and to determine the influence of writing a dissertation
on publications in the field. The results of my analysis support McCurdy and

Cleary's earlier findings. Much of the dissertation research fails to satisfy the criteria for mainstream social science research. About half of the dissertation authors did not set out to do mainstream social research. Nonmainstream research can contribute to knowledge in public administration if it is guided by alternative methodological and philosophical frameworks. Unfortunately, few of the abstracts from the nonmainstream dissertations gave any indication of this. My analysis of publications indicates that only a few of the successful doctoral candidates have contributed to academic journals. Dissertation research does not seem to be a major source of publications in public administration.

A Methodological Comment

My examination of McCurdy's and Cleary's data base offered some different results and pointed out some conflicts of interpretation. I was looking for something different in assessing validity, and I cast a wider net around topics of importance to public administrators. Also, the results of the analyses were different because we had different interpretations of the criteria, we read the abstracts differently, and the abstracts are not uniform with respect to style or informational content. The following may explain the differences in our findings for each criterion for the 1981 sample of 142 dissertation abstracts.

Determining if a dissertation has a specific research purpose may initially seem easy. Purpose can be read into the title and textual material of the abstract. Yet the difficulty of identifying a specific research purpose is something surprising. A poorly written abstract is one reason for this; another is the possibility that the dissertation really did not have a specific purpose. I counted 122 abstracts (86%) that suggested their authors had specific purposes in mind. McCurdy and Cleary (1984) looked at this differently, claiming that "a substantial number of projects were neither basic nor applied. They appeared to have no purpose at all. Thirty projects, or 21 percent, did little more than describe an existing process" (p. 52). Obviously, I read more purpose into some of the abstracts.

Determining the validity of research results from an abstract was both easy and difficult. McCurdy and Cleary (1984) were concerned with whether "the author set up the study in such a way so a reader could have confidence in the findings and infer their applicability to similar situations" (p. 50). In some cases it was obvious that a dissertation did not meet this criterion; as with one-shot case studies, histories or descriptions of some administrative or political event, reports of action research projects, political theories, and exploratory field research where no mention was made of a research design. In other cases it was just as obvious that the dissertation did meet this criterion because of explicit references to experimental designs, quasi-experimental designs, sample size and sampling techniques, and statistical controls. There was a middle ground of abstracts where it was difficult to determine the validity of research results because only one or two of these attributes of validity were mentioned. The difference between my count of 37% of the dissertations meeting this criterion and McCurdy and Cleary's count of 21% probably results from the fact that I took one or two key words as suggesting validity.

McCurdy and Cleary used theory testing and causality as two indicators of what they called Impact I and Impact 2. When a specific theory or theorist is mentioned in an abstract, it is easy to tell if a dissertation tested an established theory. It was more difficult to determine this when an abstract contained a very general discussion of the research question or problem or of the literature. By my count, 29% of the abstracts suggested that a theory was tested by explicit reference to a theory or theorist or by reference to the development of a theoretical framework from the relevant literature.

Some of the abstracts suggest that hypotheses were developed from literature reviews, field research guided by theory, or program data and information. These are legitimate sources of hypotheses for testing even though they may not be derived from a specific theoretical framework. So I added hypothesis testing as an additional independent criterion: Did the abstract make either direct or indirect reference to hypotheses that were tested? Forty-two percent of the abstracts suggested that at least one hypothesis was tested, even if only by critical conceptual analysis.

It was relatively easy to determine if an abstract contained a statement of a causal relationship in its conclusion, but McCurdy and Cleary were perhaps too restrictive in looking for specific causal statements. Several more of the abstracts contained terms such as *correlation, independent* and *dependent variables, multivariate analysis, time series analysis,* and *path analysis.* These terms are frequently associated with efforts to identify causal relationships. I used them as key words to suggest a focus on causality. By my readings, 34% of the abstracts made either direct or indirect reference to the search for causality. We may not be too far off on this criterion. McCurdy and Cleary (1984) identified 42% of the abstracts as "testing a theory or reaching a conclusion containing a causal statement" (p. 51). But it is not immediately evident that our reading of the abstracts would match up on a one-for-one basis for this criterion because I treated causality as an independent criterion.

Different people may have very different notions of what constitutes a topic of central importance. The nature of the field suggests many possible topics of central importance. The criterion of cutting-edge significance is even more difficult to pin down. Keeping current in the many and varied aspects of public administration is difficult, if not impossible. So it seems unlikely that anyone would have knowledge of a cutting-edge development much beyond his or her primary interests. In my reading of the abstracts I counted 118 topics of importance to public administration, of which 16 were of leading-edge importance. McCurdy and Cleary (1984) counted only 9 dissertations that "dealt with a major subject in public administration or were classified as 'leading edge' " (p. 51). The major difference in our readings probably turns on the notion of a "major subject" in public administration. I chose almost any subject that might be of interest to either a theorist or practitioner or that could conceivably fall within the NASPAA matrix.

These differences in interpretation should not be taken as a condemnation of these research efforts. We were faced with a difficult situation and tried to make the best of it but perhaps only to our own satisfaction. Abstracts contain limited information, and some of it is poorly presented. Although reading the entire dissertation would have been preferable, it would also have been impossible. Issues of proper purpose, method, and topic can take months to resolve in actual research situations. My repetition of McCurdy's and Cleary's work points out how difficult it is to arrive at a common definition of criteria and a common interpretation of a cultural artifact such as an abstract. But it also lends support to their original research.

Notes

1. University Microfilms International maintains an on-line data base system that allows telecommunications access to abstracts published in *Dissertation Abstracts International*. This was part of the data base for my general reading. The abstracts accessed are consecutively numbered from 1 to 350 from the latest abstract on file at the time of log on, which in this case was July 9, 1985. Unfortunately, nine dissertations had to be eliminated from the sample because only their author and title were reported. (These were produced at the University of Chicago and MIT, which do not supply abstracts to University Microfilms International.) A few dissertations did not seem to have a public administration focus. They were not excluded following McCurdy and Cleary's precedent. The data base for my general reading of the abstracts was completed by adding the 142 abstracts from the McCurdy and Cleary study. They were drawn from the 1981 monthly editions of DAI (vol. 41, no. 7, through vol. 42, no. 6).

2. The 1980 edition of DAI actually covers two volume years: half of volume 40 and half of volume 41. The set of abstracts consisted of the monthly issues from January 1980 through December 1980. In keeping with McCurdy and Cleary's precedent, a small number of abstracts from foreign universities were excluded.

3. The *Social Science Citation Index* was accessed through the Bibliographic Retrieval Service (BRS), an on-line data base search service. Authors' names were entered with last name, first initial, and middle initial. In a few cases where no "hits" were found and I recognized an author's name, I conducted a search using only his or her last name and first initial. No additional hits were found in those cases.

4. SSCI does not index *Public Administration Quarterly, American Review of Public Administration,* or *Public Budgeting and Finance.* A manual check shows that very few of the dissertation

authors from either the 1980 or 1981 dissertation years have published in these journals. For PAQ, two dissertation authors from the 1980 sample year published one symposium article each. One author from the 1981 sample year published one symposium article. For the *American Review,* one author from the 1980 sample year edited a symposium; two authors from the 1981 sample year published one article, two symposium articles, and one book review. One dissertation author from each dissertation year published one article each in *Public Budgeting and Finance.* These publications were not counted in my analysis.

The volumes checked are as follows: for the *American Review,* volumes 14 through 17 (1980-1983); PAQ, volumes 5 and 6 (1982-1983); and *Public Budgeting and Finance,* volumes 1 through 4 (1981-1984). The *American Review* has a delayed publication schedule, so volume 17, nos. 2 and 3 combined, is the latest edition of this writing. Only volumes 5 and 6 of the PAQ were checked because of the unavailability of this journal at the UMC library. It is unlikely, however, that a substantial number of dissertation authors from both sample years would have published enough items in this journal to alter the apparent existing patterns of publishing. The reader should be aware that the *American Review* was previously called the *Midwest Review of Public Administration,* and the *Public Administration Quarterly* was previously called the *Southern Review of Public Administration.*

5. Bernstein (1983) makes the fully developed argument for the practical rationality of theory choice in *Beyond Objectivity and Relativism.*

10	Revisiting the Doctoral Dissertation in Public Administration: An Examination of the Dissertations of 1990

ROBERT E. CLEARY

What do doctoral dissertations in public administration look like nowadays? Has the quality improved in recent years? Are public administration doctoral students writing dissertations that use good research designs to examine questions of importance in a way that is likely to help build the field?

The nature of doctoral education and the requirements of the doctoral dissertation—the capstone experience of the formal learning process in graduate education in most disciplines—have been the subjects of continued interest and discussion in American higher education in recent years. In April 1991, for example, the Andrew G. Mellon Foundation announced plans to spend $50 million within a five-year period to improve the quality of graduate education in social science and the humanities (McMillen, 1991, pp. 29-30). In November 1990, the Association of American Universities and its affiliated Association of Graduate Schools stated that "for most doctoral students, the preparation of the dissertation constitutes the most critical period in doctoral education. . . . The primary purpose of the dissertation is to demonstrate a student's capacity for independent work" (Association of American Universities, 1990, p. 8). In January 1991, a report of the Council of Graduate Schools reemphasized the role of the dissertation in demonstrating the ability to work independently but strongly recommended that students receive improved faculty advice throughout the dissertation process (Council of Graduate Schools, 1991).

These concerns are directly applicable to doctoral studies in public administration. In early 1984, Howard McCurdy and I published the results of a survey of the 142 doctoral dissertations that were summarized under the

157

heading of public administration in *Dissertation Abstracts* 1981. Our article included some critical comments regarding the implications of the analysis for doctoral research in particular and public administration research in general (McCurdy & Cleary, 1984).

That article engendered many reactions and responses. After reviewing dissertations from 1979 to 1984, Jay White confirmed the accuracy of our findings but argued that we had overemphasized the utility of scientific modes of research (White, 1986a, 1986b). Robert Stallings emphasized the importance of focusing research on core problems in the field of public administration (Stallings, 1986). James Perry and Kenneth Kraemer and then Stallings and James Ferris extended our study and certain of its conclusions to research reports in the *Public Administration Review* (Perry & Kraemer, 1986; Stallings & Ferris, 1988).

Although there is some disagreement in this literature on the extent and utility of key approaches and concepts, there is strong agreement that public administration doctoral research has material weaknesses that reflect problems in the field. Too many dissertations are soft methodologically, failing to use a research design sufficiently conceptual to give much confidence in the findings (and often not even testing a causal proposition). Dissertations frequently do not focus on key ideas or even on important topics in public administration. Furthermore, dissertation research as a whole is not sufficiently cumulative, tending to have little impact on the development of the field of public administration.

The problems do not seem limited to dissertation research. Stallings and Ferris's examination of research in PAR from 1940 to 1984 concluded that "[l]ittle causal analysis or theory testing has taken place over the years, and causal analyses, while significantly more frequent now than in previous decades, comprise only a small proportion of current research" (Stallings & Ferris, 1988, pp. 583-584; also see Perry & Kraemer, 1986).

The final report of the National Association of Schools of Public Affairs and Administration (NASPAA) Task Force on the State of Research in Public Administration in 1987 declared that "there are few well developed streams of research [in public administration] and research is less cumulative than in more developed fields" (National Association of Schools of Public Affairs and Administration, 1987, p. 4). Consequently, the task force suggested the need "to concentrate on (1) the distinctions between what is public and private in administration and (2) the interface between politics and administration" (p. 5; also see Stallings, 1986, on the importance of studying core problems).

Stallings and Ferris (1988) point out that public administration research continues to be "dominated by efforts to conceptualize researchable problems, delineate possible areas of inquiry, and describe objects for study" (p. 583). They conclude that "what the field of public administration needs

TABLE 10.1 Dissertations Meeting Each Criterion and Percentage Change, 1981 and 1990

Criterion	1981 (N = 142)		1990 (N = 165)		Percentage Change
	Number	*Percent*	*Number*	*Percent*	
Research purpose	91	64.1	132	80.0	15.9
Validity	30	21.1	48	29.1	8.0
Theory testing	25	17.6	36	21.8	4.2
Causal relationship	43	26.1	85	51.5	25.4
Important topic	55	38.7	53	32.1	−6.6
Cutting edge	24	16.9	120	72.7	55.8

is a strategy for coupling important questions with the techniques for answering them" (p. 585).

Given the central importance of the issues raised by Stallings and Ferris, it seems appropriate to revisit the state of doctoral dissertation research and to examine once more the quality of this research and what it contributes collectively to efforts to advance the field. The focal question of this study is, Have there been identifiable changes or improvements in dissertation quality in public administration in the past 10 years?

Findings on the Six Evaluative Criteria

Given the attention to the doctoral dissertation in the last few years, it could be expected that there has been substantial improvement in the quality of dissertations in the 1980s. Consequently, I began this research with the proposition that a substantially higher percentage of the 1990 dissertations would meet each criterion than was true for 1981. This proposition was valid for three of the six criteria: research purpose, causal relationship, and a topic on the cutting edge. In addition, small increases were recorded in the categories of methodological validity and theory testing (Table 10.1).

RESEARCH PURPOSE

Did the dissertation set out to conduct basic research? A total of 132 (80%) of the 165 dissertations from 1990 met this criterion, as contrasted with 91 (64.1%) of the 142 projects in 1981. These totals included 4 projects (2.4%) in 1990 and 8 (5.6%) in 1981 that were purely theoretical or philosophical in nature, contributing to an understanding of the nature of the field of public administration. The remainder—128 (77.6%) in 1990 and 83 (58.5%) in 1981—utilized some form of scientific or statistical methodology. The overall change is substantial, with only 33 (20%) of the 1990 dissertations classified as demonstrating no research purpose or conclusion. The number of 1981 dissertations in this category was 51 (35.9%).

The projects that met the research purpose test in 1990 were wide-ranging in topic and scope. One dissertation examined such budget deliberation variables as executive authority, program type, and formula funding to attempt to find the influence of these factors on budget outcomes. Another analyzed the impact of various social, political, demographic, and economic factors on the granting of Small Business Administration loans to minority-owned businesses. A third examined different social science paradigms to determine their explanatory ability in cases of state budgetary cutback.

METHODOLOGICAL VALIDITY

Did the dissertation have a rigorous research design? Of the 165 dissertations from 1990, 48 (29.1%) met the criterion of methodological validity, compared to 30 (21.1%) of the 142 dissertations in 1981. The projects meeting this criterion were deemed to have a careful research design—one that involved systematic exploration and analysis to test a proposition, establish a condition, or analyze a policy. Usually these projects used experimental or quasi-experimental methods or statistical techniques, as contrasted with the use of historical data or secondary sources without much attempt to infer propositions from the data or the production of individual case studies without the use of statistical controls.

THEORY TESTING

Did the dissertation test an existing theory? Of the 1990 dissertations, 36 (21.8%) met this criterion, compared to 25 (17.6%) of the 1981 projects. One study used Richard Hofferbert's model of policy making to attempt to explain such variations of municipal policy outputs as per capita expenditure and payroll spending. Another employed the Douglas-Wildavsky model of political culture to try to predict the outcomes of timber, fish, and wildlife environmental policy negotiations in the Northwest.

CAUSATION

Did the dissertation conclude with a causal statement? A total of 85 (51.5%) of the 1990 projects included at least one cause-effect relationship statement drawn from the research in their conclusions, as contrasted with 43 (26.1%)

in 1981. This is a substantial improvement. One study concluded that the increasing diversity of the American veterans population is a direct cause of a decline in the ability of the "iron triangle" concept to explain decision making in veterans' politics. Another study noted that the major factors that explain variations in examined cases of local budgeting are the economic base, intergovernmental aid, and executive leadership. A third dissertation determined that the main barriers to local governmental implementation of federal or state policies are a lack of support from the local political environment, an absence of balanced coverage from local news media, and the lack of penalties or inducements for compliance or noncompliance.

IMPORTANT TOPIC

Was the topic of the dissertation an important one in the field of public administration, as reflected by the amount of attention given the topic in current leading public administration textbooks? Only 53 (32.1%) of the 1990 studies met this criterion. One dissertation was an implementation study that examined the unforeseen local outcomes of federal medicare policy. Another investigated the performance of the Office of Personnel Management "in regard to legislative intent, the policy objectives of successive administrations, and the public interest." A third was an examination of governmental decentralization that explored the distribution of power between the central government and local governments in 25 nations. The total of 53 studies considered "important" in 1990 compares to 55 projects (38.7%) in 1981, a slight decline.

CUTTING EDGE

Did the dissertation involve the development of new questions or the creation of new experience? The biggest difference in my findings came on this criterion. A total of 120 (72.7%) of the 1990 dissertations were coded as being on the cutting edge, compared to 24 (16.9%) in 1981. This difference is so great that I feared a methodological problem on my part, a change in standards of application and classification on the criterion. To test this possibility, I resurveyed the 1981 dissertations and found a total of 26 that seemed on the cutting edge. This number is close enough to the originally reported 24 to conclude the difference from 1981 to 1990 is real indeed—an important finding. Approximately half the 120 studies on the cutting edge in 1990 were written on issues important to or central in the field of public administration.

Examples of the variety of dissertations in this category included a study of the organization and politics of the medical profession as a determinant of medical policy toward AIDS, an examination of the role of health insurers

TABLE 10.2 Number of Criteria Met and Percentage Change, 1981 and 1990

Meeting	1981 (N = 142)		1990 (N = 165)		Percentage Change
	Number	Percent	Number	Percent	
Six criteria	0	0	3	1.8	1.8
Five criteria	5	3.5	10	6.1	2.6
Four criteria	14	9.9	44	26.7	16.8
Three criteria	23	16.2	43	26.1	9.9
Two criteria	34	23.9	40	24.2	0.3
One criterion	40	28.2	16	9.7	−18.5
No criteria	26	18.3	9	5.5	−12.8
Mean	1.82		2.82		

in promoting the cessation of smoking, and an analysis of the effect of a "reformed" local government structure on economic development in urban areas.

SUMMARY OF FINDINGS ON THE SIX CRITERIA

Taking the six criteria as a group, there has been a substantial change in the nature and quality of doctoral dissertations between 1981 and 1990. The average number of criteria met in 1981 was two; the average number of criteria met in 1990 was three. In addition, in 1981, no dissertation met all six criteria, and only 19 (13.4%) met at least four; in 1990, three projects met all six criteria, and 57 (34.5%) met at least four (Table 10.2). This difference is substantial.

Other Findings

A variety of additional findings from the survey of 1990 dissertations are summarized below:

The number of Ph.D.s in public administration, as evidenced by *Dissertation Abstracts,* has increased slightly in 10 years, from 142 in 1981 to 165 in 1990.

Based on name identification, 20 women wrote dissertations listed under the heading of public administration in *Dissertation Abstracts,* 1981. For 1990, this number doubled to 41.

The number of universities granting Ph.D.s in public administration increased slightly from 57 in 1981 to 65 in 1990.

TABLE 10.3 Areas of Study and Percentage Change, 1981 and 1990

Area of study	1981 (N = 142)		1990 (N = 165)		Percentage Change
	Number	Percent	Number	Percent	
Administrative theory	36	25.4	21	12.7	−12.7
Comparative public administration	21	14.8	8	4.8	−10.0
Employee behavior and development	12	8.5	18	10.9	2.4
Finance and budgeting	3	2.1	16	9.7	7.6
Intergovernmental relations	7	4.9	1	0.6	−4.3
Management science	1	0.7	3	1.8	1.1
Organizational theory and behavior	14	9.9	42	25.5	15.6
Personnel administration	7	4.9	3	1.8	−3.1
Policy analysis	41	28.9	53	32.1	3.2

Of the 57 universities in 1981, 36 also granted at least one Ph.D. in 1990.

The average number of Ph.D.s per university was the same in both years studied: 2.5. In 1981, however, one university produced 16 Ph.D.s; in 1990, another institution produced 18.

Areas of study changed somewhat in the 10-year period. The number of dissertations in organizational theory and behavior and in finance and budgeting increased substantially, while the number in administrative theory and in comparative public administration decreased substantially. See Table 10.3 for a summary of changes in the number of dissertations in each of nine major subdivisions of public administration.

The number of purely descriptive dissertations declined sharply from 30 (21.1%) in 1981 to just 3 (1.8%) in 1990. This classification includes those dissertations that do little more than describe an existing situation or process.

The percentage of "practitioner projects" was basically the same in the two years surveyed, increasing slightly from 1981 to 1990. The 1984 PAR article defined practitioner projects as those that involved applied research on management problems with little attempt to employ a rigorous research design or methodology. We found that most of the 1981 dissertations in this category tended to be little more than a narrative description of a problem in the writer's organization. There were 21 such projects (14.8%) in 1981; there were 30 (18.2%) in 1990. One example in 1990 was a review of the "perceptions of the employees of the Ministry of Information of Iraq regarding Linguafile/Bilingual Data Base System." Another was "a descriptive study of industrial sector reconstruction plans in postwar Iran." A third was an examination of customer perceptions of the quality of contract services in an institution of higher learning in the United States. The mean number of the six evaluative criteria met by the 30 1990 practitioner studies was 1.37, as compared to a mean of 2.82 for all 165 of the 1990 dissertations. The average 1990 practitioner project, in other words, met one of the six tests.

Dissertations relying on a single-case study declined in number in 1990. In 1981, there were 37 such projects (26.1%); in 1990, 27 (16.4%). These projects were also weaker than the average on the six guidelines, with 2.33 being the mean number of criteria met.

Dissertations written in 1990 on topics that might be considered more central to the field of public administration were more likely to have a rigorous research design. Approximately two thirds of the 53 analyses coded as "important" in this study satisfied at least three of the remaining five criteria of the study. Only half the remaining 112 dissertations did this.

Programs considered higher quality by public administration academics continue to produce better quality dissertations. The study of 1981 dissertations included an assessment of general quality based on the construction of a numerical scale. The scale was composed of scores for each dissertation for validity, importance, causal relationship, theory testing, and cutting edge, with a penalty for studies whose purpose seemed essentially descriptive (McCurdy & Cleary, 1984, p. 52). Dissertation-producing schools were divided into three categories, based on the institutional rankings published in PAR in 1982 (Morgan & Meier, 1982).[1] Analysis of the 1981 dissertations led to a finding that a larger percentage of top-quality dissertations were written in the higher ranked schools. I replicated the analysis for the 1990 dissertations, with the same result (Table 10.4).

A substantially larger number of dissertations in 1990 did not deal with what this researcher deemed to be a topic or an issue affecting public administration, let alone an "important" issue. There were 26 dissertations (15.8%) in this category in 1990, compared with 13 (9.2%) in 1981. Given this finding, I added two new categories of comparison to those reported in 1984. These focused on two matters identified by NASPAA's recent Task Force on the State of Research in Public Administration as key issues in the field, namely, distinctions between public and private administration and the interface between politics and administration (National Association of Schools of Public Affairs and Administration, 1987). I wanted to discover what attention dissertation writers are paying to these key issues.

A total of 13 (9.2%) of the 1981 dissertations dealt with issues that in my opinion analyzed a distinction or distinctions or even similarities between public and private management. The comparable figure for 1990 was 11 (6.7%), a slight decline. One 1990 dissertation in this category investigated

TABLE 10.4 Quality of Dissertations Produced at Institutions, 1990, as Ranked on the Morgan-Meier Academic Scale (Grouped by Institution)

	Top 20	Ranked 21-50	Unranked	Total
Highest quality dissertations (Score of 20 to 30)	23 (35.4%)	10 (30.3%)	10 (14.9%)	43
Middle quality dissertations (Score of 10 to 15)	33 (50.8%)	15 (45.5%)	34 (50.7%)	82
Lower quality dissertations (Score of −10 to 5)	9 (13.8%)	8 (24.2%)	23 (34.3%)	40
Total dissertations	65 (100%)	33 (100%)	67 (100%)	

NOTES: Percentages refer to the proportion of dissertations in each quality rating within each category of institution on the Morgan-Meier scale. For a similar table for the 1981 dissertations, see McCurdy and Cleary (1984, p. 53).

"service quality" in the public sector, with some general comparisons to the private sector. Another examined stress and morality as determinants of behavior by public-sector employees, again with some general comparisons to the private sector. A third studied "the federal civil servant as hero: the calling to governance." A fourth explored the nature of professional education in public administration.

There was a substantial decline in the number and percentage of projects dealing with the administration-politics interface, from 80 (56.3%) in 1981 to 50 (30.3%) in 1990. An example of one such dissertation in 1990 was an analysis of the National Priorities List of Hazardous Waste Sites as a study in public and private policy making and implementation. Another dissertation explored "the impact of federal equal employment opportunity and affirmative action policies on the employment of black women in the higher grades" of the federal government. A third analyzed the use of congressional oversight to affect geographically based budget allocations in five federal agencies. A fourth studied the impact of the Reagan administration on certain state environmental policies.

Questions for Discussion

IS THE FIELD CHANGING?

There is evidence in this study that the field of public administration is changing in nature and in emphasis. As noted earlier, Table 10.3 records the number of dissertations written in 1981 and in 1990 in each of nine major subdivisions of the field. The 1990 data show substantially increased attention to topics of organizational theory and behavior as well as to public finance and budgeting and substantially decreased attention to administrative theory and to comparative public administration, along with some smaller changes.

The increase in attention to questions of organizational theory and behavior is to be applauded. These dissertations, more so than the average, study a subject using a methodology that forces attention on questions of causation and relationship to theory. Such analyses in 1990 included a study of producers' organizations in India, a reinterpretation of organizational behavior in a public enterprise in the United States in the context of how stress and a sense of morality affect the members of the organization, a study of the transition of the Peace Corps to a bureaucracy, the impact of organizational structure on administration in a foreign university, and the role of state-owned enterprises as instruments of public policy.

The increase in topics dealing with questions of financial management is also to be commended. This increase may be the result of attention given this topic by specialists in the field in recent years, including a sustained push for emphasis on this area in graduate programs in public administration by ASPA's section on budgeting and financial management (see, for example, American Society for Public Administration, 1985; Grizzle, 1985). Dissertations in this field also tend to use a research design and a methodology that leads to attention to causation and to theory. Nine of the 16 studies in 1990 in this area had such a research design, by far the highest percentage of any category in the sample. In addition, dissertations in this area met, on the average, more of the six evaluative criteria of this study than any other area.

The decline in the number of dissertations in the comparative field may be associated with increasing rigor in public administration programs at the doctoral level. Many of the comparative administration dissertations in 1981 were written by foreign nationals enrolled in unranked programs on topics in their own countries. Although public administration programs in the United States can do a real service for our colleagues in other nations by aiding some of their students with their education, we owe these students a quality learning experience, including strong offerings in comparative administration. Too many of the 1981 dissertations written by foreign students were single-case studies unsupported by a scientific methodology or any evidence beyond the case, rather than studies that tested a proposition or examined a cause-effect relationship. The former category of dissertation did not disappear in 1990, but its substantial shrinkage represents the bulk of the decline in the number of comparative dissertations.

Besides changes in areas of study, dissertation topics selected by students in 1990 also differed from 1981 in other ways. On one fundamental point, fewer dissertations dealt with specific topics I would consider central to or even important in the field of public administration. This matter is, in part, related to the issue of the quality of the dissertation. I will explore this and related matters by examining the following query: Are we doing better now than 10 years ago?

ARE WE DOING BETTER?

Doctoral dissertations summarized in the 1990 edition of *Dissertation Abstracts* are, in total and on the average, superior research projects compared to those in the 1981 edition. A substantially higher percentage of the 1990 dissertations had a research purpose, setting out to conduct basic research and report on the findings; included a cause-effect relationship in the conclusion of the study; and examined a topic that developed new questions for study or created new experience. In addition, small percentage increases were found in research design and efforts to test existing theory (Table 10.1).

At the same time, the number of descriptive studies declined sharply, while the number of unsupported case studies also declined. Both these developments are to be applauded. McCurdy and I felt it was appalling that more than 20% of the 1981 dissertations were purely descriptive in nature. Apparently, dissertation supervisors agree, because this category essentially disappeared in 1990! This finding is one of the most important changes in the 10-year period.

The reduction in the number of single-case studies is also a good sign for the field. The case study can be a useful methodology for the study of social science phenomena. It is possible to write a good dissertation, by anybody's ranking, by doing a case study. But this is most likely to be true when case studies are used as vehicles to verify concepts or to critique theories and approaches. Attaining a result beyond the specifics of the particular case usually requires a conscious attention to methodology by the researcher. Most case studies in both 1981 and in 1990 showed little or no evidence of such methodologies.

Despite the very real improvements in the quality of doctoral dissertation research between 1981 and 1990, material problems requiring attention still exist. For example, too many practitioner projects that investigate a problem in the writer's organization without much in the way of a research design or attention to rigorous methods continue to be written. In addition, the decline in dissertations dealing with important topics in public administration and even in studies dealing with matters that seem to affect public administration is troublesome. Moreover, if the topics identified by the NASPAA Task Force on the State of Research in Public Administration are as central to the field as I believe they are, the fact that there are fewer dissertations on both the question of the distinctive character of public administration and on the nature of the politics-administration interface is clearly a matter for sustained discussion by students of public administration.

I believe the generic question of what kinds of research topics are more likely to be promising subjects for doctoral study is one for priority attention in the field over the next few years. Is there any reason doctoral students cannot work on issues related to topics central to the field of public administration while they are paying careful attention to matters of research design and methodology?

Perusal of the dissertation subjects chosen for 1990 shows two distinct patterns with regard to this question. One pattern involves a compatibility of attention to matters of causation and theory, on the one hand, and to the selection of an important topic in the field of public administration, on the other. Of the 53 1990 dissertations written on topics coded as important in this study, two thirds met at least three of the remaining five criteria of the research, compared to one half of the remaining 112 dissertations on subjects not coded as important.

The opposite pattern is also present, however. Many dissertations that show material attention to questions of research design also select for study a topic that does not seem focal or even important in the field of public administration. Of the total of 112 "unimportant" studies in this research, 42 (37.5%) met at least three of the remaining five criteria of the research. This percentage is substantially lower than that in the important category, but it still represents an impressive number of doctoral dissertations.

The McCurdy-Cleary 1984 PAR article speculated that doctoral students might "have a better chance of producing a high validity dissertation if they do not address an important issue" (McCurdy & Cleary, 1984, p. 53). Given the increased emphasis on methodology and research design found in the 1990 dissertations, this proposition no longer holds, even if it did so a few years ago. Nevertheless, a sizable number of well-researched doctoral dissertations continue to be written on subjects that seem of little importance to the field of public administration. To cite just one example, would not any one of a number of other topics be more central to the field than a study of the linkage between employee satisfaction with interorganizational communication and company profitability in a particular industry in one Asian country?

The increased attention to methodology, validity, and theory testing found in 1990 is related, for many dissertations, to the selection for study of a topic that is important to or even a core issue in the field of public administration. For many other dissertations, this emphasis seems tied to the selection of a more peripheral issue that might be presumed to give students more flexibility in their study. This in turn leads to a decreased emphasis on important topics and a lack of attention to core issues in the field.

Conclusion

Public administration has taken some impressive strides on the road toward significant improvements in the use of the doctoral dissertation as a research tool to help educate students while holding promise of advancing the field. This survey of dissertations suggests that many more doctoral students are conducting quality research compared to 10 years ago. Rigorous research designs that involve attention to causal relationships are more common.

Public administration now needs to examine its subject matter with a view toward providing more careful responses to the question, What doctoral dissertation topics will allow students to write quality dissertations and at the same time hold promise of advancing the field? All of us concerned with dissertation quality, especially faculty advisers, need to look again at the possibilities for dissertation topics on such core issues as the characteristics that make the field distinctive and the interface between politics and administration. If topics central to the field lend themselves to quality research as well as and perhaps even better than fringe topics do, why should we not ask students to focus on important or even core issues for study? Increased attention to the choice of topics for analysis in terms of their possible contributions to the field is now called for in doctoral research as well as in public administration research generally.

Appendix: The Survey

This chapter reports the results of a survey of dissertations published in 1990. In order to be able to compare the findings with those on the 1981 dissertations, I replicated the McCurdy-Cleary (1984) methodology in this survey. I used the following six criteria to analyze the abstracts of the 165 dissertations included in the Dissertation Abstracts (1990) under public administration: research purpose, methodological validity, the testing of theory, causal relationships, importance of topic, and topic on the cutting edge.

To do this, I posed the following six questions:

- Did the study have a research purpose; that is, did it set out to conduct basic research and report on the findings?
- Did the study have a rigorous research design?

- Did the research test an existing theory?
- Did the study conclude with a causal statement?
- Was the topic of the study an important one in the field of public administration?
- Did the study involve the development of new questions or the creation of new experience? (For an explanation of these questions and their use as criteria of research quality, see McCurdy & Cleary, 1984, p. 50.)

Before applying the criteria to the 1990 dissertations, I did a fresh analysis of a sample of 1981 dissertation abstracts to test my judgments. The test judgments coincided with the earlier conclusions in more than 95% of the cases sampled. It seems safe to conclude, therefore, that the judgments I made on the 1990 dissertations were closely analogous to those originally made on the 1981 dissertations and that the two studies are comparable.

I also reviewed a sample of 10 dissertations in order to check the validity of the proposition that reading a public administration dissertation abstract allows investigation of whether the dissertation satisfies the six evaluative criteria used in this study. In no case did the review of a dissertation change a rating judgment made on the basis of analysis of the abstract.

Note

1. I realize that more recent rankings of quality in public administration programs now exist, but I used the Morgan-Meier ratings because I wanted to make as parallel a comparison with the 1981 ratings as I could. Also, as an experiment, I did explore one somewhat different set of rankings for the 1990 dissertations, the rankings set forth by Ferris and Stallings in the *American Review of Public Administration* in 1988, with virtually no change in result.

11

Doctoral Programs in Public Administration: An Outsider's Perspective

ROBERT A. STALLINGS

The debate over the content and quality of doctoral education in public administration has once again appeared in the pages of the *Public Administration Review* (McCurdy & Cleary, 1984; White, 1986a).[1] A key issue in this debate is the nature and role of research in the field, especially the research conducted by students in pursuit of their doctorates. Underlying the various positions on this controversy are some key assumptions that are seldom articulated. The purpose of this article is to make these assumptions explicit and to offer a rationale for the kind of inquiry that is central to the field of public administration.

The article is divided into two sections. In the first, confusion over whether public administration refers to practice in the public sector or to the study of the public sector is noted. Because the study of the public sector seems to be the only defensible role for a doctoral program in the field, firsthand knowledge of practice is not sufficient as a method of study at the doctoral level.[2] A qualitatively different form of knowledge, with different skills and training, is required for the study of public administration. The second section deals with assumptions about the core problems of the field. The practical problems of day-to-day activity in the public sector do not automatically produce significant questions for meaningful scholarly examination. A distinction between the form and content of human conduct based on the work of the German sociologist Georg Simmel is presented as a device for identifying the types of problems central to doctoral study in this field (Wolff, 1950).[3]

The perspective taken in this article is that of the "outsider." It may seem that someone with neither background in managing public agencies nor an academic degree in public administration (the author's graduate degrees are in sociology) would have nothing useful to say about doctoral education in the field. After all, how can an outsider understand "our" problems? But Merton (1971) argues that by this reasoning, it would then appear . . . that only French scholars can understand French society and, of course, that only Americans, not their external critics, can truly understand American society. Once the basic principle is adopted, the list of Insider claims to a monopoly of knowledge becomes indefinitely expansible to all manner of social formations. . . .

   Insider doctrines maintain that, in the end, it is a special category of Insider—a category that generally manages to include the proponent of the doctrine—that has sole or privileged access to knowledge. (pp. 13, 28-29)

In fact, assuming the posture of an outsider has its advantages. Most important is the detachment that comes from being less thoroughly permeated with the world-taken-for-granted of a group than are insiders.[4] One of the most useful descriptions of early American society, for example, was provided by an outsider—Alexis de Tocqueville (1945). Some have even claimed that being at the margin of differing social groups provides a keener insight into the culture of those groups than being central to any one.[5] No such superior insight is claimed here, for it is not necessary to choose between insider and outsider points of view. Quoting Merton (1971) again: "We no longer ask whether it is the Insider or the Outsider who has monopolistic or privileged access to social truth; instead, we begin to consider their distinctive and interactive roles in the process of truth seeking" (p. 36)

In recent years, the nature of doctoral education in public administration has once again become a much discussed issue. Most attention focuses on the role of research, in particular the function, type, and quality of research by doctoral students. This is not a new issue; clearly debate over the role of research in public administration has appeared in the literature during most of this century.[6] But these recent papers merit looking into because they disclose two issues that, to an outsider, appear to determine both the nature and the content of doctoral programs in public administration. These issues are the selection of appropriate problems for study and the selection of methods of study appropriate for those problems.

Not surprisingly, these papers reflect a variety of points of view, and their authors reach vastly different conclusions about the nature and role of research. On the negative side, Howard McCurdy and Robert Cleary (1984) used mainstream social science methods as a measuring stick and found that the vast majority of doctoral dissertations completed in 1981 neither dealt with significant issues nor were conducted in such a way as to produce findings in which one could have much confidence. They conclude: "Based upon our sample, it appears that a sizeable number of people in the field do not believe that the doctorate should be a research degree" (p. 52). Jay D. White (1986a) replicates the McCurdy-Cleary analysis and examines some 300 dissertations for the period 1979-1984. Even allowing for a wider variety of types of methods, he finds the state of dissertation research to be similar to that described by McCurdy and Cleary and concludes pessimistically that current dissertations contribute little to the knowledge base of the field (White, 1986a, pp. 12-13).

A more optimistic point of view is contained in another conference paper by Robert Biller (1982) in which he contends that the problem with evaluations such as the one by McCurdy and Cleary is that the definition of research is too narrow. He argues instead that everyone working in the public sector is a researcher and that what they do every day is research. In fact, he states that everyone in this society is a researcher (1982, p. 6); hence, there are in the United States alone 230 million researchers in the field of public administration. If we can take literally these statements, which may have only been intended for the sake of argument at a professional conference, they seem to assume the following: Human social activity involves choosing among appropriate courses of action when confronting a problem; the choice is made after information about the problem is gathered and assessed; because this information-gathering and information-assessing activity is really a type of research, everyone—especially those in government who make choices in a highly formal way—has research skills, and everyone is a researcher.

If this is a reasonable interpretation, then the argument is reminiscent of comments sociologists frequently hear from their undergraduate students. The beginning student in introductory sociology, for example, often confidently informs his instructor that, because he is a member of society and of many of its principal social groups, he will undoubtedly get an "A" in the course. Similar comments are sometimes heard from married students enrolling in a course in the sociology of marriage and the family, from minority students in the sociology of ethnic relations, and so on. Each, by the way, is a mild form of the insider's claim to knowledge (Merton, 1971). The problem, of course, is that the student confuses subject matter with the perspective used to understand that subject matter. As Berger stated (1963) so succinctly, sociology is not society; it is only a way of looking at society.

The same confusion permeates the field of public administration and is a key feature defining both the nature of doctoral education and the place of research in it. There is widespread confusion of the public sector (the object of study) with public administration as a field devoted to the study of the public sector. Such confusion is frequently evident among doctoral students who, when asked on a qualifying examination to write an essay on the role of theories of organizations in the field of public administration, often mistakenly respond by attesting to the importance of organizations in the public sector. But this tendency is not limited to doctoral students.

This same confusion permeates White's description of the knowledge base of the field. White (1986a, pp. 18-19, 22) equates the logic of the explanatory, interpretive, and critical modes of research with the tasks of the public manager. He thus confuses the study of the field with practice in the field. This represents the confusion of two types of knowledge that William James (1932) called "acquaintance with" and "knowledge about." The former is characteristic of direct familiarity with phenomena gained through firsthand experience; the latter involves more abstract formulations some would characterize as theory. The problem of defining a field of study such as public administration on knowledge of the "acquaintance with" type is that no one can judge another's competence because no two people belong to the same field of public administration. No examinations are possible, but then no degree is necessary because firsthand experience does not need to be certified by an academic diploma.

This confusion of public administration with the public sector is central to discussions of research methods appropriate for the field. Methods basically have to do with how we know something. Actually, how we know is a function of cultural rules rather than positions debated in conference sessions or professional journals. Reichenbach (1963) uses the term *scientific philosophy* to describe the rules that characterize knowledge in Western European civilizations and their cultural descendants. The logic of science is merely a formalized version of this cultural positivism. It is essentially a confrontation between empirical evidence (with rules governing its accuracy and reliability) and causal hypotheses (informed guesses about what affects what in the real world). Another manifestation of this cultural tradition is found in the slogan, "I'm from Missouri; show me!" A reasonable translation would be, Provide me with some empirical evidence for your assertion that if this is done, then that will result.

The problem with a field based on "acquaintance with" as a method of research can now be stated more technically. It is that the data, and the findings based on them, of these practitioner-researchers are so individualistic that they do not meet the minimal criteria of replicatability and falsifiability. Therefore, the products of such research, whether its producers are faculty, students, or laypersons, will never contribute to the accumulation of knowledge about the public sector, not because arrogant, dogmatic social scientists say so, but because such products are unconvincing when judged against the more fundamental cultural standards of knowing that we Westerners possess. Firsthand experience alone cannot therefore be the primary method of knowing (i.e., research) in a doctoral program.

"A question well-stated is a question half-answered" (chapter heading in a research methods text widely used by graduate students in professional schools, Isaac & Michael, 1981).

It is frequently said that the principal weakness of the field of public administration is the absence of theory. But theories are merely clusters of statements that explain something. Before there is a need for theories—borrowed or otherwise—it is first necessary to establish what needs to be explained. What are the core problems in the field to which theories can be applied? Several recent works contain systematic arguments on this point.[7] Nothing nearly so definitive is attempted here.

One common response to this question is to argue that the core problems of the field of study known as public administration are the practical problems of public administrators. Although such a position may work adequately in structuring practitioner-oriented master's degree programs, it in fact creates rather than resolves difficulties when applied to doctoral education.[8] There are several reasons for this.

Foremost is the fallacy, noted in the previous section, of creating countless unique fields of public administration, each with slightly different core problems. There is also considerable evidence that a field based on practical problems resulting from firsthand experience would continually reinvent the proverbial wheel. Several examples come to mind, but one is so nearly universal that it is representative. Considerable research in sociology, social psychology, and psychology dating back to the early 1940s clearly shows that panic is an extremely rare phenomenon that occurs only under unique circumstances even in a crisis. We know from the research literature that people do not panic when disaster warnings are given; in fact, this literature clearly shows that the real problem with warning is how to get recipients of warning messages to do anything (McLuckie, 1973; Mileti, 1975; Williams, 1964). For more than 20 years, several federal agencies as well as the National Science Foundation and the National Research Council have been disseminating findings such as this to local and state practitioners. Yet most practitioners at the local and state levels, whether elected or appointed, remain convinced that the real problem in a disaster is how to issue information, including warning messages, in ways that will not panic the population. Serious discussions are frequently held in which public servants conclude that fewer negative consequences would result if the public were not told anything whatsoever about an impending catastrophe.[9]

There is a more general reason why the problems of practitioners should not automatically be taken as the core problems of the field. The substance or content of a particular practical problem does not make it theoretically important. Such daily concerns as how to control a recalcitrant subordinate, how to diffuse angry citizens, how to deal with a mayor who is more interested in his or her political future than in a particular city department, and so on are not by themselves theoretically valuable research topics. To be so, they need to be reconstituted so that they are subsumed under more general patterns having the same form. Furthermore, their study must be carried out in such a way that something further will be known about the problem in the end beyond a mere descriptive, historical anecdote.

One popular way of thinking about the practical problems of the public sector is to treat them as some sort of loosely defined problem-solving experiment. The problem is defined by the parties involved, a solution is proposed and carried out, and an evaluation of the results is conducted. If this so-called experiment (i.e., the practical problem and its resolution) is to be of any more than immediate local interest, however, it must be designed so that the following questions may be definitively answered: Did the intervention really work, or was its successful outcome the result of other forces (i.e., the problem of spuriousness)? How do we know that it worked (i.e., what independent evidence is there that things have changed)? Why did it work? If it worked, was it because the situation contained a unique mixture of elements, or can the intervention be exported to other similar situations (i.e., the question of external validity)? But this is seldom done. Few administrators and even fewer politicians have the interest or the patience to support the research design implications of these questions (multiple cases, control groups, measurements at several points in time, etc.). If the immediate problem is solved, they proceed to the next problem.

A fourth reason for not letting practitioners' problems automatically define an agenda for doctoral education concerns the fundamental difference between running a particular department, organization, or city and acquiring knowledge that is generalizable (i.e,, universal) to a majority of departments and so on of the same class. To be useful, core theoretical principles must subsume the most typical instances of the phenomenon to which they are addressed. Their very power, in fact, resides in the ability to make sense of the particular through reference to the general. Necessarily such general principles fail to capture all the detail of the particular case. But this is not the function of an explanation anyway.

Fifth, letting the problems of practitioners set the intellectual agenda for a university-based faculty in the field of public administration, while perhaps an effective marketing and recruitment tool, seems more like followership than leadership. Is the recalcitrant subordinate the only subject worthy of the resources of the intellectuals in the field? Or the department with its dwindling budget? Or the city with its disputes with neighboring jurisdictions? What does one say to doctoral students who choose for their dissertation research such topics as the criminal justice administrator who wanted to do a door-to-door survey of a low-income Hispanic neighborhood to determine if residents thought the police were doing a good job and were an asset to the community? Or the foreign student who wanted to conduct an empirical analysis of corruption and how to eliminate it in the government of her native country? These students were committed; they know such problems are important to administrators in the real world. Nevertheless, in their stated form, neither of these is a theoretically significant research problem.

This question of defining core problems may not be unique to the field of public administration. Other professional fields such as education seem to have similar difficulties. Describing the results of a study of doctoral programs in schools of education at 42 research universities, Winkler (1982) quotes the dean of one of these schools: "Too often, we encounter [doctoral] students in education who have difficulty even finding serious questions worth addressing" (p. 11).

A related issue surfaces here. It is often said that professional fields are "borrowing" fields, that is, they borrow from other disciplines, presumably the social sciences. Public administration is a professional field; therefore, it is one of the borrowing fields. Of course this begs the question of what is borrowed and for what purpose, but the focus here is strictly on core problems of the field. Are these problems also to be borrowed from the social sciences? Presumably not, because it is widely accepted that the mainstream social sciences (principally economics, political science, sociology, and psychology) are primarily interested in knowledge for the sake of knowledge. If this is so, then there is no reason at all to trust the social sciences to be interested in "our" problems. It is more likely that these "pure" sciences will only occasionally wander into our territory, and even then for other purposes. But if the public sector is worth studying at all, who should be studying it? Why should a university-based faculty abdicate its responsibility for growth of knowledge in its own field to outsiders? No one else is better equipped or more vitally interested.

If the critical question in the field is not, then, the absence of theory so much as the absence of a set of core problems, and if programs of public administration housed within research universities are the logical (indeed, the only) choice to best inquire into those problems, how can such a set of core problems be derived? Once again, an outsider has an advantage here, especially if the outsider is from sociology. The reason is that sociologists, especially since Simmel (1909), have been especially conscious of the distinction between form and content. A rough translation of the terms would be that content designates the more readily apparent aspects of some activity or behavior usually described by terms familiar to all laypersons, while form refers to the analytical properties of those same activities or behavior visible only through application of constructs contained within a theoretical framework. In countering the historicism of early 20th-century German social science, which held that human affairs could only be studied as a series of unique events, Simmel pointed out that although there were an infinite number of specific historical events and activities, only a few finite forms of sociation were involved in them (Coser, 1971, p. 181). Churches, police departments, and radical political parties differ in content but have similar form (for example, in their structure of superordinate and subordinate relationships). The study of form rather than content requires a cognitive style, abstract and analytical in nature, that psychologists refer to as field independence (Witkin, 1962, 1976). The role of theory in such studies distinguishes the result as knowledge about rather than acquaintance with.

A focus on form rather than content provides for a clear-cut distinction between the practitioner-focused master's degree program and the doctoral degree. Although courses at the master's level properly deal with the unique detail of issues in the public sector and with the techniques for dealing with them (i.e., content), the focus of doctoral education on the formal properties of these issues is qualitatively different. This may be illustrated with an example involving a current public-sector issue, that of toxic waste. The master's student would be instructed in the details of the toxic waste problem as defined by practitioners, the state of the art in governmental policies and programs for dealing with hazardous materials, and the principal actors—organizational and individual—on both sides of toxic waste controversies.

The student in a doctoral program, however, would face a qualitatively different set of questions that extend beyond these particulars. Why does a toxic waste problem exist at this particular time and place in human history? Are problems of this type endemic in the technological substructures of industrial societies? How are technological problems dealt with in societies with other types of economic and political structures? To what extent do class interests drive technological problems? How have governments in societies with differing political cultures dealt with technological problems of this sort? These are merely illustrative and as such are far from exhaustive, but they make the point that the skills involved in the study of practical problems such as governmental efforts in regard to toxic waste are different from those involved in working every day in a middle management position in the Environmental Protection Agency, for example.[10]

To sum up, the core problems in the field of public administration for a doctoral program must rise above the individual and particular problems of day-to-day practical administration. They should be the sorts of things that overworked public officials seldom have time for during normal working hours.[11] The function of the university doctoral program should be to provide an intellectual "sanctuary" in which doctoral students, regardless of their occupational roles, may step back and contemplate the meaning of public activity and its relation to the rest of society.

The distinction between the form and content of public activity, loosely borrowed from the work of German sociologist Georg Simmel, was suggested as one way of clarifying the nature and purpose of research involved in the doctorate. This distinction highlights the difference between analytical skills and the world of everyday experience. Hence the skills required for doctoral research will differ from the managerial skills possessed by the practitioner.

This implies, furthermore, that the relation between theory and practice is more complex than commonly assumed. Many students of the public sector look only to theory for guidance of practice or to the world of practice as a "test" for theory. Henry Mintzberg (1973) points out the major stumbling block here: So-called theories of management rest on a false picture of what managers actually do. Herbert Simon (1976, p. 20) labels these theoretical notions "proverbs." Another stumbling block is that other types of theories bear only remotely and indirectly on practice. In any case, the argument here is not over the separation of theory from practice (or vice versa), but rather for a three-way relationship among practice, theory, and method, where method refers to techniques of theory elaboration and clarification rather than the techniques of everyday management.

Finally, the arguments in this article do not identify any specific research technique as the one best way to approach the study of problems defined by form rather than content. Simmel's own research on the types and processes of sociation could hardly be described as positivistic. The present author's personal experience suggests that the most successful studies combine the quantitative data of the positive tradition with the qualitative data of the phenomenological tradition. The latter are especially useful in identifying the "rationale" for why causal structures hang together (Labovitz & Hagedorn, 1981, pp. 11-12). It is the rigorous and systematic application of method—of whatever type—that creates the detachment of the outsider in the research process, a detachment otherwise difficult to achieve when the researcher in all other respects is really an insider.

Notes

1. My thanks to Ken Kraemer for his helpful suggestions and to the anonymous reviewers who took the time to offer thoughtful and extensive comments on an earlier draft of this article.

2. The arguments developed here do not deal with similarities and differences that one might envision for the DPA degree as contrasted with the Ph.D. Although an important issue, the position recently adopted by NASPAA that, whatever its title, the doctorate should be a research degree is the position assumed here.

3. See the papers by Simmel in Wolff (1950), especially pp. 21-23 and 40-57; for a good overview of Simmel's work, see Coser (1971, pp. 177-199).

4. As the term is used in Berger and Luckmann (1966). See, for example, the discussion of the role of the stranger in Schutz (1944).

5. For example, see Park's (1931) discussion of marginality in race relations. The passage is from Park (1928, p. 892): "There appeared a new type of personality, namely, a cultural hybrid, a man living and sharing intimately in the cultural life and traditions of two distinct peoples;

never quite willing to break, even if he were permitted to do so, with his past and his traditions, and not quite accepted, because of racial prejudice, in the new society in which he now sought to find a place. He was a man on the margin of two cultures and two societies, which never completely interpenetrated and fused."

6. See, for example, Dahl (1947); also Gaus, White, and Dimock (1936), Mosher (1956), and White (1926). More recent contributions have been McCurdy and Cleary (1984), Perry and Kraemer (1986), and White (1986a, 1986b).

7. See, for example, Ostrom (1974); also Guerreiro-Ramos (1981) and Marini (1971).

8. This is not to say that master's candidates are not students of the field, but rather that the MPA has historically had as its goal the improvement of the student's management skills. Providing research training is another matter.

9. Yes, there is even research on why, despite widespread dissemination of these research findings, many key organizational officials continue to believe otherwise; results suggest that they trust their own "experience" more than ivory tower researchers. See Dynes, Quarantelli, and Kreps (1972); also Quarantelli (1985).

10. For a clear description of the differences between the world-taken-for-granted of the risk analyst as a practitioner on the one hand and of the study of risk as a formal property on the other, see Douglas and Wildavsky (1982).

11. Behavioral studies of managers, whether in the public or private sector, provide vivid evidence of the difference between the menial activities of practitioners and doctoral students. Managerial work is superficial, frequently interrupted, involving primarily verbal communication and focused, immediate detail rather than abstraction. In contrast, the doctoral student seeks large blocks of time free from interruption in order to think analytically and reflectively on written documents. For a behavioral description of the nature of administrative work in the private sector, see Mintzberg (1973); for a replication with a sample of five city managers, see Hale (1983).

PART 4

Research and Knowledge Development in an Applied Professional Field

In Chapter 5 Richard C. Box raised the question of whether the mainstream social science disciplines (such as sociology or economics) are appropriate standards of comparison for an applied field such as public administration. He suggests that comparisons with other applied fields such as planning, management, or social work might be more appropriate. In raising these questions, Box nudges our attention to an important issue: To what extent are knowledge and theory development—and therefore research—different within applied, professional fields? The chapters in Part 4 offer an extended discussion of just this issue.

In Chapter 12, Mary Timney Bailey comes to the defense of the often-maligned case study approach to research. She cogently argues that case study methods are central to the work of physics, chemistry, and other "hard" sciences, which is precisely the model many of the research critics seek to emulate in the study of public administration. She argues that properly structured case studies will live up to the scientific standards of rigor, including generalizability, transferability, and replicatability. In addition, Bailey refutes the argument against practitioner-focused research by reasserting Dwight Waldo's contention that a bond exists between theory and practice in public administration.

Marisa Kelly and Steven Maynard-Moody offer an insightful alternative to the traditional methods of program evaluation in Chapter 13. They note that evaluation research relies on methods rooted in a detached scientific positivism. Recently, a growing number of evaluation research analysts have used a postpositivist approach based on understanding agency operations from insiders' or stakeholders' perspectives. This calls for greater involvement by the analyst in facilitating discussions among insiders. The authors show how these new methods were used in a nationwide study of the Economic Development Districts Program.

Mary R. Schmidt in Chapter 14 shows what managers can learn from ordinary workers and people. Beginning with a story of a dam that failed, she describes four alternative kinds of knowledge that differ from the mainstream concept of scientific knowledge. Referring to these types of knowledge as "a feel for the hole," "intimate knowledge," "passive-critical knowledge," and "a feel for the whole," Schmidt argues that science, engineering, and bureaucratic institutions, under a common model of reality, often ignore and suppress these kinds of knowledge. Examples from biological science and ideas from organizational theory suggest a richer notion of nature and of human-constructed reality and a broader concept of rationality in decision making. She concludes with the general characteristics of such knowledge and an application to public administration.

Finally, in response to critics who argue that the knowledge base of public administration is too unscientific, Ralph P. Hummel in Chapter 15 offers a defense of the way public-sector managers acquire and use knowledge. In contrast to those who contend that public administration needs to generate and use knowledge based on "objectivity" and "pure reason," Hummel contends that the way managers interpret their world—"storytelling"—is a valid means for producing and accumulating knowledge. He argues that this source of knowledge is as credible for scholars and students of public administration as it is for practitioners.

12

Do Physicists Use Case Studies? Thoughts on Public Administration Research

MARY TIMNEY BAILEY

Research methods in public administration have been the subject of ongoing discussion in *Public Administration Review* in recent years. Articles on this subject include McCurdy and Cleary's (1984) study of doctoral dissertations in public administration, White's (1986b) replication and enhancement of their study, and Stallings's (1986) assessment of doctoral programs in public administration from the perspective of an outsider. White (1986a) also examined the theory-building potential of interpretive and critical research, and Kraemer and Perry (1989) studied the institutional setting for academic research in public administration.

Three issues run through all of these articles: (a) the quality of doctoral programs in public administration as measured by the quality of research produced from them, (b) the proper methodology for public administration research, and (c) the proper research questions for public administration as a discipline. Kraemer and Perry add a further dimension to the discussion by focusing on doctoral programs in public administration and providing a set of conditions needed to improve research quality and quantity. In general, the authors exhibit concern over use of the case study as a research methodology, in particular single-sample case studies used by practitioners as dissertations.

Specific concerns focus on the nature of the research questions addressed, the accumulation of knowledge in the field, theory testing and development, scientific rigor, and the development of public administration as a mature field of study. An underlying concern, more explicit in Stallings, is the question of the scientific quality of that research identified as "practitioner-oriented," the principal manifestation of which is the case study.

Throughout this literature and, indeed, across the discipline, there is a fundamental bias, an unarticulated value, favoring the acceptability of empirical or quantitative research methods over qualitative. Empirical, or "hard" methods, are considered a priori to produce more scientific, and thus better, findings than "soft" methods. The result is a hierarchy of researchers based solely on their methods rather than the significance of their work. Scholars who utilize quantitative methods, the "numbers crunchers," are revered, while those performing qualitative or case study research, which, done properly, can be much more intricate, are devalued, if not scorned.[1]

These are critical concerns for the field and for academicians seeking success on university faculties. Increasingly, researchers are pressured to move away from case studies as a research methodology and to utilize the positivist social science methodologies thought to be associated with "mature disciplines."

This article argues first for reconsideration of the abandonment of the case study (or its relegation to second-class status) and for a focus instead on the development of criteria to ensure scientific rigor in any research methodology that is appropriate for the study of public administration. I further argue that public administration should be practitioner-oriented in the sense that business, medicine, and engineering are practitioner-oriented, and that researchers need to define what that means for the field. The principal theses here are that case studies are an appropriate means for addressing many research questions in public administration and that case studies, even those that are practitioner-oriented, can be designed to pass tests of scientific rigor. Finally, if the problem lies with doctoral schools and lack of emphasis on rigor in dissertation research, these more rigorous standards may help to overcome that problem as well.

The Research Problem in Public Administration

In their 1984 study, McCurdy and Cleary attempted to develop data on the quality of research in public administration. To limit the study population, they narrowed their focus to doctoral dissertations. They reviewed the abstracts for 142 dissertations in public administration published in the 1981 edition of *Dissertation Abstracts International* (DAI) and concluded that few of the doctoral projects met "the criteria that conventionally define careful, systematic study in the social sciences" (McCurdy & Cleary, 1984, p. 50).

White (1986b) later replicated their study and added the 163 abstracts published in the 1980 edition of DAI. He reached generally the same conclusions, although he used somewhat different operational definitions for his criteria. Both studies used a conventional statistical model to collect and evaluate the data, and both contained an inherent bias against the case method.

McCurdy and Cleary were fairly explicit about their bias. Their study involved analyzing the abstracts using such criteria as validity, theory-testing impact, causal relationships, and cutting-edge importance. In defining the criterion "validity," they noted, "A study that was carefully designed—it might use experimental or quasi-experimental methods or statistical techniques—generally met this test. Case studies generally did not" (McCurdy & Cleary, 1984, p. 50). Not surprisingly, only 15% of the abstracts reviewed met the standards of this criterion. Further, in interpreting the data, McCurdy and Cleary "incorporated under the heading of significant research those projects which utilized generally accepted social science methods to test propositions or analyze phenomena." They purposely "omitted applied management projects (even those that used scientific methods, such as the evaluation of a specific program)" (McCurdy & Cleary, 1984, p. 52).

White, although allowing that the research topics of public administration may be suited to alternative methodologies, nonetheless used criteria with a mainstream bias. His criteria included validity, theory testing, hypothesis testing, and causality, which were generally defined to favor empirical studies (White, 1986b, p. 227).

Both studies attempted to correlate quality of dissertation research with quality of graduate programs in public administration. McCurdy and Cleary ran correlations with graduate schools ranked by Morgan and Meier (1982). They found that "overall, public administration graduate programs that ranked high on the Morgan-Meier scale did not consistently produce dissertations of high quality" (McCurdy & Cleary, 1984, p. 52).

White attempted to measure the influence of dissertation research on the field by tracking the authors through the *Social Science Citation Index* (SSCI) from 1978 to 1985. He found that, in each of his sample years, only 22% to 27% of the authors had published at least one item. He concluded that "most research from the 305 dissertations was not communicated beyond a small group of people, namely, the dissertation committee" (White, 1986b, p. 230).

White's findings seem to corroborate McCurdy and Cleary's conclusion that "most public administration dissertations are not set up in such a way that they can make much of a contribution to the development of our conceptual base or even to our base of information," leading to a further concern that "students are not researching anything really important in public administration" (McCurdy & Cleary, 1984, p. 54).

Both of these studies raise serious concerns about the quality of research in public administration, the emphasis on research in doctoral programs, and the role of research in expanding knowledge in the field. Both studies are also flawed in that the use of mainstream social science methodology limited the measurement and interpretation of their data. Only tentative conclusions can be drawn from these studies, given the biases built into the research designs and the limitations of the mechanisms used to collect the data.

It is still possible to agree, however, that a research problem exists in public administration. Underlying that problem is the issue of what should be the questions of central importance to the field and the appropriate ways of answering them. This is the primary issue addressed by Stallings in his assessment of doctoral programs in public administration.

Stallings begins by making a distinction between doctoral programs and "practitioner-oriented" master's degree programs. He asserts that "the study of the public sector seems to be the only defensible role for a doctoral program in the field" and that "there is widespread confusion of the public sector [the object of study] with public administration as a field devoted to the study of the public sector" (Stallings, 1986, p. 236).

Stallings is highly critical of public administration programs and research that he describes as being based on "acquaintance with" rather than "knowledge about." He is particularly concerned that acquaintance with data and findings are individualistic and "do not meet minimal criteria of replicatability and falsifiability" (Stallings, 1986, p. 236).

He argues further that the focus on practitioner problems dooms the field to "continually reinvent the proverbial wheel" and prohibits the development of a set of core problems appropriate for an academic field. The way to develop these core problems, Stallings believes, is to make the distinction between form and content.

A rough translation of the terms would be that *content* designates the more readily apparent aspects of some activity or behavior usually described by terms familiar to all laypersons, while *form* refers to the analytical properties of those same activities or behavior visible only through application of constructs contained within a theoretical framework (Stallings, 1986, p. 238).

The difference between the practitioner-focused master's degree program and the doctoral degree allows the courses at the master's level to deal with content, "the unique detail of issues in the public sector and the techniques for dealing with them," whereas the doctoral program provides "an intellectual 'sanctuary' in which doctoral students, regardless of their occupational roles, may step back and contemplate the meaning of public activity and its relation to the rest of society" (Stallings, 1986, p. 238).

Stallings' separation of theory and practice neatly distinguishes between the skills required for doctoral research and the managerial skills possessed by the practitioner. Unfortunately, it does not occur to him that these theoretical scholars may not be equipped to be teachers of practitioners. If the master's program is to have a focus on skills development, where are the faculty who possess these skills to come from if not from the doctoral programs in public administration? Although "acquaintance with" practice is not a sufficient criterion for doctoral programs and research, neither is "knowledge of" theory alone sufficient for teaching master's degree students.

This distinction made by Stallings is reminiscent of the politics-administration dichotomy and just as intellectually damaging. As the development of professionalism in the field has been hampered by an unrealistic image of administrators as apolitical generic managers, so too has the development of theory been inhibited by the inappropriate application of criteria derived from the "pure" disciplines of social science where theory does not have to have practical value.[2]

In public administration, unlike the mainstream social sciences, a bond exists between theory and practice. Moreover, Waldo has observed that public administration, unlike sociology and political science, is both a study and an activity, and both are "intended to maximize the realization of goals" (Waldo, 1955, p. 11). He has developed his own notation to distinguish between the doctrines and discipline, Public Administration, and the activities of government managers, public administration. The existence of the theory-practice bond sets Public Administration apart from other social sciences and implies the need for a specialized set of research questions and research designs appropriate to address them.

Science, Social Science, and Research Methods

Professor Stallings identifies himself as an outsider (he is a sociologist) and asserts that this enables him to take a less-biased view of the field of public administration. I, too, am somewhat of an outsider, having come to social science from a background in chemistry, one of the "real" sciences. It has frequently struck me that those social scientists who would limit research to mathematical models have misunderstood "real" science and overlooked critical features of human interaction that make social science research worth doing.

The conventional model of social science research is generally understood to be drawn from the natural sciences, especially physics (Lieberson, 1985, p. 234). The principal attributes of the results of scientific rigor are that they are generalizable, transferable, and replicable. A primary concern of researchers in both natural and social science is the control of extraneous variables. In physics, this is done by carefully controlling the laboratory conditions under which experiments are conducted. These conditions are made explicit so that experiments can be replicated. The findings of a given experiment are then tested and challenged by other scientists in other laboratories looking for conditions or results that differ from those reported by the initial researcher. The outcome of an experiment, then, is essentially a hypothesis, and each experiment is, in reality, a case study. A set of case studies can be used to challenge dominant theories or for applied research projects in fields (medicine, engineering, etc.) that are derived from the "pure" disciplines.

Social science research designs begin with a hypothesis, and data are then collected to test it. The outcome of the research is essentially predetermined, and the interpretation of the data is limited by the statistical methods used to test the hypothesis. Unlike natural science, where a cause-and-effect relationship can be established with some confidence, social scientists must accept "lack of falsification" as the closest they can come to verification.

Experimental control in social science is achieved by limiting the influence of variables through research design, definitions of terms, measurement methods, and selection of statistical techniques. The more distant the researcher and his or her methods are from the subject at hand (values), the more scientific the data will be (facts), and the closer the researcher will come to verification or scientific truth. The social scientist aims to eliminate the influence of unique variables and concentrates instead on variables that are common across all subjects under study.

Social scientists rarely carry out experiments where causes and effects can be systematically tested. Instead, empirical research generally produces nonexperimental data, which, as Lieberson (1985, p. 4) notes, "are treated as far as possible as if they were truly experimental data," capable of explaining why something is happening. Yet in the best of circumstances, empirical data can only tell us what is happening.

Lieberson (1985) argues further that when empirical research is used for theory testing, it cannot provide insights into the relative importance of different theories. "We can learn only whether or not the consequences of causal propositions occur, not whether one is more important than another" (p. 223). Moreover, the variation in some phenomenon can be readily identified quantitatively, but not the principle behind its existence. Thus "variation explained is not existence explained" (p. 224).

Social science research is rarely replicated. Indeed, replication in the natural science sense is impossible because conditions can never be the same twice. Changes in context; time; political, social, and economic conditions; or the possibility of Hawthorne effects make research projects involving human beings singular events. Empirical research, then, is as time- and context-bound as case studies are. While natural science deals with inanimate objects or controlled subjects with high degrees of predictability and replicability—one molecule of oxygen is pretty much like all the others—social science deals with social processes and human beings who are infinitely different and continually changing. A common belief among natural scientists is that, when one introduces the human element, science goes out the window.

Social science has attempted to overcome this problem by using statistical analysis of objectively measured data. To collect these data, it is necessary to construct research questions in such a way that the answers can fit the instrument of analysis. This requirement has several drawbacks. First, the data that are most adaptable to the model—that is, they can be measured— may also be the most trivial. Second, the research cannot produce new information, only existing data.[3] Third, the data are collected out of context and cannot account for variations related to context, although these may be of critical importance. Finally, the model eliminates anomalies altogether. The limits of the quantitative research model are such that the social scientist risks producing reliable but insignificant "so what" results. Indeed, Lindblom and Cohen (1979) describe "Professional Social Inquiry" as ritualistic, like dancing in tribal societies, which produces assurance even when the exercise is futile (p. 84).

These shortcomings are most serious if research aims at theory building. White (1986a) has noted that philosophers of science use the hermeneutic method, which involves interpretation and criticism, for the development of theory (p. 21). Empirical methods aim to control conditions that could create interpretive variances, thus eliminating the possibility for theory building as an outcome of the research. Similarly, anomalous findings are usually treated as outliers and excluded from statistical analyses. Yet it is the accumulation of anomalies that leads to the identification of new scientific paradigms, according to Thomas Kuhn (1970). Without anomalies, it is questionable that theory development can occur in social science. What is left, as White (1986a) argues, is research that is little more than "rule-following behavior" (p. 21). Casanova (1981, p. 10) argues, moreover, that quantitative methods are more likely to be employed by researchers who wish to preserve the status quo of the political and social systems.

One way out of this problem is through the use of case studies. In simple terms, a case is a study of people, events, or organizational processes in situ, which incorporates a "process of discovery" (Lofland, 1971, p. 4). Yin (1990, p. 4) offers the following more technical definition:

A case study is an empirical inquiry that
1. investigates a contemporary phenomenon within its real-life context;
2. when the boundaries between phenomenon and context are not clearly evident; and
3. in which multiple sources of evidence are used.

Case studies can be descriptive, critical or interpretive, problem solving, or theory building. They can range from purely practitioner-oriented to esoteric scholarly studies. For public administration, the ideal case study will have value for both academics and practitioners.

Case studies, prima facie, do not meet the test of being scientific because they are too close to individual subjects with too many variables. Case studies are limited in time and space, as are statistical analyses, and descriptive single-agency case studies without a broader conceptual base can also produce "so what" results. At the same time, case studies have the potential to produce valuable information about the richness of human interaction. The case study, properly structured, may actually come closer to the physics model than does conventional social science, at least for the field of public administration.

Case study findings, because they deal inherently with time and space, can be examined in their own context. These conditions can be made explicit in the same way that a physicist reporting research results makes the laboratory conditions explicit. Any interpretations or conclusions drawn from these studies can be studied in other contexts to determine if, in fact, commonalities are to be found in different places with different groups of people. A simple analogy here is Newton's study of gravity. In developing his law, Newton dropped "apples" in several places under different conditions. Only after having conducted several "case studies" did he publish his theory of gravity. Lieberson used Newton's gravity studies as a backdrop for criticizing the study of variation by social scientists. Where Newton could apply a strong control, a vacuum, to eliminate the effects of variations in objects such as density and shape, social researchers can only measure the variations and could, hypothetically, explain all of the differences without ever considering gravity (Lieberson, 1985, p. 100).

The laboratories of public administration are the offices of practitioners. Moreover, according to Landau (1973, p. 539), organizations are intended to be solutions—decision rules—which are therefore predictive in character. The information that practitioners own is needed by scholars to develop and test theories, which can then be applied by practitioners to improve the practice of public administration and by scholars both in further theory development and for the teaching of public managers. Following Landau, a case study may also take the form of a postaudit of the organization or decision rule. This is not an argument favoring the use of single-agency case studies, because such research without a rigorous methodology may only provide descriptions of limited reality. It does not follow, however, that case studies a priori lack value for the development of theory.

Public administration research can become more scientific, that is, more like the laboratory sciences, by identifying replicable conditions and using research designs that incorporate rigorous case methodology. What is needed is to identify the factors that are necessary to obtain measures of scientific rigor.

Scientific Rigor and Case Study Methodology

If case studies are to pass the test of scientific rigor, they must produce results that are generalizable, transferable, and replicable, as with the natural sciences laboratory cases. If case methodology does not meet these criteria, it is not science.

Generalizable refers to the ability of a case to be uniform across organizations or events. Yin argues further that "case studies, like experiments, are generalizable to theoretical propositions, not to populations or universes." A case study does not represent a "sample of one" but provides the opportunity to "expand and generalize theories (analytic generalization) and not to enumerate frequencies (statistical generalization)" (Yin, 1990, p. 21). As an example, consider that all public organizations, departments, or agencies are subject to the requirements of the budget process. Regardless of what system of budgeting is used—simple, program, zero-based, and so on—the theoretical concept of budgeting in relationship to agency management is pretty much the same everywhere.

Transferable means that the findings or research solutions can be applied in other similar organizations, either in toto or with minor modifications for a situation's conditions. Examples would be the development of a problem solution—a productivity improvement—or an interpretive analysis, which can inform practitioners in and academics studying similar organizations. An excellent example of the latter is the work by Irving Janis, which led to the identification of groupthink (Thomas, 1983, p. 57).

Replicable refers generally to being able to reproduce the method of experimentation and analysis. Given the same conditions and using the same methods, the same or similar results should be obtained in other studies or with other organizations. To facilitate replication, Yin (1990) prescribes the use of a case study protocol as part of a carefully designed research project. The protocol contains the case study "instrument but also contains the procedures and general rules that should be followed in using the instrument" (p. 70). A protocol should include the following sections:

- overview of the case study project (project objectives and auspices, case study issues, and relevant readings about the topic being investigated);
- field procedures (credentials and access to the case study "sites," general sources of information, and procedural reminders);
- case study questions (the specific questions that the case study investigator must keep in mind in collecting data, "table shells" for specific arrays of data, and the potential sources of information for answering each question); and

- guide for the case study report (outline, format for the narrative, and specification of any bibliographical information and other documentation).

Replicability can be built into case studies through the use of multiple cases, where each case is selected to produce either "similar results (literal replication) or contrary results but for predictable reasons (theoretical replication)" (Yin, 1990, p. 53).

Good case studies will identify those features of the case or set of cases that are uniform and generalizable. This is precisely what is done in management science and policy analysis. The inherent assumption in these methods is that all organizations are pretty much the same; thus scientific, value-free management skills can be applied in any setting, private or public.

At the same time, case studies will also identify those features that appear to be relatively unique. The basis for such distinctions may be drawn from the literature or through comparison with similar organizations in other places. For example, in doing a study of police departments, it could be argued that they are all alike in certain respects and are all different in others. Could a study of, say, management styles or organization culture reveal findings—patterns or interpretations—that could provide practical insights for city managers about police administration and also for scholars about the theoretical concepts themselves? Going further, could such a study have value for the development of a political theory of the citizen-public administrator interface?

Some pitfalls exist with case study research, the greatest being researcher bias. Good case researchers must be able to step away from preconceived notions if the discovery process is to work. This condition may circumscribe that research that has been described as "the most frequent form of case study dissertation in public administration: a study conducted retrospectively or concurrently on an organization by one of its employees."[4]

Yin recommends that researchers should continually discuss their research design and interpretations with colleagues in order to guard against error and bias. Lofland (1971, p. 112) argues that researchers must self-consciously evaluate their own observations. Questions that they should ask include, How direct is the observation? How did the location of the report contribute to potential bias or skewing? What influence would my relationship with the interviewee have on the data? Can I detect self-serving error and bias—that is, did I find only what I wanted to? How accurate have my observations been in the past? Is the report internally consistent? Is there external consistency, across cases or in relation to a standard? He concludes that "truthful observation depends heavily on the sincere good faith, open-mindedness, and thoroughness of the observer" (Lofland, 1971, p. 113). The same maxim applies equally to empirical researchers.

The Case Study as Theory-Building Methodology

The principal indictment against the case methodology as charged by McCurdy and Cleary and Stallings is that it does not add to the growth of knowledge in the field through theory building and theory testing. Case studies are seen as unique, noncumulative events that cannot meet the requirements of scientific methodology.

Elsewhere, it has been argued that critical case studies have advantages for theory-building purposes because "they avoid the 'inductive fallacy' which assumes that theories lie in phenomena and can be derived through data processing" (Thomas, 1983, p. 57). White (1986a) concluded that "theory building is fundamentally a practical activity in explanatory, interpretive, and critical research" (p. 21), for which the primary methodologies are the case study, descriptive histories, philosophical analysis, or social critique. Yin argues that case studies are the preferred strategy "when a 'how' or 'why' question is being asked about a contemporary set of events, over which the investigator has little or no control" (p. 20).

I would argue further that public administration theory could not have developed as it has without the theory building derived from case studies. The field has been enriched by important case studies such as Philip Selznick's (1949) study of the Tennessee Valley Authority, Herbert Kaufman's (1960) study of forest rangers, Graham Allison's (1971) analysis of the Cuban missile crisis, and Daniel Mazmanian and Jeanne Nienaber's (1979) study of the Corps of Engineers.

Despite their long-term value to the field, these studies would fail the scientific tests established by positivist social science. To underscore the point, White noted that even Dwight Waldo's (1948) classic *The Administrative State,* which was his doctoral dissertation, would not meet "Cleary and McCurdy's criteria of causality, testability, and validity" (White, 1986a, p. 22).

More recent examples of the use of cases for theory building include Karen Hult and Charles Walcott's (1990) analysis of the space shuttle Challenger disaster to develop a theory of governance networks and institutional design, and John Burke's (1986) use of the case of Environmental Protection Agency whistleblower Hugh Kaufman, among others, for his theory of bureaucratic responsibility.

Other cases that appear to offer rich opportunity for theory building or testing include the Iran-Contra affair, the Department of Energy's management of nuclear weapons facilities, the scandal at the Department of Housing and Urban Development, and the massive regulatory failure in the savings-and-loan industry. The lessons to be gained from these examples can be derived only through case methodology.

Ultimately, resolution of the research question in public administration will require further attention to the purpose of research for both public administration and Public Administration. Because of the practitioner-academic interface, research has two purposes: (a) to improve scholars' understanding of the dynamics of public organizations and their impacts on clientele, employees, and the polity; and (b) to develop information to improve the practice of administration by practitioners within the American political context, including the identification of theories and models that can be applied in problem solving.

The second purpose is extremely hard to achieve through empirical research because the internal and external environments of public organizations are at once common but at the same time unique. Each agency, bureau, or city hall is unlike every other one, although all may be fundamentally alike in all unimportant respects. Hummel (1988) argues, in addition, that no two problems are ever exactly the same.

The only way that empiricists can study these problems and organizations is by adjusting the research design to exclude the uniqueness as much as possible. It is more likely through some form of case methodology, however, that the variables that make these organizations work can be identified and examined. It is through cases, carefully developed and rigorously analyzed, that academicians and practitioners can jointly work to advance the knowledge of the field.[5]

What is needed for public administration to resolve the research issue is the redefinition of the field in terms of its practitioner orientation, like engineers or physicians, and the delineation of a theory-based conceptual methodology to facilitate creative and theoretically significant case studies. By legitimizing the case study as a scientifically rigorous method, researchers can enhance both the theory and practice of public administration.

Public Administration and the Case Study

As public administration advances toward fruition as a mature field, it is necessary to resolve the research issue. The recent focus on narrowly defined positivist social science, because of its inherent biases, may impede this resolution by creating a hierarchy for research and scholarship. If research leads to reducing the field to numbers, it risks losing the substance of public administration and reinforcing the barriers between academicians and practitioners. Public administration researchers who strive for a dynamic relationship between theory and practice will continue to be relegated to second-class status in university faculties, their research denigrated as "practitioner-oriented," while they are held to a mainstream social science standard that impedes the advancement of theory in the field. To avoid this fate, public administration must embrace a practitioner orientation, rather than apologizing for it, and develop a scientifically rigorous research methodology appropriate for the field.

One of the basic problems in the discipline, which may partly explain why case studies are generally regarded as weak scientifically, is that social science programs do not generally stress the development of analytical or critical thinking skills.[6] In the natural sciences, analytical skills are developed along with substantive knowledge through laboratory courses that are linked with classroom lectures. Thus developing skill with the scientific method is an integral part of the learning process for all science courses.

In the social sciences, in contrast, students take research methods as a discrete course and various tool courses—regression analysis, factor analysis, and so on—are also studied separately, often as electives, with little connection to the substantive or theory courses of the discipline. Because these are discrete courses, students tend to think of research as something set apart, and, for many, the courses to be put off as long as possible. As a result, I submit, they do not develop a critical eye when examining the basic literature of the field or the events or organizations that they encounter.[7]

It is this lack of capability for critical observation as much as anything that may account for poor quality in both research and practice in public administration. The fundamental challenge for public administration educators is to move students away from right-wrong truth-seeking research and practice to the acknowledgement of bias as a feature of all research and in every research outcome. If we are to train researchers and practitioners to make significant contributions to the discipline, then we need to envelop them in a learning environment that emphasizes critical analysis and the integration of research throughout the curriculum. Graduate schools must take the lead by making research a more prominent feature of doctoral programs.

In adopting this model, however, care is necessary to avoid uncritical acceptance of a self-limiting mainstream social science methodology. The appropriate methodology for a given research project depends on the question and situation being studied. The development of a rigorous case methodology offers the potential for enriching the public administration theory literature and strengthening the theory-practice linkage that is fundamental to the field.

Scholars in public administration and the positivist social sciences need to understand that the case study method does not necessarily equate with practitioner research, that applied research does not equate with lack of theory development, and that theoretical research does not equate with usefulness. If advancement of the field is the goal, then all are equally important.

Notes

1. Although case studies are often categorized as qualitative research, Yin (1990) distinguishes the case study as a research tool with a distinctive research design.

2. This is not so clearly the case with the "pure" natural sciences. Theories of chemistry and physics appear to have a more fundamental role in practice than do theories of the social sciences.

3. Researchers may note serendipitous findings on occasion, but these may also be regarded as a failure of research design.

4. I am indebted to an anonymous reviewer of a draft of this article for this observation. He or she goes on to argue, "In its worst form (and worst-case examples occur frequently) it is analogous to conducting research on the American family by using as data recollections from one's childhood."

5. There seems to be a practitioner-academic dichotomy developing in the field. This is particularly apparent at meetings of the American Society for Public Administration.

6. I have no empirical evidence to back this up, only informal observations from my own graduate education and the departments with which I am familiar as an academic.

7. For a method of teaching critical observation, see "The Administrative Journal" in Denhardt (1984, pp. 188-197).

13

Policy Analysis in the Postpositivist Era: Engaging Stakeholders in Evaluating the Economic Development District's Program

MARISA KELLY

STEVEN MAYNARD-MOODY

Policy and policy analysis define each other. When reforms are seen as experiments, policy is considered a form of causal argument, and analysts look to experimental methods for guidance. When policy is viewed as a social good, analysts turn to economics for help. In recent years, views of policy have been evolving: We now conceive of policies as symbolic and interpretive rather than as efficient solutions designed to solve society's ills. Policy is now defined as after-the-fact interpretations (Lynn, 1987, p. 30), stories (Doron, 1986; Stone, 1988, Chap. 6; 1989), and arguments (Dunn, 1982). The policy process is seen as a struggle over the symbols we invoke and the categories into which we place different problems and solutions, because ultimately these symbols and categories will determine the actions that we take. Interpretation and argument are increasingly seen as playing primary roles in the policy process (Feldman, 1989; Weiss & Gruber, 1984). Furthermore, policies themselves are now considered as largely symbolic, a way to give voice to latent public concerns: "Rather than responding to pre-existing public wants, the art of policy making has lain primarily in giving voice to these half-articulated fears and hopes, and embodying them in convincing stories about their sources and the choices they represent" (Reich, 1987, p. 5).

AUTHORS' NOTE: An earlier version of this article was delivered at the 1992 annual meeting of the Western Political Science Association, San Francisco, March 19-21, 1992. We would like to thank Dvora Yanow, Martha Feldman, Dennis Palumbo, Michael Hallett, and the anonymous reviewers for their helpful comments. Many helped in this research; we would especially like to thank David Elkins for his creativity and hard work on this project.

These new understandings or conceptions of policies themselves have shaped and been shaped by new conceptualizations of the practice of policy analysis. Policy analysts have traditionally used positivist methods to carry out their research, but such methods are incompatible with interpretive and symbolic conceptions of policy. In recent years, policy analysts, and researchers throughout the social sciences, have become aware of the limits of such methods (Bernstein, 1982; Guba & Lincoln, 1987; Hawkesworth, 1988; Lindblom, 1990; Weiss, 1991).

If, as these critics demand, positivist methods are rejected, then the knowledge base of traditional policy analysis is threatened.[1] Is there an alternative epistemological foundation from which policy analysis can draw its legitimacy? Is there still a role for the policy analyst, the discredited expert? The claim made in this article is that we can answer Yes to both of these questions, but to do so requires new methods and a new conception of the role of the analyst. An evaluation of the Economic Development Administration's (EDA's) Economic Development Districts program (EDD) is used to illustrate one conception of this new role and the results it can yield, an important step because most postpositivist critiques rarely move beyond the theoretical debate to practical application.

Critiques of Positivist Methods

Positivism is based on the assumption that we can best comprehend and evaluate the world by striving to escape our own historical and culturally constructed presuppositions. As positivism first developed in the 19th century, the basic assertion was that sense perception is the basis of all human knowledge and that through objective observation we can discern facts such that they correspond to reality itself. Empirical verification is all that is needed to validate the truth claims of any given assertion. Anything that is not observable (anything, in other words, based on "theological, metaphysical, philosophical, ethical, normative, or aesthetic" foundations) is dismissed as meaningless, as having no valid knowledge claims (Hawkesworth, 1988, p. 38). Interpretation and judgment classically conceived of by philosophers, such as Aristotle, have no validity and no role to play in the positivist world. Value neutrality is essential. Neutral observation will allow the facts to speak for themselves unaffected by history or context, which ultimately only distort reality. Only objectivity, as obtained through the use of an inductive scientific method, can allow us to see the external world as it really is.

Later, Karl Popper (1959) revised this conception, arguing that we always make sense of the world through theories, and these theories affect the phenomena we are attempting to observe. Rather than trying to use inductive methods to build theories, he believed that we should use empirical obser-vations to test them and attempt to falsify them. No theory can be absolutely true, but all can be absolutely falsified by the observation of unexplained phenomena. According to Popper, the method of falsification allows us to eliminate inadequate theories and to have an increasingly better grasp of reality. For Popper, objective truth exists, but it lies beyond our grasp. We can, however, come close to attaining it by following the falsification method.

Although Popper recognized the cognitive limits of the human mind, which the original positivist tradition does not, his methodology is now often thought of as orthodox positivism, and the two schools do share a great deal. As M. E. Hawkesworth (1988, p. 47) has noted,

> both positivist and Popperian conceptions of science are committed to the correspondence theory of truth and its corollary assumption that the objectivity of science ultimately rests upon an appeal to the facts. Both are committed to the institutionalization of the fact-value dichotomy in order to establish the deter-minate ground of science. Both accept that once safely ensconced within the bounds of the empirical realm, science is grounded upon a sufficiently firm foundation to provide for the accumulation of knowledge, the progressive elimination of error, and the gradual accretion of useful solutions to technical problems.

Positivist and Popperian methods have traditionally dominated the field of policy analysis. The analyst's claim to knowledge is based on the value-neutral observation of facts that can then be employed by decision makers as they formulate and implement policies. The more scientific or objective the analyst, the more credible his or her claims (Jennings, 1987, p. 15).[2] Scien-tific principles applied to the world of politics can solve our problems, or such is the claim of adherents to this tradition. "Science provides a neutral ground upon which people of all creeds and colors might unite, on which all political contradictions might be overcome. Science is to provide a balance between opposing interests, a source of unity amidst diversity, order amidst chaos." (Proctor, 1991, p. 8)

WEBS OF SHARED MEANING

In contrast, the postpositivist critique put forth by some philosophers and social scientists is rooted in the idea that no objective truth is "out there" waiting to be discovered. Rather, all "reality" is socially constructed. As Richard Rorty (1982, 1991) asserts, from the moment of birth we begin to construct webs of beliefs, desires, and sentential attitudes that are, though variable from person to person, the very foundation of the self and of reality.

These webs grow and change as we encounter new phenomena, but there is no way to interpret those phenomena without these webs. Our webs allow us to interpret the world; meaningful reality would not exist without them. If the changes become extensive, then we have undergone a process of recontextualization: Our webs can now be thought of as a new context (Rorty, 1991, p. 94). The new text or web, however, is still historically situated and still theoretically shapes our world. We cannot escape our historically and culturally determined theoretical positions. Thus the search for objective truth is misguided, for no such thing exists. By this criteria, even Popper's falsification test is inappropriate. If "there is no tenable distinction between theoretical assumptions and correspondence rules, if what is taken to be the 'world,' what is understood as 'brute data' is itself theoretically constituted (indeed constituted by the same theory which is undergoing the test), then no conclusive disproof of a theory is likely" (Hawkesworth, 1988, p. 50).

IMPORTANCE OF HISTORY

Similarly, that which we attempt to study is also uninterpretable outside of its own context. We cannot separate a "thing" from a thing's context, because context creates meaning. Thus, as opposed to the ahistorical framework of positivism, postpositivism emphasizes the importance of history. The social world is a narrative composed of many subnarratives. Everyone and everything is a part of that larger ongoing narrative even as each plays the primary role within its own narrative. We are active coauthors, not sole authors of our own narratives, sharing this position with the authorship of history and of those who share or have roles in our narratives as we have roles in theirs.

> We enter upon a stage which we did not design and we find ourselves part of an action that was not of our working. Each of us being a main character in his own drama plays subordinate parts in the dramas of others and each drama constrains the others. . . . An action is a moment in a possible or actual history or in a number of such histories. The notion of a history is as fundamental a notion as the notion of action. Each requires the other. (MacIntyre, 1984, pp. 213-214)

We can understand the actions of others only if we understand this conception of narratives and their historical, embedded character. We can make sense of what we attempt to study—be it the effects of particular public policies or the specific actions of members of an organizational unit, or anything else—only if we explore the history of our subject.

Of course, this is not to imply that our vision of any given narrative or history is objectively derived. Again, our explorations of history are themselves contextualized phenomena within the webs of our understanding. History is not objective fact but itself interpretation and memory. Our version of history reflects our values and theoretical presuppositions more than the "facts" (Neustadt & May, 1986). In other words, history and our webs of meaning are interdependent, each simultaneously shaping the other. As James Clifford (1986) writes, "the poetic and the political are inseparable; . . . science is in, not above, historical and linguistic processes" (p. 2).

Thus all analysis is interpretation, not ahistorical objective observation of the facts. This discussion applies to both the natural or so-called hard sciences as much as it does to the social or soft sciences. In any field of inquiry we are engaged in the search for a language that will help us make sense of the world. That language is developed through the process of interpretation, not objective observation. Richard Rorty illustrates this with a brief discussion of an artifact of the natural sciences, fossils. According to Rorty (1982),

> if we think of the fossil record as a text, then we can say that paleontology, in its early stages, followed "interpretive" methods. That is, it cast around for some way of making sense of what happened by looking for a vocabulary in which a puzzling object could be related to other, more familiar objects, so as to become intelligible. (p. 199)[3]

From this perspective, interpretation means casting about for a vocabulary that helps us to make sense of things. Such vocabularies, as Rorty notes, are not more or less objective, they are simply more or less useful, no matter what our subject of inquiry (Rorty, 1982, p. 205). New useful vocabularies are incorporated into our existing webs, for "anything is, for purposes of being inquired into, constituted by a web of meanings" (p. 199). The interdependence of our webs of meaning and our observations is reflected in the very process of so-called positivist objective knowledge construction, as interpretations of inquiry in action reflect.[4]

Postpositivism, however, is not an endorsement of radical subjectivity or of analysis reduced to advocacy. Interpretive social science attempts to spin a web that is wider and more complex than existing webs by bringing more information into view and by opening up the possibility of recontextualization. As Bruce Jennings (1987, p. 145) argues, interpretive social science "seeks to transform thin particularity into thick particularity." Objectivity is reconceived as attempts to achieve intersubjective agreement through the outsider's facilitation of recontextualization. The desire for objectivity thus becomes "the desire not to escape the limitations of one's community, but simply the desire for as much intersubjective agreement as possible, the desire to extend the reference of 'us' as far as we can" (Rorty, 1991, p. 23).

This conception of inquiry as recontextualization aiming at intersubjective agreement requires "probing, not proving" (Lindblom, 1990).

New Methods, New Roles

Postpositivism is a young intellectual movement, whose assumptions pose many unanswered questions for the practice of policy analysis. What form is a break with positivism to take, particularly within the policy studies field? If analysis is interpretation, who should be empowered to interpret? Is there still an epistemologically valid role for the policy analyst, and if so, what form should that role take? The preceding discussion of postpositive assumptions foreshadows some of the possible answers to these questions.

The assertion here is that rational understanding can be pursued in policy analysis if we conceive of the analyst as an "outsider" who will work inclusively with "insiders" or stakeholders. Analysts are outsiders not because they stand above the process but because they are not primary characters in this particular larger narrative. Outsiders can facilitate the recontextualization of the insiders' webs by bringing together different subnarratives so that all concerned can gain a better understanding of the larger narrative of which they are all a part. Also, this process pursues objectivity as intersubjective agreement among the insiders while simultaneously allowing the understanding of the outsider to add new vocabularies for possible incorporation by insiders. Once we accept that all interpretations are necessarily value-laden (including the positivist interpretations of reality), then we can accept the debate over interpretations as a valid approach to policy inquiry. Thus "social analysis that survives an open and nondistorted process of collective deliberation can be said to be 'objective' in the relevant sense" (Jennings, 1987, p. 29). Our views are similar, but not identical, to those of Guba and Lincoln (1987). They see the policy analyst (or evaluator) as subservient to the stakeholders. In their view, the analyst must accept "at face value" (p. 212) the insiders' views, while we argue that the analyst must challenge the insiders to move beyond their narrow interpretations.

Two specific activities can help policy analysts to engage in this postpositivist inquiry. First, they must engage in practical reasoning. As originally discussed by Aristotle, practical reasoning (or phronesis) attempts to discern the best course of action in any given situation by consciously considering values and cultural understandings. Practical reasoning as conceptualized by postpositivists is a rational and critical reflection on actions or potential action that accepts the cultural embeddedness of policies. Practical reasoning makes use of "creativity, deliberative judgment, and evaluative assessment"

(Hawkesworth, 1988, p. 55) to work toward intersubjective agreement. In Hawkesworth's (1988, p. 89) view, rational deliberation requires holding on to assumptions while examining problems and understanding from different frames of reference and competing explanations. We argue that policy analysis has a positive role in broadening the interpretive frame out of which more reasoned judgments emerge.

Of course, practical reasoning used on behalf of policy analysis requires situations in which the analyst can attempt to facilitate this whole process. The proposal here is to conduct policy analysis within interpretive forums. These forums are meant to bring together various stakeholders and the policy analysts, who then engage in inquiry as recontextualization by bringing together the various pieces of the historical puzzle and by engaging in practical reasoning. Thus the postpositivist role for the policy analyst is to facilitate rational deliberation, to bring together multiple perspectives, to assist in the process of exploring alternative courses of action, and to aid policy makers and, perhaps, citizens in understanding the possible limitations of their current perspectives. The policy analyst is not an expert but a facilitator, who lends his or her own subjective but outsider perspective to the evaluation process.

The appropriate insider participants in any such forum, of course, are context or policy specific, and practical reasoning must itself assist the analyst in making such decisions. In the sections that follow, we describe our efforts to apply postpositivist thought to a policy analysis of the Economic Development District Program, one of the Economic Development Administration's (EDA) major programs. We begin, as the analysis began, by describing the context. Rethinking the EDD program requires some understanding of the history of EDA; the stories of the individual EDDs are part of the larger narrative of EDA. We then describe the analysis process. The discussion is meant to take those of us interested in postpositivism beyond the theoretical realm to the application of these new conceptions to the applied world of policy studies.

EDA: An Agency in Turmoil

In the spring of 1990, at the beginning of our study of the EDD program, the EDA had endured the most difficult decade of its tumultuous 25-year history. From President Reagan's first budget in 1981 through President Bush's administration, funds for EDA were first slashed and then, from fiscal year 1983, eliminated from the president's budget request. EDA has survived only because of congressional support, but that support has not shielded EDA from severe cutbacks. By fiscal year 1983, EDA's budget had been cut from the $625 million allocated in President Carter's last year in office to a little less than $200 million. This 60% cut required major reductions in personnel; during the early 1980s, several waves of reductions in force reduced EDA's staff by 30%.

The cutbacks went beyond losses in funding and staff. Also cut, or at least undermined, was the legitimacy of the federal role in promoting substate regional economic development. EDA was created in 1965 as a division of the U.S. Department of Commerce to promote, in President Johnson's words, economic growth where jobs are too few and incomes too low. In 1981, President Reagan's first Secretary of Commerce, Malcolm Baldridge, wrote in the preface to the EDA annual report, "President Reagan has called for a reduction in Federal spending as part of his overall Economic Recovery Program. . . . Within this context, the President proposed phasing out the Economic Development Administration (EDA)" (U.S. Department of Commerce, 1981, p. ii). In 1965, EDA was created to lead the nation's poor regions out of poverty. In 1981, the Reagan administration saw it as a barrier to economic growth; the administration felt that EDA could best fulfill its mission by disappearing.

Although partisan struggles over the funding, role, and existence of EDA reached a peak during President Reagan's first term, the conflict began in the early years of the Nixon administration. President Nixon denounced EDA as a failure when it was only a few years old.[5] He tried to shift the emphasis from public works to business loans and to replace programmatic grants with block grants. He vetoed an expansion of EDA and, in 1971, impounded $1 million in public works grants. President Carter expanded EDA's role in urban economic development, changes that were reversed a few years later when President Reagan took office.

PROGRAM EVOLUTION

Although EDA programs were always politically controversial in Washington, local support for them grew steadily throughout this period. This was especially true of the EDD program. Congress designated more and more regions as eligible for EDA grants and loans, and these regions established EDDs as conduits for federal grants. EDDs are substate regional economic development planning districts that are encouraged and regulated by EDA. EDDs are not local EDA offices but semiautonomous agencies. They require state and local involvement, involvement that translates into strong support in Congress.

Despite the general criticism of EDA coming primarily from Republican presidents, the number of EDDs grew dramatically. In 1969 there were 24 EDDs, mostly in the Deep South.[6] While the Nixon administration was trying to cut EDA funding, the number of EDDs multiplied sevenfold in the first five years of his presidency. By 1974, 157 EDDs had spread throughout the Southeast and Appalachian regions; they were also beginning to form in the Northeast and older industrial states. By 1976, the number reached 211. By 1990, there were 261 EDA designated EDDs, of which 244 were funded by EDA.[7]

As EDDs expanded to cover much of the nation and as federal support waned (in inflation-adjusted dollars), the form, activities, and mission of EDDs evolved. Most EDDs began with a narrow focus on job creation and retention and relied primarily on EDA funds. Many EDDs quickly became multipurpose, grant-getting agencies, and the narrow focus on unemployment gave way to the more amorphous goal of economic development. In many regions, emphasis shifted from helping the poor to helping businesses. Over this period, EDDs worked ever more closely with state and local governments as federal funding diminished in importance. Some see this evolution from a federally directed, narrow-focused program to a largely independent, multipurpose agency as a dilution of mission. Critics denounced EDA and EDDs as pork barrel, as existing merely to hand out largess to congressional districts. This evolution, however, is adaptive to both the increasingly harsh political and funding climate and the local needs of diverse communities.

This recent history left EDA and the EDD program in a difficult position. The budget cuts and layoffs demoralized EDA. One high-level career employee said the work force spent the decade of the 1980s cleaning out their desks. As the decade ended, the agency continued to survive, and with the confidence of survivors, it was ready to do more than endure. Many within EDA wanted to take a fresh look at its programs, such as the EDD program. At the same time, the local programs had grown increasingly independent of EDA and were not ready to follow Washington's lead. They were frustrated by the lack of resources and emboldened by their collective power: They had endured not because of EDA's support, but rather EDA had survived because support for local programs translated into congressional support. Government agencies often restrict policy analysis to standard methods; they turn to outside analysts not for their ideas but for their techniques. Positivism provides a gloss of legitimacy, of scientific objectivity, for their choices. In this case, EDA looked to the evaluation not to judge the success or failure of a specific program but to rethink its role and direction: The administrators hoped the evaluation could help rebuild collaboration with local programs. This openness gave us the opportunity to experiment with method.

From Theory to Practice

Several basic ideas guided our study of the EDD program.[8] The first was to elevate the importance of stakeholders in all phases of the research. Practically, EDA administrators understood that any decision, no matter how reasonable, would lead nowhere without the support of various program stakeholders. Local programs had too much autonomy and clout in Congress to accept orders from Washington. For example, when the Washington office of EDA made minor changes in budgets to local programs, the local programs convinced Congress to change the EDA reauthorization bill to forbid EDA from reducing the budgets of local EDDs. Local stakeholders circumvented even routine administrative control.

Engaging stakeholders is also important for theoretical reasons. The presumption of objectivity embedded in standard policy analysis deemphasizes the personal: As long as methods are scrupulously followed, the findings of positivist analysis are supposed to speak for themselves. Interpretive policy analysis strives to articulate intersubjective understanding through the deeply personal process of historically conscious recontextualization. Who gets to interpret policy has, therefore, both political and research implications. At a minimum, engaging stakeholders creates a dialectic between the outsiders, such as the research team, and the insiders. In our study, we sought the broadest range of insider and outsider views that was feasible: We sought the greatest manageable diversity.

To contribute to reasoned discussion, interpretations must be focused. The study design started with broad questions but became increasingly narrow. Because winnowing is part of interpretation, the stakeholders guided this narrowing process. The research team played two major roles in this regard. First, we convened and guided discussions, and second, we gathered and organized information that could strengthen or challenge emerging interpretations. In other words, we acted as facilitators of a recontextualization process, one that included our own texts or webs of understanding.

Within these general guidelines, the study went through five stages.

STAGE 1: SELECTING PARTICIPANTS

Participants in this research included the research team and stakeholders. The research team included faculty and researchers from two universities[9] and from diverse disciplines including public administration, political science, regional planning, economics, and business. Stakeholders included those directly involved with the EDD program at the federal and local levels, various individuals from state and local governments, and private organizations with an interest in the EDD program. Stakeholders came from all regions of the country; some were from rural and others from urban programs.

How many stakeholders are enough? Stakeholders are included in the analysis process to broaden the interpretive base, to spin a more intricate web. In a large and diverse program, such as the EDD program, only a small proportion of stakeholders can be included; including some means excluding many more. Including stakeholders in policy analysis raises concerns about representation that complicates all democratic decision processes. Lively discussions and close working relations require small groups, but no small group can reflect the whole. This is a dilemma that can never be entirely overcome.

We chose 24 stakeholders. They were selected to maximize diversity in region and type of program and because their individual views were widely respected by EDA and local officials. The selection of stakeholders who represent diversity and are credible to others is crucial to the success of a study. In interpretive policy analysis, designing the forum and selecting the participants are primary, if novel, roles for the analyst.

STAGE 2: FIRST FORUM

The first forum included the research teams, stakeholders, and EDA officials and lasted a day and a half.[10] On the first day, after introductions and an explanation of the process, the stakeholders were divided into three groups of eight. Also present, but not participating, in each group were one EDA observer and members of the research teams. Participants stayed together as a group, but the focus-group facilitators changed three times during the day. The facilitators were experienced group leaders and did not participate in the subsequent research. The three sessions covered three general topics: the mission of the EDD program, the operations of the districts, and the evaluation of the districts.

These focus groups were assigned the responsibility of defining and articulating the range of important issues facing the program. Facilitators and stakeholders were free to examine other issues, but they were charged with helping articulate the scope of the policy concerns, not with making judgments about programs or policies.

On the second day, the views of the three groups were presented to all of the participants, and the issues were discussed once again in this larger setting. EDA observers participated in these discussions. The result of these additional discussions was a charge to the research team. This charge included a range of topics that, in the view of the stakeholders, warranted further attention; relevance to the stakeholders was more important than coherence or ease of research.

STAGE 3: RESEARCH

The university-based research teams sought to gather and organize whatever information was relevant to the topics.[11] We scavenged EDA records and budgets for historical trends and patterns and gleaned the scant research literature for a few relevant insights. By positivist standards, we had no design: We rarely worried about operationalizing definitions and never stated hypotheses or tested causal arguments. We defined our research role as bringing to the surface evidence and observations that could enrich interpretations.

We also used the research as an opportunity to expand participation. We feared that 24 stakeholders were too narrow a base, that we would overlook important perspectives, and that the final interpretations would prove myopic. Although we could not involve more people in the direct deliberations of the policy forums, we interviewed more stakeholders as part of the research.

Sampling EDDs

We divided EDDs into those above and below the 24-month unemployment rate and randomly sampled 15 EDDs from each group. To ensure geographical dispersion, we randomly dropped two EDDs from the South—the region with the most EDDs—and randomly added two from the West.

We then conducted detailed interviews with the directors of each sample EDD. All agreed to participate, and the open-ended interviews lasted between 30 minutes and 2 hours. These 30 EDDs were in 20 states, and the research team also interviewed a state official in each of the 20 states, who worked directly with the sampled EDDs. The director and state official interviews were similar: Both followed a script but allowed wide latitude in response. All interviews were tape-recorded and transcribed. We also asked the EDD directors to forward local documents such as their regional economic plan.

The sample EDDs also narrowed our search for demographic information. The 30 EDDs encompassed 209 counties, and for these counties, we examined census data on (a) resident characteristics, (b) economic characteristics, and (c) federal funding.

Draft Report

The research teams then wrote a draft report. This report sketched the history of EDA and the EDD program, describing the changes in mission and services over its 25-year life. As with many federal programs, many stakeholders tend to view the EDD program from a singular perspective. From Washington, the EDD program is viewed through the lens of mandates, regulations, and reports; in the districts, the EDD program as a whole is seen as a reflection of local experience. Based on the interviews and census information, we drew an enlarged and detailed portrait of the EDDs, one that highlighted the many differences among and within them by bringing these many subnarratives together. One major problem in policy analysis is getting participants to look beyond their own valid yet parochial views and interests. By describing the common history and variation in local problems and programs, we attempted to provide a shared yet broader background to the stakeholders. By articulating the context and highlighting the larger narratives of which each EDD subnarrative was a part, we hoped to enhance the deliberations of the second forum.

After discussing context, the report more directly addressed the policy concerns raised in the first forum. We described three theoretical models of the mission for the EDD program: These models were defined to articulate questions rather than specify goals. We then reviewed the different policy questions. We did not include policy recommendations in the draft report. Taking the information in the draft and making recommendations was the primary task of the second forum. The draft report was circulated among the stakeholders prior to the second forum.

STAGE 4: SECOND FORUM

Approximately six months after the first forum, the stakeholders and observers reconvened.[12] In four working groups, this time led by stakeholders selected by the groups, and in plenary session, the second forum reviewed the report and developed a set of policy options. The draft report was the shared text that guided interpretations, but stakeholders freely pointed out limitations in the report and introduced new topics. Stakeholders and researchers argued about errors, omissions, and wording until agreed-upon interpretations emerged. We did not achieve consensus on all points. The web of interpretation need not be without flaws: Ours had numerous broken and unconnected strands. We were, however, able to articulate areas of agreement and disagreement. When discussing and revising recommendations, specific terms, such as *economic distress,* were important to stakeholders; their interpretations were worth arguing about.

Stakeholder interpretations existed on at least two levels. They read and discussed the draft report as a way of rethinking their program. The report encouraged stakeholders to look at themselves from a broader perspective; they began to examine their program from a more collective view, expanding their web of understanding. They also saw the act of reviewing the report and articulating recommendations as a means of guiding the reinterpretation of their program. Many of their interpretations were strategic.

STAGE 5: FINAL REPORT

We revised the draft report based on the discussion during the second forum. The major revision involved adding the recommended policy options and then organizing the discussion around those recommendations. The stakeholders who led the work groups formed an editorial board; they reviewed the revisions, with the final report reflecting their suggestions. The final report was then formally sent to EDA. Copies were also sent to all EDD directors and the participants in both forums.

This evaluation did not radically change the EDD program or EDA. Programs and agencies are embedded in their own routines and history and are difficult to redirect. A year after its completion, the report is still discussed, however. According to several officials, it provides a basis for ongoing review of the programs. Although officials and stakeholders care little about the epistemological arguments that surrounded our methodological choices, they do express the belief that the report is more credible, more worthy of attention, because it is based on the views of people in the field. One official suggested that academic studies are usually dismissed because they never deal with the truth of programs. The insiders' epistemological instincts are keen indeed.

Comments

Positivist methods have a life of their own. Regardless of the issue or the knowledge base, they have come to define sound policy analysis. This often leads to absurd research. For example, in 1982 the Subcommittee on Economic Development of the House Committee on Public Works and Transportation conducted a survey of recipients of EDA funds to help them in their assessment of the agency. One of the survey questions asked fund recipients whether or not the "EDA is a 'pork barrel' Federal agency whose programs generate little or no job impact that would not otherwise occur at the local level" (U.S. Congress, 1982). Ninety-six percent of the respondents replied that it was not. The study reported these perceptions as facts, never recognizing the self-interest of the respondents. This parody of quantitative research illustrates the mindlessness of defining good research as the blind application of quantitative methods. Such devotion to method is clearly counterproductive and can be avoided if postpositive assumptions can reshape the policy studies field.

Postpositive conceptions of policy analysis recognize the importance of history and the interpretive nature of policy and our assessments of it; they recognize the need to engage in interpretive research that seeks to expand

and thus to recontextualize our webs of understanding, seeing objectivity as the process of striving to enhance (even if never reaching) intersubjective agreement. The policy analyst is not above this process but rather is submerged within it, facilitating recontextualizations and connecting his or her outsider text to those of the insiders or stakeholders. This is not to suggest that quantitative methods must be set aside never to be used again; some things are better represented as numbers than words, such as unemployment rates or local economic output. Our report included statistical and graphical analysis. Such methods, however, must play only a part in the larger analytical process; they may be used in the process of inquiry as interpretation but not as a substitute for it.

The use of interpretive forums is, we believe, one of the best ways to engage in policy analysis in the postpositist era. The epistemological problems posed by positivism can be avoided without abandoning policy analysis. Such forums, however, may also assist us in overcoming other problems posed by traditional research methods. First, in some cases, they could be used to enhance democratic practices by involving concerned citizens in the forum process. Welfare policy, for example, might be greatly improved and formulated more democratically if even a very small percentage of welfare recipients were engaged in program analysis, with a policy analyst acting as a facilitator and lending his or her own interpretation to the deliberative process. Second, interpretive forums encourage analysts to consider local context and recipient needs, thus enhancing the likelihood of successful implementation, a point made by Peter deLeon (1992). For a variety of reasons, then, the postpositivist conception of policy analysis suggests a new methodological paradigm for the policy studies field. Of course, this requires that we begin approaching substantive policy studies from this postpositist perspective rather than remaining solely within the confines of the theoretical debate. We have tried to move in this direction with the EDA study discussed here.

Notes

1. In addition to epistemological doubts, critics of positivism have also argued that policy analysis threatens democracy by promoting technical over citizen knowledge and expertise over participation (Fischer, 1987, 1990; Lindblom, 1990; Weiss, 1991).

2. See Bozeman (1986) for a discussion of the importance of credibility in policy analysis.

3. For an account of how the interpretations of fossils have changed with historical and social context, see Gould (1989).

4. See Kuhn (1970) and Latour (1987) for studies on science in the making. The fact that positivist methods are questioned even in the hard sciences illustrates that the attempt to copy their methods in the social sciences to avoid being deemed inferior is a misguided project.

5. The image of failure was reinforced by Pressman and Wildvasky's (1984) a classic study of EDA programs in Oakland, California.

6. Many of the EDDs evolved out of the Appalachian Regional Councils.

7. EDA provides a modest planning grant to all funded EDDs. As funds were frozen and then cut, they continued to identify regions eligible to become EDDs but were unable to award planning grants. These districts are "designated" but not funded.

8. For a complete discussion of the project, see Maynard-Moody, Burress, Ambrosius, and Weisenburger (1991).

9. The University of Kansas and Kansas State University. The project was run through the Kansas Center for Community Economic Development, a joint university center.

10. The first forum was held in Lawrence, Kansas, in June 1990.

11. We divided into four teams. Steven Maynard-Moody led the Background and Evaluation Team, David Burress led the Funding Issues Team, Margery Ambrosius led the Intergovernmental Issues Team, and Raymond Weisenburger led the Regional Planning Team. Steven Maynard-Moody was the overall research director.

12. Also in Lawrence, Kansas, in December 1990.

14

Grout:
Alternative Kinds of Knowledge
and Why They Are Ignored

MARY R. SCHMIDT

In 1975, as the federal Bureau of Reclamation was filling the reservoir behind an earthen dam just completed on the Teton River in Idaho, the structure unexpectedly collapsed. Eleven people died, 3,000 homes were damaged, 16,000 head of cattle drowned, and 100,000 acres of newly planted farmland were flooded. The property damage was estimated at more than $1 billion (U.S. Congress, 1976, p. 8).

What had gone wrong? Several blue-ribbon committees investigated the causes—just as was later done after the accident at Three Mile Island and the explosion of the space shuttle Challenger. The investigators concluded that the failure was the result of inadequacies in the engineers' design and overconfidence in the bureau, both ignoring safety factors. The remedy was a set of general administrative guidelines (Interagency Committee on Dam Safety, 1979) to govern all facets of work on dams in a dozen federal agencies.

Everyone acknowledged that the site was poor; the rock on which the dam was built was highly fractured, crisscrossed with narrow cracks, and peppered with larger holes. The project engineer had been confident that extensive use of grout—a mixture of cement and water—could seal these holes. However, the bureau's own grouting expert testified before Congress after the failure that grouting is not an exact science and that absolute certainty is impossible. Grouting is more like an art and requires a certain "feel" for the work (U.S. Congress, 1976, p. 24).

A Feel for the Hole

To appreciate the grouters' feel, one must understand the context and details of their work. Grouters are often expected to stabilize the material under the

213

foundation of a structure. On this particular project, they worked 450 feet down at the bottom of a steep, walled canyon more than 3,000 feet across. Their job was to pump grout under pressure into closely spaced holes drilled 300 feet farther down in the bedrock to create a subsurface "curtain." This solid underground wall was to prevent water from undermining the dam. As a clue to subsurface conditions, before they grouted each hole, the workmen first measured the amount of water they could pump under pressure to fill these holes to overflowing. However, the rock was so porous that the water often disappeared as into a bottomless pit, only to surface later far downstream.

To prevent wasting grout flowing too far through narrow cracks, the bureau specified that salt be added to harden it more rapidly, a fairly common procedure. If the grouters suspected larger holes, they were to add sand instead. The bureau had made preliminary tests to analyze how fast the grout would set with various proportions of salt but could not discover a formula relating salt to setting time because of the complex interactions among many variables (U.S. Department of Interior, 1976, Appendix G). So the decision on whether to add salt or sand, and how much of each, was left to the grouters and their mysterious "feel for the hole."

What kind of knowledge is this? Obviously these workers could not directly observe conditions deep below the surface nor know with any certainty where the grout had traveled, how soon it had set, or what voids remained. Unlike most artisans and skilled craftspeople, whose work can be judged by others, they alone could evaluate their work. Yet the integrity of the dam depended on it. Their knowledge seems more like that of an old-time doctor who diagnoses an illness by palpating the patient, listening to his heart and breathing, and asking about his life and family.

The grouter's knowledge in practice is difficult to put into words. It cannot be measured and represented by formulas or subjected to rules or standards. It cannot be taught in a classroom, but only learned in the field, by direct hands-on experience in specific situations, under the guidance of a master craftsperson.

The art of grouting appears to require continuous attention to a host of subtle qualities, such as the resistance of the rock to drilling, the color and even the smell of the water flowing back, the pressure of water and grout at the pump, and the humidity in the air. These data cannot be treated as independent or separate from the context or subjected to analysis, as the bureau discovered.

Instead, the grouter must combine data from many senses, including kinesthetic ones. These senses may be sharpened with time, as the newly blind learn to hear sounds that sighted people miss. This synthesis, the essence of art as opposed to science, must be further understood in the context of particular local conditions.

I posit that over time grouters build up a repertoire of strategies for treating various kinds of rocks in specific situations and acquire a kind of general knowledge. Because, as was said, each site, each hole, and even different stages of a single hole, is unique, grouters can never rely on formal models or general rules of thumb or recipes. If they settle into a mindless routine, they will jeopardize the quality of the work. They must constantly be alert to the "back talk" of the specific situation.

Ralph Hummel addressed such issues in a short article entitled "Bottom-Up Knowledge in Organizations" (Hummel, 1985). He too posited that craftspeople working directly with their hands have a special kind of knowledge in their mundane understanding of their tools and material. A sensitive worker without preconceptions or a priori notions may acquire a feel for the object of his or her work, apprehend its unique qualities, and come to know it "in its own terms" and "how it wants to be handled." Such workers become attuned to the qualitative phenomena that seem to emanate from an object and thereby overcome the subject-object dichotomy typical of the scientific attitude.

Underlying this kind of knowledge, Hummel wrote, is an assumption that reality is more than what is known through analysis, under a unilateral approach with the intent to control materials. This richer view of reality requires a worker to interact with an object, understand it in the context of the work, and synthesize that understanding with a feel for and receptiveness to the back talk of the object and the opportunities it presents. This description captures the grouters' knowledge. But there is more.

A Feel for the Whole

The grouters' feel for the hole is not the only kind of knowledge essential in securing a dam's foundation. In this case, the cracks and holes in the surface of the foundation also had to be tightly sealed with a thin slurry grout to prevent the hard-packed fill, which would form the core of the dam, from sinking into fissures, leaving voids through which water could later tunnel. A larger and less professional crew worked, on three shifts around the clock, on the irregular surface of the base and then up the steep slopes. Each shift encountered unique conditions; sometimes workers could fill 10 holes in eight hours, at other times, barely one. These surface crews worked under pressure to avoid delaying the laying of fill. But several times they had to stop work and flee swarms of bats emerging from caves through narrow holes (U.S. Department of the Interior, 1976, Appendix D, p. 6).

Although these workers might sense the extent of a hole by the feel of cold dank air—or bats—coming out, they had more superficial knowledge than the grouters. As they worked on the irregular surface, they would each have observed details of individual fissures and areas around them. Over time, these workers collectively must have acquired a more complete knowledge of the heterogeneous surface than anyone had before or would be able to ever have again.

The designers had known local conditions only indirectly from core samples taken before the site was excavated. The project engineer, high in an office on one bank, had largely secondhand knowledge from formal reports filed by supervisors after each shift. Indeed no one person on these grouting crews observed all of the surface conditions. During the four years of construction, each worker acquired only a fraction of the knowledge that they collectively possessed. Communication was limited by the organization of crews into separate shifts and, on any one crew, by the noise from heavy trucks and compression equipment echoing off the canyon walls. The only time and place these workers might have shared their individual knowledge was in a local bar on weekends.

From a social perspective, this collective knowledge can be called a "feel for the whole," but it was disaggregated by the formal organization and working conditions. Moreover, this fine-scaled knowledge was ephemeral: It would soon be forgotten. It would also become obsolete as tons of fill covered the surface, settled into cracks, and shifted with the inevitable seepage of water through the dam. Such knowledge is like that of witnesses of an automobile accident; no one sees it all, but each may contribute to a fuller picture.

Passive and Critical Knowledge

A third kind of knowledge emerged as these same workers were finishing surface treatment high on one bank. They received "orders from above" to stop their work. They were at first bewildered, because the rocks there were as fractured as those below. They tried to construct an explanation and finally accepted a plausible one that was "floating around." The pressure of water at the bottom of the reservoir is always greater than at the top, where the water pressure "would be low enough to allow quitting" (U.S. Department of the Interior, 1976, Appendix C, p. 15). Although these workers lacked formal training in dam engineering, they understood this hydrological principle. They attributed its use to their superiors as a valid basis for stopping work. They were right in principle, but wrong in giving credit for such reasoning to those above. Bureau officials far off in Denver were unaware of these site conditions; they were simply in a hurry to complete the dam (Independent Panel, 1976, pp. 10-12).

These workers demonstrated a kind of passive knowledge, as when one understands a language but cannot speak it or appreciates a good design but cannot create it. An interested amateur may have the critical ability to distinguish between a masterful and sloppy performance and offer evidence in valid arguments as sound as any expert's to support his or her judgment.

Top engineers were unaware of the critical knowledge of these lowly workers, who stopped sealing the surface where the water later tunneled and undermined the dam. The investigators never spoke with the grouters or other workers but took statements from supervisors, made tests at the site, and reviewed formal records on construction. Based on these, they absolved the contractor and crews from responsibility because they had faithfully adhered to the specifications (U.S. Department of the Interior, 1976, p. v).

Why were these three kinds of knowledge ignored? (A fourth kind will be given later.) A simple explanation might lie in the lowly status of these workers, both physically at the bottom of the site and organizationally at the bottom of the hierarchies of engineering practice and the bureaucracy in which that practice took place. A complex explanation seems more valid. For it is science that dismisses knowledge expressed as feelings, engineering that scorns the knowledge of uneducated laborers, and bureaucracy that disaggregates such knowledge. Thus the reasons seem to lie in the context of these three overlapping institutions.

The Institutions of Science, Engineering, and Bureaucracy

These institutions interact in complex ways. Engineering is said to depend on science, drawing on and applying scientific principles in its practice. It uses bureaucratic forms of organization for large projects and also works within the federal bureaucracy. The government in turn builds and supports large, engineered public works as a matter of public policy. It also depends on technical experts for analyses and advice in making rational decisions on policy matters. It sponsors scientific research and development, which usually requires engineering. Science, with its freedom to do pure research, seems to be at the top of a hierarchy among these institutions. I will describe the stereotypical characteristics of each one, starting with science, its structure, view of the physical reality, goals, way of acquiring knowledge, and concept of valid knowledge.

The structure of science itself is hierarchical, headed by an elite corps, notably theoretical physicists. As a model for other sciences, physics has claimed to know and represent the physical reality directly with general theories couched in abstract terms. Observed regularities have been expressed as deterministic causal "laws of nature"; physicists seek one unifying law (Keller,

1985). These laws act as structuring principles to describe the material reality below in ways that differ radically from the flux of heterogeneous phenomena we perceive in everyday life.

Science suggests a universe unfolding progressively over time, in causal sequence, under uniform laws that governed the past and will continue eternally. The past is assumed to be a reliable guide to the future and the basis for making predictions. Indeed, a goal of science is to make reliable predictions, eliminate uncertainty, and, through technology, bring nature under control.

Science has claimed that the only reliable knowledge is obtained by the scientific method, which involves deduction, pulling hypotheses down from theories, and testing them in experiments under controlled conditions. Such experiments generally utilize analysis, removing objects from contexts and dividing them into independent parts, which are then manipulated to test hypotheses and strengthen theories. Here the assumption is that the whole is nothing more than the sum of the parts, and that partial knowledge will add up to reliable knowledge of the whole. Thus the everyday world of our senses is transformed, reduced to abstract forces and unobservable essences.

Engineering, in turn, is said to derive its knowledge from science and to apply scientific principles. However, many competent and forthright civil engineers admit that their practice also involves a kind of artistry. They are artists in the sense that they must closely attend to the unique characteristics of a specific site and also consider economic, social, and even political factors before they design a project. Such a synthesis transcends scientific principles (Office of Science and Technology Policy, 1978).

Top engineers then send the design down to less-seasoned specialists, who flesh it out with details of components that worked well in projects at other locations, on the assumption that various kinds of sites are basically alike, all salient features are known, and again that the parts will add up to a reliable whole. Midlevel engineers write specifications for these details and make schedules so that construction can adhere to a predetermined causal-like sequence. A contractor with the lowest bid will then apportion parts of the job to specialized subcontractors. Such institutional arrangements create constraints of time and money, which preclude attention to any new information available after excavation and during construction, and inhibit costly changes in the design, which acquires an almost sacred status. Thus artistry remains at the top, the exclusive property of the chief engineers.

Bureaucratic organizations have their own kinds of knowledge and ways of distributing it. Ideally, top leaders use complete information from analysis of problems to make rational decisions on the best means to achieve clear ends, much as causes determine effects. In this way, they produce general policies, which serve as a kind of reality to those at the top. These broad statements are sent down through stratified layers to lesser officials in specialized offices, who subdivide them and spell them out with written rules and regulations and transform them into standard operating procedures, the "how to" knowledge of bureaucracy. Lowly workers can then be trained and held accountable to perform these tasks by rote.

Communication flows down, but little flows up unless it is written on proper forms that confirm that work has conformed to specifications. These forms have no place for the sensory knowledge, aggregate observations, or critical judgments that were found among the workers at the dam. Bureaucracies thus rationally structure and suppress information and disaggregate knowledge of the whole.

All three institutions are led by artists, in a sense, who express reality in the form of general theories, designs, and policies. Such elites tend to act like disembodied heads, sending down hypotheses, specifications, or procedural rules to control the specialized functions below. This division of head from body is reflected in the split of theory from practice, design from construction, and policy from programs of implementation, and in other dualities. These reified entities take on a temporal dimension, a life of their own, to make things orderly at the bottom and predictable over time, through the control of nature or of public life. However, they greatly oversimplify reality, as will be illustrated next by an example from science.

Another Model of Science and Reality

The kinds of knowledge found in engineering can also be found in science. Many competent scientists develop a feel for the phenomena they study, building on the collective observations of their peers and sometimes drawing on a passive critical understand of other fields; such practices are rarely discussed. They were most evident in the work of Barbara McClintock, a geneticist who won a Nobel Prize, who offers an alternative view of the physical reality (Keller, 1983).

McClintock's style of research contrasted with that of her peers. When most geneticists were interested in the mechanism and structure of genes, she wanted to understand their organization and functions in relation to the rest of the cell, within the organism as a whole; she sought a kind of feel for the whole. Rather than dismissing exceptional cases as irrelevant to general theory, she focused on anomalous pigmentation of individual plants. Instead of starting with an hypothesis prescribing what she expected and framing the questions for the material to answer, as in most controlled experiments, she felt the need to "let the experiment tell you what it wants to do" and to "listen to the material" (Keller, 1985, p. 162).

She followed each unique seedling through its life in the field, relating to it as a friend and ally. At times, she became so engrossed in examining individual cells in a grain of corn through her microscope that she felt as if she were down there within the cell, the same size as the chromosomes, and could see how they were interacting (Keller, 1985, p. 164). In such ways, she developed what she called a "feeling for the organism," akin to the grouter's "feel for the hole."

Her unique understanding led her to question the genetic theory of Watson and Crick: The DNA contained a cell's vital information, which was copied onto the RNA and acted as a blueprint for genetic traits. She thought that this "master molecule theory" claimed to explain too much and did not acknowledge the differences between small simple organisms and large complex multicellular ones. More important, it treated DNA as a central autonomous actor, sending out information one way, through a genetic organization structured hierarchically, like a classic bureaucracy (Keller, 1985, p. 170). McClintock showed that genetic organization is more complex and interdependent. The DNA itself adapts to outside factors and can be reprogrammed by signals from the environment to meet the survival needs of the organism. In essence, information flows both ways.

These findings confirmed what McClintock viewed as "the resourcefulness of nature" (Keller, 1985, p. 171). For her, nature is not simple and deterministic. The universe is richer, more bountiful and abundant than can be captured in formulas or put into words, than we can describe or prescribe. Within that a priori complexity is a "natural order" of patterns, regularities, and rhythms, with a kind of facticity that challenges scientists to go on. The complexity of this order transcends our capacity for ordering and dwarfs our scientific intelligence (Keller, 1985, p. 162).

This view of science shifts the focus from an hierarchical model of a relatively simple static system to more interactive models of complex dynamic systems. Picturing nature as generative and resourceful also allows it to become an active partner in reciprocal relationships with an equally active observer. That observer, however, must assume an attitude of humility, patience, and open attentiveness that allows one to listen to the material in an inquiry based on respect rather than on domination (Keller, 1985, p. 135).

Keller draws out the implications of such a view. Science has fostered dichotomies: knowledge and belief, objective and subjective, reason and feeling, eternal truth and transient phenomena. The search for universal laws and consistency imposes a rank order on these, transforming differences into otherness, inequalities, and ultimately into exclusion (Keller, 1985, p. 163), such as many women in science, engineering, and public administration have experienced. This new view of reality, which respects differences and interactive relationships without hierarchy, threatens the authority of a particular form of science, and, by extension, of engineering that depends on the laws and principles of science, and of bureaucracy as the organizational expression of the rational scientific approach.

Rather than pursue epistemological and ontological questions, I emphasize only that this new picture of the physical reality allows for great diversity in local expressions of nature, in particular places and specific objects, and is even more relevant to the social and cultural reality. Such diversity seems to require alternative ways of knowing. I now suggest a fourth kind of knowledge drawn from dam engineering, which was also evident in McClintock's science.

Intimate Knowledge

After construction, a dam must be monitored for signs of damage or aging. In the hills of California, forest rangers often monitor dams within their territories and are said to develop an "intimate knowledge" of each one over time. It takes time to acquire this kind of knowledge (which McClintock displayed in her patient study of individual plants). After a heavy rain or hard winter, rangers would look for signs of weakening. If they spotted something unusual, they would discuss it with their supervisor in the central office to determine if it merited a more extensive field check.

When the U.S. Corps of Army Engineers (1976) was considering a national dam-inspection program in the 1970s, few engineers were competent to inspect the 10,000 dams across the country in a timely manner. Yet no one set of uniform guidelines would be adequate for less competent people inspecting the details of a wide variety of dams. So a decentralized bottom-up approach was devised. Each state received a brief set of general guidelines with a checklist for earthen and less-common concrete structures (Appendix D). Dam safety officers should use discretion and refine the guidelines for large or particularly hazardous structures. Other dams would be inspected in stages, by reviewing written records, then through field surveys by low-level people, like the forest rangers, and then with detailed sophisticated analyses by top engineers, if warranted. Few of these were needed.

Translating the checklist into simple English reveals that almost anyone could recognize signs of weakness in an earthen dam, such as an irregular alignment, surface cracks, or fresh springs at the base. Ordinary people who regularly fish or hike around a dam may, like the rangers, acquire a familiarity or intimate knowledge of it over time. They would know it in the way one knows a spouse or fellow worker, well enough to recognize when something is amiss and even how to cope with it.

People who live in a floodplain below a dam should be motivated to act on such knowledge, because a failure could destroy their homes or even their lives. They may fail to act for many reasons: They do not understand the significance of what they see, or do not feel responsible, or even know who is. More likely, they will assume, like those who quit work at Teton, that the people in charge already know about these conditions. Outside amateurs may also rightly fear that if they voice their concerns, the people in charge will dismiss them as unqualified meddlers. Those at the bottom of an organization who speak out on the basis of intimate knowledge or other information risk more than humiliation; like whistleblowers, they risk being fired.

On the other hand, if people in organizations would listen and check and then deem such observations valid, they could prevent a disaster. Even if no cause for concern existed, they could at least commend laypeople for their sense of responsibility and tell them what to look for in the future. In this way, local people would acquire critical knowledge to assist officials in watching over potentially hazardous structures, transforming rare and costly national inspection programs into continuous monitoring.

Social Rationality

After studying Teton and other disasters, Charles Perrow concluded that some kinds of accidents may become so common that they should be treated as normal, especially in certain types of systems, both technological and organizational. The very nature of some systems transforms minor incidents into major accidents. For instance, in complex interactive systems with tightly coupled components, small unexpected failures can occur in invisible ways and proliferate before they can be contained (Perrow, 1984). Components could be decoupled in some systems, but Perrow would eliminate others, such as nuclear power plants, altogether. In a few, greater top-down control is needed, but many should be decentralized so that those closest to anomalies can stop work, move about, ask questions of others, reflect, and make unauthorized changes to contain the errors. This exemplifies the value of alternative kinds of knowledge.

Perrow recognizes that the reality of many human-made organizations and technologies, like nature itself, is more complex than can be imagined. The knowledge and action of lowly workers is often vital in coping with unforeseeable events. Such a bottom-up approach horrifies the technical elite, who deem the public, and lowly workers, irrational. Nonexperts do not use logic and statistics to make rational decisions about risks the way experts do. On the other hand, studies show that ordinary people consider many technologies in a larger context, with a sense of "dread," which combines their feelings of limited control and fears about the long-term future with skepticism about the ability of experts or institutions to avoid potential catastrophes (Perrow, 1984, p. 328). Such studies aggregate the feel for the unknown, the hole, and passive critical knowledge and even intimate knowledge into a kind of knowledge of the whole, to provide an understanding of the context of public dread.

Perrow also points out that choosing a context, framing a problem, is a predecision process, which experts also do, but usually within the limited framework of their specialized disciplines, selecting solutions to fit their methods. Indeed, everyone has cognitive limits and special skills, some with numbers, others with words, still others in visualization. Because of our different perspectives and limited abilities, we need one another. In working together, we enrich our view of the world and increase the possibilities of solving problems. For such reasons, Perrow sees the limits of rationality in decision making not as a liability but as an asset, for it points to our need for interdependence and suggests a broader concept, which he labels "social rationality" (Perrow, 1984, p. 321).

Social rationality acknowledges the limits of human understanding and the value of people's feelings, such as fear of the unknown and unknowable. It transforms both reason and feelings from dichotomies, divisions contending as opposites, into a synthesis that respects and retains the differences and gives them equal voice. Thus it seems rational to take account of alternative kinds of bottom-up knowledge, to supplement and complement, but not necessarily replace, the top-down knowledge of science, engineering, and bureaucracy.

Conclusions

Certain general characteristics or family resemblances link these alternative kinds of knowledge and set them apart from the traditional view of scientific knowledge. One characteristic is that this knowledge is usually of specific phenomena, as opposed to the general knowledge about abstract classes of objects in science. Another is the need for direct, bodily involvement in acquiring such knowledge, in contrast to the tendency of science to use impersonal instruments to acquire objective data. Related to this characteristic is the need for a synthesis of data from several senses, for a feel for the hole, over time in the case of intimate knowledge, or from several individuals for knowledge of the whole; this contrasts with the analytical approach attributed to science. The qualitative nature of such knowledge is another characteristic that sets it apart from science, which seeks to reduce its knowledge to quantitative terms. Finally, although verbal communication may contribute to the acquisition or expression of alternative kinds of knowledge, these are often difficult to describe completely in words; "we know more than we can say."[1]

The value of such kinds of knowledge to public administration may be illustrated by a hypothetical case. An unfamiliar male field-worker unexpectedly staggers into a central office, raving incoherently about a local program. Using a kind of feel for the hole, or a person, the administrator looks him over, helps him into a chair, and even sniffs his breath for alcohol. The administrator telephones his local supervisor, who has intimate knowledge of this employee but cannot explain his bizarre behavior and denies his story. The administrator then calls the regional office, which has only indirect passive knowledge of the local program but a plausible hypothesis to explain the story, based on experiences with unrelated programs. Sending the man to a hotel, the administrator flies to his city, talks with caseworkers and clients there to gain a bottom-up knowledge of the whole situation, and confirms the regional office's hypothesis. The administrator is then able to prevent a scandal that could have undermined a national program.

To conclude, such kinds of knowledge are not necessarily mutually exclusive, the list all-inclusive, or the characteristics complete. As our awareness of global diversity expands, we need to be alert for and respect other ways of seeing the world and other kinds of knowledge, such as that of rainforest inhabitants on the medicinal value of plants. We need to remember that all kinds and sources of knowledge are not superior or inferior but simply different ways of perceiving and organizing our limited understandings of a rich and complex reality.

Note

1. The author wishes to express her thanks to Donald A. Schön for his quote and his critical research support.

15

Stories Managers Tell: Why They Are as Valid as Science

RALPH P. HUMMEL

> Public administration is dying. It is dying because people
> in the field are not producing enough scholars capable of
> producing significant research.
> McCurdy (n.d.)

> I suspect that public administration is not going to disap-
> pear. Whether you call it a profession or not is maybe a se-
> mantic term more involved with our egos than what is
> going to be happening. Since people do act, either explic-
> itly or implicitly, on the basis of theory part of the time
> or most of the time, the job of the theorist is in large part
> to ascertain first of all what is it that we're operating on
> and how can it be improved.
> Ambassador, 1989

In the last several years, a small but vociferous group of critical scientists has conducted a concerted attack on how public managers acquire knowledge (McCurdy & Cleary, 1984; Perry & Kraemer, 1986; Stallings, 1986; Stallings & Ferris, 1988).[1] In addition, they condemn how public administration professors guide research and how students write dissertations. The upshot of this criticism is that neither practitioners nor academicians know what they are doing because they are not scientific enough. The implication is that more use of science among managers and in public administration curricula can cure what ails public administration, namely, an alleged deficit of valid knowledge. The extreme penalty for failure to comply is, in the words of one scientist (McCurdy, n.d., p. 1), the supposed fact that "Public Administration is dying."

There is, however, another possibility besides epidemic stupidity among public administrationists: It is that public managers and teachers and students know what they are doing. This article explores that possibility.

Until scientific critics do what they themselves have never done—explore the possibility that the prevailing form of knowledge acquisition is basically healthy and functional for public administrators' own purposes—it may be time to declare a moratorium on further attacks.

The defense of knowledge acquisition in public administration is possible on several grounds:

1. Managers live and work in an environment different from that of scientists.
2. Managers need knowledge for purposes different from those of scientists.
3. Scientists themselves have uncovered an alternate way that managers use to obtain knowledge, one that critical scientists have deprecated but have failed to investigate.
4. Managers themselves, far from being naive, can consciously question whether the assumptions of science apply to their situation.
5. Managers themselves are concerned with and utilize validity standards for their own preferred way of communicating and acquiring knowledge; in other words, their form of knowledge acquisition is for their purposes as valid as science.

The major alternate means of acquiring knowledge that managers use is storytelling, in written form: the case study and descriptive narratives. The critics themselves admit this when they note that most of the field's research, as reflected in studies of its leading journal, relies on deductive reasoning, recalled experience, or case studies (Perry & Kraemer, 1986). A similar tendency was observed by critics of dissertation research (McCurdy, n.d., p. 6): "Case studies were frequently used, but not as often as purely descriptive studies and more porous alternatives to social science research which outnumbered case studies in our study of dissertation work two to one."

In the private sector, we have known since the studies of Aguilar (1967) and Mintzberg (1973) that managers "favor verbal channels—face-to-face contact and the telephone and, to a lesser extent, direct observation as means of supplementing (and often replacing) formal sources of information" (Mintzberg, 1975, p. 3). In addition, Kanter (1977) found that managers spent about half their time in face-to-face communication, concluding that the manager's ability to win acceptance and to communicate was often more important than their substantive knowledge of the business. Aguilar found that personal sources exceeded impersonal sources in perceived importance for providing information by 71% to 29% (Mintzberg, 1975, p. 4). Further,

Mintzberg (1975) reports that managers seldom spend more than a few minutes on any given event, making it problematic that a manager can engage in lengthy scientific analysis before needing to come to a judgment of what is going on and what can be done about it (pp. 51-52). In the public sector, much of the evidence on managers' preference for personal communications over scientific reports comes from the utilization literature in policy analysis. For example, the most recent study of four agency heads in each of the 50 states found that they rely more on talking with the people they deal with and make little direct use of scientific policy analysis (Lester & Webber, 1990).[2]

The trouble that critics have with formal written echoes of such communications—for example, case studies—is that these generally do not meet scientific validity standards. For example, one pair of critics posed the test question, "Did the author set up the study in such a way so a reader could have confidence in the findings and infer their applicability to similar situations?" (McCurdy & Cleary, 1984, p. 50). This general criterion already begs the question of what managers are supposed to learn from case studies; it begs the question because it predefines knowledge in an analytic scientific way.

In contrast, in-depth conversations with managers show that they are quite capable of defining their reality, judging what kind of knowledge is useful to them, and developing validity standards relevant to their world. Even initial research into the appropriateness of science and scientific validity standards for managerial knowledge acquisition shows that both analytic science and its standards may not be appropriate for providing the fundamental kind of knowledge and confidence in it that managers need. The knowledge they seek must answer the question "What is going on here?" before any scientific attempt at measuring what goes on where and when.

The following two sections explore how managers see their world differently from the way scientists see it and how managers rely on stories to provide them with what is in their context valid knowledge.

How Managers Define Their World

When managers are asked how they determine what is going on in their world, they refer to "intuition," "judgment," "flying by the seat of your pants." Typical is the comment of an Apollo moon astronaut, who said this about selecting facts for a report: "You choose only by drawing on the most intuitive and most deeply buried recesses of your mind" (Thayer, 1980, p. 135). In the past, testimony of this kind has been the terminal point of inquiry about how managers think.[3]

However, conversations with managers show that they can critically think about their own thinking. They can judge the utility of basic assumptions of science and rationalistic inquiry for their work world. Managers can be engaged not only in counterposing their own assumptions against those of science and pure reason but also in suggesting valid alternatives to these forms of inquiry. To the surprise of their critics perhaps, their responses are as profound as—and fit with—similar fundamental propositions about what is real and how it can be known in the philosophy of science itself. For example, in problem formulation, managers seem to operate in a world that is often quite different from the kind of world to which analytic science can apply but a world not much different from that of the great original scientists who set up paradigms that define the research paths of their successors. Like the original scientists' world, the manager's world seems to be a world founded on synthesis, not analysis.

But managers' needs also differ from those of paradigm-setting scientists. Managers question the need for all-pervasive objectivity; to them a reality is constituted not by consensus of all imaginable detached observers but by the present community of those involved in a problem who must be brought along to constitute a solution. They question the relevance of the analytic scientific tenet that experiences pile up into an aggregate about which rules then can be formed; to the manager this still leaves the problem of judging whether a rule about bygone experiences applies to a new situation at hand. They question the principle of the separation of reality and observer; that the observer is separate from what is observed, can usefully be detached from what is observed, and can leave the observed undisturbed. In short, managers who were engaged in conversations about the foundations of knowledge— about what is real (ontology) and how we get to know it (epistemology)— juxtaposed tenets of their experience against the tenets of science and pure reason. To get knowledge about what is real:

- Managers question the value of mere objectivity. Managers prefer hearing from participants in a problem rather than from an objective outsider, such as a consultant. They find they can work better with intersubjectivity rather than mere objectivity.

- Managers question the direct relevance of mere science and pure reason in problem solving. They express a concern for the difficulty of judgment. To them aggregated facts or rules drawn from these do not directly address a new problem but must be judged for their applicability.

- Managers question the value of scientific or rationalist detachment. They value the skill of sensibility that comes from being in touch with events rather than being detached from them.

INTERSUBJECTIVITY
VERSUS OBJECTIVITY

A manager is challenged to explain why she would accept five different reports on an event rather than a single scientific report.[4] The manager's response: "By us, by each one of the five of us, by each one of the five of us coming up with a different thing and listening to each other, it would actually be better" (Military contracts manager, 1989). What can explain this answer?

Managers find themselves in social situations in which they do not have the power to set up a way of looking at a problem so that the problem will appear the same to all involved, what scientists would call *objectivity*. Instead, when the problem is created by the interactions of people, it exists in a work group, and different participants in it will look at it differently. The practical solution for the manager is to permit and encourage participants to help define the problem—not in an objective way in which all can agree on the same objective definition of the problem, but in an intersubjective way. In intersubjectivity, all agree to respect one another's definition of the problem and, by respecting this, puzzle out a synthesis that leads to a solution. To do otherwise would often mean to ask participants to surrender their position, of professional standing or of power or of entitlement, that sets the perspectives from which each views a problem.[5]

In asserting that "coming up with different things and listening to one another would actually be better" than waiting for a scientific report with a single viewpoint, the manager confronts directly analytic science's claim that what she needs is "objectivity." Objectivity may be won—that is, an object is grasped with accuracy and certainty—when an investigation is so designed that different observers will agree, not disagree. But the point here is that a problem in management often arises exactly because different people involved in a situation cannot agree. This is not because they are people of ill will, irrational, or antiscientific, but because they are so placed in the organization that their roles give them specific perspectives and responsibilities that are not necessarily compatible. The division of labor, for example, or position in hierarchy, divides work and the approach to work; such design assumes that different roles' approach to and role inhabitants' knowledge of the work ought to differ. In short, organization design is also the design of conditions of knowledge, or in Frederick Thayer's words, "any epistemology is an organization theory, and vice versa" (1980, p. 113).

The manager is, by structural impact of the institution as knowledge system, precisely not in that situation which the scientist makes a precondition for establishing the nature of an event; the manager cannot become the "author" of a single method for establishing reality. She has some authority and some discretion. But the institutional framework does not provide the total latitude necessary to permit her the scientific freedom to "set up" (McCurdy & Cleary, 1984, p. 50) a way of looking at the problematic event that would, according to scientific analytic method, guarantee one way of seeing it. She does not control the variables of observation that might guarantee seeing an event in an objective sense according to a single standpoint to which all viewers would previously have agreed. Rather, she is caught in an organization structure involving hierarchy and division of labor that, by design and for the original purpose of the specialization of work and of control, guarantees that people see the same event from different perspectives. Given the shortness of time for dealing with most events, the manager must deal with perceptions as they are structured by the institutional environment.[6]

UNIQUENESS VERSUS REPLICABILITY

Another manager took on another assumption of science. It is assumed that aggregate data-analysis produces rules governing a type of event. It is then assumed that users can directly benefit from established scientific knowledge because they will be ready to apply the scientific rule governing an event when the event comes along again in the future. Asked whether she believed that things that happened in the past ever repeat themselves in just that way in the future, she at first tried to be accommodating. "Yes . . . ," she said, but there was an ellipsis in her words. "But?" asked the interviewer. "Things are always different," she said. "There's different people. There's different mind-sets" (Office manager, 1987).

Even if an event—and we know by now how varied these can be in real life—should repeat itself, the manager would still have to make a judgment as to the degree to which past scientifically established variables could be used to affect the situation today. An astute manager might ask, If the problem is patterned enough for science to study it, what is it doing on my desk? Clearly, for patterned problems there are organizational routines that can be installed to handle them.

What makes an event a problem is that it does not fit into existing routines. This is true even and especially in the context of institutionalized routines of a bureaucratic structure. If an event does not fit into established routines, it is in that context unique. Even if a general pattern of scientific findings is available about this kind of problem from research elsewhere, the manager must still make a judgment as to how the general and repeated pattern of the past fits this event of the present with an opening toward a future solution. As Robert Denhardt and Jay White (1986) put it, "Effective public administration requires not only technique but balanced judgment, broad understanding, and a good sense of future possibilities" (p. 316). The world of problems that surrounds the manager is not one of routines but of particular events—this event or that. About each event, judgments must be made as to how general knowledge can fit it, and, if not, what kind of knowledge can help: "We are not paid for doing what we are told to do . . . but for doing rightly that part of our job which is left to our discretion" (Vickers, 1984, p. 200).

INVOLVEMENT VERSUS DETACHMENT

Another manager questioned the scientific assumption that the observer can be detached from what is observed. An engineer by training, he referred to the engineering concept of the undisturbed sample. "What I'm saying: The civil engineer knows there is no such thing as an undisturbed sample" when a core sample is pulled out of the ground. Pointing to an organization chart, he then drew this analogy: "the practitioner up here being part of the problem, therefore being part of the solution." "So you carry this over to management?" he was asked. "Hell, yes," he said. "You assume that people are shaken by your presence?" "Disturbed," he answered, "or, uh, varied or wavered or somewhat deviated from their original course just by the fact that I'm there" (Former city manager, 1987).

In bringing this description of the managerial world to light, the manager simply reflects the practical fact that a manager is never an individual by and for him- or herself but is an individual who lives in an already preexisting context. In that context, subordinates are as aware of the manager as he or she is of them. They are not objects to be moved around; they are sentient subjects who respond to the mere presence of the manager, to say nothing of his or her subliminal signals or expressed words and actions. The manager does not have the luxury of detachment that the scientist tries to gain. Even doing nothing or not appearing will be interpreted by the members of the manager's organization, and responses will result from unintended and unexpressed positions of the manager.

Managerial World Definition
and Philosophers of Science

Survey research will still have to show to what extent these findings can be generalized.[7] But assume that managers find themselves in a world in which they are participants rather than detached observers. Grant, for the moment, that their knowledge is intersubjective rather than objective when it comes to problem definition. Stipulate that even where there are rules summarizing past experience, a judgment must still be made as to whether those rules apply in this situation. If all this is true about managers in general, not just those we have talked with, then does this not add up to a picture of a world deficient in every crucial aspect of any capacity for producing the certain knowledge that analytic science or rational calculation can produce? What, then, can make any managerial claim to knowledge, much less valid knowledge, legitimate?

Here managers find a perhaps unexpected ally, and analytic scientists a long-ignored foe, among those who have thought as deeply as human reason can about knowledge and how it can be acquired: philosophers and theoreticians of science.

KANT

How can we know when to apply a scientific finding to a new situation? This is one problem posed by managers. In the philosophy of science, Immanuel Kant, who thought through the operations of science down to their basic assumptions, said an answer to this question requires a prior operation of synthesis, not analysis. Before any empirical research can be applied, before any "fact" can be fitted into problem, a "concept" must be developed for the mind to catch in the abstract an event that occurs in the concrete.[8] Concept and event relate to each other the way a hand shapes itself to grasp a stone. The stone must be small enough to fit the hand; but for the hand to grasp it, the hand itself must take on a shape that will fit the contours of the stone. This sounds surprisingly like what managers do. As in synthesis they try to determine what is going on before analyzing it. For them as for Kant, "the synthesis (the making) of concepts always precedes," in the words of one commentator, "their analytic relationships. Concept formation always precedes the analysis of already formed concepts" (Gendlin, 1967, p. 278).[9]

Now, what analytic scientists do is to take apart already formed concepts and operationalize the testing of elements of them against reality. They do not spend much time studying how a concept comes together, and even less on validating concept formation prior to empirical testing.[10] Yet judging rightly how a concept comes together within which the facts of a problem can be captured and brought to a solution is everything to the manager. The office manager cited above recognizes the priority of concept formation over analysis when she says, "Things are always different. There's different people. There's different mind-sets" (Office manager, 1987). She implies that different mind-sets have to be taken into account before a judgment can be made as to whether findings about past situations can be fitted, along with other knowledge, to a present situation that may constitute a problem.

Kant (1965) himself calls such concern for the combination of factors in the consciousness of the observing individual the "supreme" (p. B135) and "first" principle of human understanding (p. B139), "[f]or without such combination nothing can be thought or known" (p. B137).

HEIDEGGER

Kant (1965) also opens up science's position on objectivity to subsequent criticism. He warns that all knowledge, even knowledge under the categories of space and time, depends on the presence of the human observer. For example, "If we depart from the subjective condition under which alone we can have outer intuition . . . the representation of space stands for nothing whatsoever" (pp. A46, B42). Under the influence of subsequent philosophy of science, Kant (1965) can be taken as a point of departure for the city manager (above) who noted that, "the practitioner up here [is] part of the problem." What is out there must already, in Kant's words, become "an object for me" (p. B138). The philosopher Martin Heidegger takes up the suggestion that scientific laws may be universal but whether they apply to specific situations depends on the presence of an acting and perceiving subject and the approach he or she takes toward the object.

Further, Heidegger, following Edmund Husserl,[11] proposes that, when we are at the point of approaching an object, knowledge is never knowledge apart from an object but is always "knowledge of" something. An object shows itself, but only if properly addressed. To properly address an object a subject must become attuned to it with a certain concern or care. As the approach changes, the object changes also, yet there is a limit to approaches; the approach must be adequate to the object. Again, a manager is legitimated by the philosopher of science when, as in the case of the former city manager (1987), he suspects that his mere presence in the field constructed by himself and his subordinates alters their relationship: People are "varied or wavered or somewhat deviated from their original course just by the fact that I'm there" (Former city manager, 1987). Heidegger (1967) calls this process the constitution of "the thing" (p. 5). By this he means the field within which subjects and objects, managers and colleagues or subordinates find themselves.

A military contracts manager (1989) suggests that a better sense of what is going on is mutually constructed by participants in a reality: "by each one of the five of us coming up with a different thing and listening to each other." Her philosophy of how reality is constructed parallels that of Heidegger's premise that a thing, or state of affairs, is constructed by mutual attunement between subject and object. Only if their views are taken into account is it possible to construct a thing that is held in common. Beginning with the initial premise that even physical objects must be so approached that they can reveal themselves in their own terms, Heidegger (1976) leads us to the definition of a social object: Things as they stand between us are created when we so address our partner in a social relationship that he or she can freely take part in defining what is to be talked about.[12]

WEBER

On the level of method, Max Weber offers perhaps the most easily understood solution to the problem of the relative place of analysis and synthesis. As one of the founders of social science, he placed at the center of his investigations what things mean to people. This move addresses the experience of managers who find themselves in situations in which their colleagues or subordinates exercise the freedom to define what is going on. This is the familiar problem that in real life things are defined by talk among different subjects in different positions—intersubjectively—rather than by scientists conveniently able to take the same position. Weber shows how such intersubjectivity can be achieved with an explicit set of methods that refer the action of a fellow social actor to core values of a situation or culture to establish their meaning. Weber (1968) concludes that until the definition of what is going on is undertaken, all further analysis or statistical operation is meaningless: "[W]herever there exists the possibility of interpretation in principle, there it should be completed; that is, the mere relating of human 'action' to a rule of experience that is simply empirically observed, be it ever so strict, does not suffice us in the interpretation of human 'action' " (p. 69).

In this conclusion, Weber develops on the methodological level and in the realm of culture Kant's tenet that our seeing is blind without concepts and anticipates Heidegger's tenet that objects held in common—things as they stand between us—are mutually constructed.

An End to an Embarrassment

All three thinkers concerned with how knowledge is acquired, and what can make it valid, stand critically opposed to the corps of critical scientists that argues that all knowledge acquisition must meet analytic validity standards.

The question "Why can't we resolve the research issue in public administration?" has an embarrassingly simple answer. It is because some analytic scientists confuse two operations: the analytic operation of taking a reality apart and the synthesizing operation of putting a reality together.

It is to the eternal credit of managers that despite the pressures of a scientific culture and a rationalist-scientist education, they have stayed realistic. The best of them—those with the longest track record and those most highly educated—explicitly rely on sources of knowledge other than the mere scientific (Lester & Webber, 1990). They thus resist the importuning of scientists that managers need to get in line with analytic validity standards when managers are well and appropriately engaged in their prior task of putting and keeping the world of work together.

The question remains, Are there validity standards for synthesis? It can be argued there are. If there are, and to the extent that managers exercise them, their knowledge of how a world is put together must be considered as potentially as valid for its purpose as analytic scientists' knowledge of how a world can be taken apart.

Asserting the Usefulness of Stories: How Managers Use Stories and What Their Standards Are

There is at least some evidence—much of it unintentionally gathered by those who criticize public administration research for not following the canons of analytic science—that managers care first and foremost about putting a problem together, in a way that makes sense to those concerned, before taking it apart. In the synthesis of construction, immediate concern for objective determination of scientific facts takes a back seat. In the driver's seat is the need to construct intersubjective agreements defining particular events in which self and others are, and remain, involved. To steer their work group in the right direction, managers talk to one another and their subordinates; the story and storytelling emerge as the prime means of orienting oneself (Mitroff & Kilmann, 1975; Rein, 1976; White, 1987). Stories can take many forms, including the recalled experiences, case studies, or purely descriptive studies so decried by analytic scientists.

It is not possible to give an account of all kinds of stories available as sources of knowledge to the manager. Here, only two types of story are used to illustrate how stories work: the engaging anecdote and a biographical anecdote. The engaging anecdote directly invites the listener to practice reality construction by taking an active part in the story. Second, the biographical anecdote—a "recalled experience"—serves the function of making a new situation part of the listener's previously experienced world, broadening the parameters of his or her world and deepening or intensifying the meaning of its contents. Examining the story can show how it works to do at least two things:

1. Including listeners in a storyteller's world; that is, engaging them in helping define a situation or problem and winning their commitment to its solution.
2. Expanding the listener's own world, or definition of reality, by allowing him or her to tentatively include the storyteller's different and even strange experience.

The Story as a Tool of Engagement

Jay White, in the original draft of his research on the growth of knowledge in public administration, told a story about a manager. As reproduced elsewhere (Hummel, 1987b, p. 83), what happened went like this:

> A middle manager is called upon to "do something quick" by her executive assistant who bursts into her office announcing: "Your people are killing each other on the fifth floor."
> The manager rushes into the elevator, takes it down to the fifth floor, flings open the door to the claims bureau and finds a fistfight in progress among ten of her employees.

What is the first thing the manager says?

She might say, "Get me a consultant to do a scientific study to explain what happened here!" though this is unlikely. Or she might say, "Get the operations research unit to do a trend projection on how long this is going to go on." Unlikely also. More likely, perhaps: "What the hell is going on here?" Or, as many practitioners in our classes have said, "Stop!" Or, from those at the more advanced levels of administrative sophistication, "Who's in charge here?"—thereby both allocating blame and distancing oneself from the problem.

What function does this kind of story serve? Note that no matter what the manager says, the events are not given their managerial meaning until she says it, and the story is not complete until she says it (Searle, 1969, p. 47). Further, as we hear the story, the events are not meaningful for us until we have read ourselves into the story. This is how a story, and the telling of it, functions in a fundamentally different way for us than does analytic science. Analytic science gives us events that are objective fragments of reality and leaves us detached from them; the story always gives us events that are intended to be coherent and meaningful to us, something that cannot happen unless we become involved with them.

The story is a tool of engagement. But engagement in what? Engagement in this context means participating with others—the storyteller as well as those about whom the story is told—in the construction of the reality that the story opens up. In the case of the open-ended anecdote, the invitation to become involved in "making up" a reality is explicit.

For the manager there is no "right answer" to the problem posed by the story until she has committed herself to participating in the co-definition of the event in question. Only the commitment of the individual to both the perception of the problem and possible efforts directed at a solution can bring about an answer that "fits"—fits not merely the past "facts" of the situation but also its future resolution. Any validity standard applied to this active synthesis will have to answer the question: Can the story so engage the listener that he or she will contribute to co-defining what the story is about—the problem—and work on solving it? The ultimate test is that a new and desired reality is jointly created. Clearly, managers are first in the creation business, not the analysis business.

For us as listeners, the best we can do with such a story is to judge this: Given who the manager is, did he or she do the right thing by him- or herself, by the situation, by others involved as these were coherently involved in the situation?

The case of the engaging anecdote is our first occasion for showing how the structure of a story appeals and draws in the listener by its congruence with the structure of the world of practice. The story is a report about an event, a situation, a little world, as seen through the eyes of the storyteller who reports about his relations with an object or objects in that world. In the case of the engaging anecdote, the listener is asked to step into the manager's shoes and provide a point of contact between the story world and his or her own. This point of congruence gives the listener who has now become a participant in the story a vantage point into a larger reality. From it, he or she can see that the structural characteristics of his or her own world and the story world are the same. Both will be marked by an observing subject, at least one object, and the relations between the two; and these markers will constitute a coherent field. What this experience minimally tells the listener is that the storyteller's world is essentially just like your world—even though the story content is different—as you prove to yourself by being able to feel at home in either. Managers are able to understand this quite well when pressed on the point. In the words of one manager asked about what could be learned from the story of another dealing with an entirely different work situation, "You're looking for somebody that has the, that shares—this is a contradiction in terms—that shares a unique experience" (Parks and recreation manager, 1989). Pictorially, the point of contact and the congruence that becomes visible from it is depicted in Figure 15.1.

As the listener steps into the position of the manager and faces the task of how to deal with the fight, the fight becomes thematic to him or her and moves into the foreground of his or her concern. Meanwhile, the objects of his or her own world become temporarily hazy and move out of focus. In putting him- or herself in the manager's position, the listener not only construes what the manager's world would mean to him or her but also in fact is enabled to reenact the structural steps of world constructing that the manager in the original story would have had to go through. Even though the listener's solution might be different, the listener touches base with the same structural elements in the story that construct his or her own world:

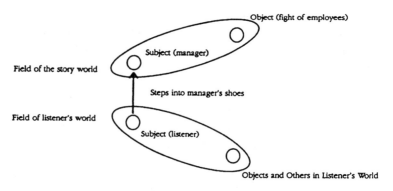

Figure 15.1. Listeners and Storytellers: Worlds Apart

subject involved in relationship with an object and through this relationship constituting a field (Schon, 1983, pp. 150-151; Weber, 1968, pp. 4, 22, 26).[13] In short, the structure of the story, because it is congruent with the structural elements of the world described above by managers as the elements of their world, inspires a trust in being able to move back and forth between one's own experienced world and the world represented by storytellers.

This moves us already to the question of validity. The reference points for any questions of validity applying to a story told do not lie originally in the facts of the story; rather, they are constituted by its structure. Each structural element of the story must stand up to scrutiny: subject, object, relationships between subject and object. Ultimately, the question is raised whether all of these together constitute a coherent and therefore plausible field for action. By referring to the structures of subject, object, relationships, and field, the unfamiliar can become familiar because it can be assigned to structural categories already mutually understood between two subjects, each belonging to different worlds.

Contrary to the analytic scientist, who takes for granted the existence of a shared world that has relevance to all who use his approach, the manager listening to a story is concerned with the prior problem of establishing the relevance of the world told about to his own world and his interests in it.[14] The fundamental criterion of validity for a story is therefore the ability of the listener to literally "re-cognize"—in the original sense of knowing again—the familiar even in an unfamiliar story. On the level of practice there is no mystery in this; this is simply how human beings expand their horizons of knowledge.

But, what can be familiar in what is strange? Except the structures of the storied world when compared to the structures of one's own. The validity the listener seeks is a structural validity. Its key question: Are there those structures in the story told that the listener needs to orient himself or herself in the new world the story announces? Structure by structure, the subordinate questions can be formulated like this:

- Is there a subject, and can I identify with him or her?
- Is there an object, and is it likely that such an object as is told about could exist? If the object is a person, or persons, a recognizable bit of personality will help make the connection to the newly involved listener. If the object is a physical substance, the question is whether there is something whose familiarity or even contradiction to familiarity provides a handhold.
- Is there a relationship between subject and object that is likely between such a subject and such an object? Practically, this may simply mean referring the relationship between subject and object to a previous similar or contrasting experience the listener has had.
- Does the field of the story told hold together? This is a question of whether the story makes sense as a totality.

The validity standards applied to a story are relevance standards first and factual standards second. This is not to say that relevance standards are not epistemological standards, just as scientists claim factual standards are. In fact, relevance standards are epistemological standards of the first order, because they ask the question, "Does this ring true?"

The emerging relevance standards test the relevance of all parts of the story both to each other and to me and my world. They are further distinct from factual standards in that they open up a world, when they are met, while factual standards can only foreclose what is not fact and thereby close worlds. Beyond ringing true, a story well and properly told opens up possibilities of action for me, rather than foreclosing them; it broadens and deepens my world.

The primacy of structural elements of the story as points of contact between worlds experienced by different subjects and their primacy as referents for validity questions becomes explicit in the words of a senior foreign service manager recounting a biographical anecdote.

Parallel Experience and
Structural Congruence in a Biographical Anecdote

All stories invite us to become engaged with the reality they represent. But why should we believe in anything that is represented in the story being told? Beyond the very fact that the story engages our attention and concern, do we apply validity standards or criteria that give the story strength and command us to believe it? And what is it that we are being asked to believe?

A high-ranking foreign service manager (Ambassador, 1989) tells a story about Colonel X in a foreign army who, instead of prosecuting two soldiers who had mistreated civilians,

> had them drop their trousers and their underwear. He removed his Sam Brown belt, ordered them to lean over and grab his desk, and he beat them 'til they had welts on them. He gave them more verbal hell, telling them that he would apply the law if they ever repeated such behavior, and he sent them to their quarters.
>
> Now those men went out and they told that story. They loved Colonel X. The adoration was shared by all other men in the unit who heard the story.

Although there is no space to report this story in full, it can be used to point out two things. First, the manager considered the story a tool not only to widen understanding of Colonel X by his men but also to widen understanding back home of the nature of the forces allied with the United States in its foreign policy. He had begun his story with the comment,

> Colonel X, whom everyone accuses or alleges to be someone who at least turns his head to human rights abuses by his men, if he does not in fact encourage them, is important politically and in the conduct of the war. It is important that American policy makers and diplomats understand him. Now, by the time I get through I won't be able to articulate to you all that I learned from the story, but you will have learned something and I will have learned something.

Second, the manager expressed concern for validity standards and was able to produce at least two:

> The story had a particular relevance to me because when I was a brand new Marine lieutenant with my first platoon, one of my Marines came in drunk and took a poke at the Company First Sergeant. Believe me, that is not acceptable behavior in the Marine Corps. The First Sergeant wanted to bring charges under the Universal Code of Military Justice. I did not let it happen. Instead I took that Marine on an all-night training exercise, I made him carry that 54-pound radio plus all his 782 gear, and made him run up and down mountains until he was vomiting between lamentations that he would never drink whiskey again. But I did not permit my Marine to be thrown in jail. As things ended up, he became one of my most loyal supporters and as a shave-tail lieutenant I won the admiration of my men.
>
> I could empathize with Colonel X, and I understood him better. When I heard that story about Colonel X it meant something to me. I had a certain amount of empathy for him and his situation.

Why would he believe that story?

"Well, I believed that story because of the person who told me, who was present. But, without my having had my own experience—I've told that story to other people in trying to help them understand Colonel X, and it added to their understanding, certainly."

What the manager has done here is build himself a framework within which the personality or the actions of the individual in question can be understood. Clearly, reliable tests for the further analysis of the individual's character can be applied through science. But it is only once a previous framework exists and is validated as reflecting events in reality according to its own validity standards, that any kind of action, including scientific investigation, can proceed.

Are there such criteria for the frameworks that stories become, and is the person who hears a story aware of them? In the words of the same manager, "Sure there are. Criteria of coherence: whether it's credible in terms of your previous experience, whether it's comparable to other experience. There are all kinds of standards." Interviewer: "Is the person a notorious truth-teller or a notorious liar?" Manager: "What is his previous history?" Interviewer: "Things like that. So there are standards." Manager: "Sure there are."

It is interesting to see how the manager here paints a picture of points of validation that correspond to the structural reference points of reality developed above. Managers can think not only about the structure of their world but also about validity standards.

Summary

In sum, managers first and foremost communicate through stories that constitute or construct their world. How could it be otherwise? When problems arise in life or at work, people tell each other what is going on. Lois High (1990) of the Department of Veterans Affairs says in a pointed way what most managers know: "As managers, our people are our only resource. We must know our people" (p. 70).

Getting access to what people in their shop think is going on is the first, and perhaps the biggest, problem for the manager. Judging the validity of stories about what is going on is perhaps the toughest. When the manager at Morton-Thiokol ignored an engineer's warning that the space shuttle's O-rings might fail at low launch temperatures, the resulting disaster was not directly caused by scientific or technical faults. It was mediated by a failure of interpretation, a failure of a previous problem formulation to include scientific facts as one source of reality definition. The manager simply did not believe the engineer's story, so scientific analysis could find no place in the construction of reality.

People in management everywhere—including public management—could do worse than hone their skills in storytelling and in story validating.

In a highly technical workplace, science and rational calculations have their place. But the manager must also develop a felt sense for what it is that his or her subordinates and co-workers are talking about. It has been argued that this requires developing a special aesthetic sensibility that reaches beyond the confines of the manager's desk,[15] and it may involve occasional re-apprenticeships in which managers develop a feel for how the work gets done at the physical or hands-on level.

But, ultimately, what managers must judge is not what has been scientifically calculated in the past or even what trends a computer can project into the future. They must judge whether the data of science and rational calculation fit into a future no one has yet seen.

In the words of the secretary of state of a Southwestern state, who was asked about whether science can drive policy, "That's not how we operate in a cabinet meeting. Sure we hand the [scientific] reports around, but then we have to see if they fit with what we can do" (Secretary of State, 1989). This means not only puzzle solving that requires hearing from many sources—technical, scientific, rationalist, interpersonal, psychological, political, ideological, cultural, and so on—but also the art of feeling one's way with all one knows across a great divide to open up the potential of an unknowable future.

The questions closest to the manager are what constitutes good work and what constitutes good management. With their eyes firmly fixed on the hands-on or street-level knowledge that comes from knowing one's workers and the integrative knowledge that is the synthesis of management itself, managers have been founding and refounding the practice of public service every day while academicians have been fighting over the definition of a discipline that can teach future managers. There is no doubt that, as our foreign service manager interviewed said, "Public administration is not going to disappear" (Ambassador, 1989). But the academician's task, as this manager said, "[is] to ascertain first of all what is it that we're operating on and how can it be improved."

Whether public administration in the tradition of Franklin Delano Roosevelt can survive is not the issue here, though that survival faces a challenge and a crisis. Public choice or privatization may or may not appeal to the efficiency and economy oriented and may succeed traditional public administration or not. Implementation studies and policy analysis with their focus on outcomes rather than administrative processes may appeal to those concerned with whether what emerges is in tune with the law's intent. Top administrators may continue to spread the literature of their lofty experience. Excellence or quality management may be the future, with more lessons from the private sector, or an entirely new concern for the public enterprise may develop out of disappointment with deregulation and the failure of controls.

Whoever legislates the delivery of public goods and services with whatever means, there will still be those who manage and those who work. We could do worse than study and give full credence to the knowledge of those who manage and work to maintain not so much public administration but public service. They and their realities are the only possible foundation for a renewed or new discipline.

Notes

1. My rebuttal to this attack has, I believe, been greatly helped by comments on earlier versions of this article from members of the Project on Reviving the Case Study (Mary Timney Bailey, Richard Mayer, and Robert Zinke) as well as the many questioners at meetings of the Public Administration Theory Network, which spawned the project. I was also helped by concurrent studies on how managers think undertaken by Richard Herzog, on how city managers newly perceive their relation to policy and politics by John Nalbandian, and by the usual critical support of Dwight Waldo. Anonymous managers gave freely of their time and deeply of their thought. Gregory Brunk, David Carnevale, C. Kenneth Meier, and Richard Wells, in my own department, provided the kind of collegial support that the academic enterprise demands. I consider Professor Brunk, in his role as scientific methodologist, the moral coauthor of my current position between scientific-analytic and synthesizing thought. Finally, my thanks to analytic scientists who made it all possible.

2. In a review of utilization literature, Lester and Wilds (1990) conclude that "early utilization research suggests that governmental decision makers make little direct use of this [policy analysis] research" though "[m]ore recent trends are somewhat more optimistic about the utilization of policy analysis by decision makers."

3. For an alternate path of inquiry, see the work of Agor (1989). I would like to thank Patricia Ingraham for bringing this work to my attention.

4. The following three sections are based on exchanges with managers that I would like to describe as exploratory conversations rather than interviews. In these conversations the author challenged managers to agree or disagree with assumptions underlying science and rationalist inquiry and to judge whether these could be accepted in the management world. They were also pressed to admit to and assert other ways of knowledge acquisition they might be using. The use of stories was explicitly brought up and, if managers admitted to their use, they were asked about validity standards for these stories. In the conversations, the author made a special effort to engage those he talked with in full partnership of dialogue, pushing his points as hard as he could and encouraging or even provoking managers to push theirs as hard as they could. The sources for citations from conversations with managers include military contracts manager, 1989; former city manager, 1987; parks and recreation manager, 1989; office manager, 1987; secretary of state, 1989; and ambassador (career foreign service officer of ambassadorial rank), 1989. Interviews

reported as 1987 were conducted in the period 1986-1987. Interviews reported as 1989 were conducted beginning 1989.

5. Accepting here a general principle of the sociology of knowledge.

6. It may be argued that different locations in an organization may give different people different power to insist their view of reality is the correct one, and that therefore power becomes a determinant of knowledge among managers while among scientists this does not happen. Thayer (1980) refers to the literature that establishes that power is also a factor in the determination of which scientific paradigms or methods become official standards (1980, pp. 119-121).

7. Any survey instrument, however, will have to be open to offering respondents a choice between defining problems and procedures of knowledge acquisition according to at least three paradigms: that of science, that of pure rationalism, and that of storytelling.

8. The best known Kantian comment on concepts is perhaps this:

> Without sensibility no object would be given to us, without understanding no object would be thought. Thoughts without content are empty, intuitions without concepts are blind. It is, therefore, just as necessary to make our concepts sensible, that is, to add the object to them in intuition, as to make our intuitions intelligible, that is, to bring them under concepts. . . . We therefore distinguish the science of the rules of sensibility in general, that is, aesthetic, from the science of the rules of the understanding in general, that is, logic (Kant, 1965, pp. A51-52, B75-76. Original editions: A is 1781, B is 1787).

The application here is that managers are more concerned with the rules of sensibility that govern the problem of how to get access to reality, while scientists are more concerned with the rules of logic that govern the problem of how to get clarity about that which one has previously gotten access to.

9. Similarly, another commentator observes that "Kant has made the discovery that there are judgments which are both a priori and synthetic, and that they are the presuppositions of science." In synthesis, putting the case in philosophical terms, "the predicate was not got by analysis of the subject, but by somehow going out of or beyond the subject and coming to connect it with what it had not hitherto been seen to be connected with." Even in mathematical discovery, previously held to be the result of analysis, Kant insists that discovery is not a mere matter of analysis: "It always involves a synthetical element: even the result of a simple sum is not got by analysis, but by counting or some kind of construction" (Lindsay, 1936, pp. 57-58).

10. For example, one current textbook on research methods (O'Sullivan & Rassel, 1989, p. 6) gives two paragraphs to the heading of "Ideas" and where they come from ("insight," "experience, knowledge or opinions") out of 450 pages of text.

11. For example, Husserl (1970) suggests that most of our propositions about the nature of reality in daily life are "occasional propositions" whose meaning depends on the occasion, the person speaking, and his situation (p. 125). Knowledge based on these, Husserl adds, constitutes "a realm of good verification and, based on this, of well-verified predicative cognitions and of truths which are just as secure as is necessary for the practical projects of life that determine their sense" (1970, p. 125).

12. The guiding principle to the conversations with managers here reported.

13. The idea of a managerial reality as a field, dating back to Kurt Lewin, has been most fully developed in the organization development consulting movement and its resulting action research approach.

14. Up to a point, my model here parallels the work of Alfred Schutz. For the contrast between science's and managers' constructs of the world, see specifically Schutz, 1967, pages 38-44. On relevance structures, see also Berger and Luckmann (1966, p. 45). See also, for a later update of relevance into interests, Habermas (1971, p. 212).

15. The exercise of such sensibility is advocated in concepts like that of "managing by walking about" in Peters and Waterman (1982). For empirical evidence that mental operations establishing a "felt sense" for things can be distinguished from other mental operations, see Gendlin (1973). On executive apprenticeships, see Hummel (1987a).

References

Abel, T. (1948-49). The operation called Verstehen. *American Journal of Sociology, 54,* 211-218.

Adams, G. B. (1992). Enthralled with modernity: The historical context of knowledge and theory development in public administration. *Public Administration Review, 52,* 363-373.

Adams, G. B. (1993). Ethics and the chimera of professionalism: The historical context of an oxymoronic relationship. *American Review of Public Administration, 23,* 117-139.

Adams, G. B., Bowerman, P. V., Dolbeare, K. M., & Stivers, C. (1990). Joining purpose to practice: A democratic identity for the public service. In H. D. Kass & B. L. Catron (eds.), *Images and identities in public administration* (pp. 219-240). Newbury Park, CA: Sage.

Adams, G. B., & Ingersoll, V. H. (1990). Culture, technical rationality and organizational culture. *American Review of Public Administration, 20,* 285-302.

Adams, R. N. (1988). *The eighth day: Social evolution as the self-organization of energy.* Austin: University of Texas Press.

Agor, W. A. (ed.). (1989). *Intuition in organizations: Leading and managing productively.* Newbury Park, CA: Sage.

Aguilar, F. J. (1967). *Scanning the business environment.* New York: Macmillan.

Aldrich, H. (1979). *Organizations and environments.* Englewood Cliffs, NJ: Prentice-Hall.

Allaire, Y., & Firsirotu, M. E. (1984). Theories of organizational culture. *Organizational Studies, 5*(4), 193-226.

Allen, W. H. (1907). *Efficient democracy.* New York: Dodd, Mead.

Allison, G. T. (1971). *The essence of decision: Explaining the Cuban missile crisis.* Boston: Little, Brown.

American Society for Public Administration (1985). *Graduate curriculum in budgeting and financial management.* Working papers (mimeograph), section on Budgeting and Financial Management, National Task Force on Curriculum Reform. Washington, DC: Author.

Apel, K.-O. (1984). *Understanding and explanation: A transcendental-pragmatic perspective* (G. Warnke, trans.). Cambridge: MIT Press.

Arendt, H. (1954). *Between past and future.* Cleveland, OH: World.

Arendt, H. (1958). *The human condition.* Chicago: University of Chicago Press.

Argyris, C., & Schon, D. A. (1978). *Organizational learning.* Reading, MA: Addison-Wesley.

Aronson, S. H. (1964). *Status and kinship in the higher civil service.* Cambridge, MA: Harvard University Press.

Asher, W. (1987). Editorial: Policy sciences and the economic approach in a post-positivist era. *Policy Sciences, 20,* 3-9.

Association of American Universities and the Association of Graduate Schools. (1990). *Institutional policies to improve doctoral education.* Washington, DC: Author.

Axelrod, R. (1987). *The evolution of cooperation.* New York: Basic Books.

Babbie, E. R. (1973). *Survey research methods*. Belmont, CA: Wadsworth.

Backoff, R. W., & Mitnick, B. M. (1986). Reappraising the promise of general systems theory for the policy sciences. In W. N. Dunn (ed.), *Policy analysis: Perspectives, concepts, and methods. Vol. 6: Public policy studies* (pp. 23-40). Greenwich, CT: JAI.

Bailey, M. T. (1989). Minnowbrook II: An end or a new beginning? *Public Administration Review, 49*, 224-225.

Bailey, M. T. (1992). Do physicists use case studies? Thoughts on public administration research. *Public Administration Review, 52*(1), 47-55.

Barley, S. R. (1983). Semiotics and the study of occupational and organizational cultures. *Administrative Science Quarterly, 28*, 393-413.

Barley, S. R., Meyer, G. W., & Gash, D. C. (1988). Cultures of culture: Academics, practitioners, and the pragmatics of normative control. *Administrative Science Quarterly, 33*, 24-60.

Barnard, C. A. (1938). *The functions of the executive*. Cambridge, MA: Harvard University Press.

Barrett, W. (1979). *The illusion of technique*. Garden City, NY: Anchor Doubleday.

Bauman, Z. (1989). *Modernity and the Holocaust*. Ithaca, NY: Cornell University Press.

Bell, D. (1976). *The cultural contradictions of capitalism*. New York: Basic Books.

Bellah, R. N., Madsen, R., Sullivan, W. M., Swidler, A., & Tipton, S. M. (1985). *Habits of the heart: Individualism and commitment in American life*. New York: Harper & Row.

Bendix, R. (1956). *Work and authority in industry*. New York: Harper & Row.

Berger, P. L. (1963). *Invitation to sociology: A humanistic perspective*. Garden City, NY: Doubleday.

Berger, P. L., Berger, B., & Kellner, H. (1973). *The homeless mind*. New York: Vintage.

Berger, P. L., & Kellner, H. (1981). *Sociology reinterpreted: An essay on method and vocation*. Garden City, NY: Doubleday.

Berger, P. L., & Luckmann, T. (1966). *The social construction of reality: A treatise in the sociology of knowledge*. Garden City, NY: Doubleday.

Berlinski, D. (1976). *On systems analysis: An essay concerning the limitations of some mathematical methods in social, political and biological sciences*. Cambridge: MIT Press.

Bernstein, R. J. (1976). *The restructuring of social and political theory*. Orlando, FL: Harcourt Brace Jovanovich.

Bernstein, R. J. (1982). *Beyond objectivism and relativism*. Philadelphia: University of Pennsylvania Press.

Bernstein, R. J. (ed.). (1985). *Habermas and modernity*. Cambridge: MIT Press.

Bernstein, R. J. (1992). *The new constellation: The ethical-political horizons of modernity\ postmodernity*. Cambridge: MIT Press.

Biller, R. P. (1982, October). *Research and the public sector: Choices for NASPAA*. Paper presented at annual meeting of the National Association of Schools of Public Affairs and Administration, Portland, OR.

Blalock, Jr., H. M. (1979). *Social Statistics* (rev. 2nd. ed.). New York: McGraw-Hill.

Blankenship, V. L. (1967). Theory and research as an act of faith. *Public Administration Review, 27*, pp. 262-271.

Bobrow, D. B., & Dryzek, J. S. (1987). *Policy analysis by design*. Pittsburgh, PA: University of Pittsburgh Press.

Boulding, K. (1981). *Evolutionary economics*. Beverly Hills, CA: Sage.

Box, R. C. (1992). An examination of the debate over research in public administration. *Public Administration Review, 52*, 62-69.

Bozeman, B. (1986). The credibility of policy analysis: Between method and use. *Policy Studies Journal, 14*, 519-539.

Brodbeck, M. (1968). Explanation, prediction, and "imperfect" knowledge. In M. Brodbeck (ed.), *Readings in the philosophy of the social sciences*. New York: Macmillan.

Brown, R. E., & Pyers, J. B. (1988). Putting teeth into efficiency and effectiveness of public services. *Public Administration Review, 48,* 735-742.

Brunner, R. D. (1982). The policy sciences as science. *Policy Sciences, 15,* 115-135.

Buckley, W. (1967). *Sociology and modern systems theory.* Englewood Cliffs, NJ: Prentice-Hall.

Burke, J. P. (1986). *Bureaucratic responsibility.* Baltimore, MD: Johns Hopkins University Press.

Burrell, G., & Morgan, G. (1979). *Sociological paradigms and organizational analysis.* London: Heineman.

Bush, P. D. (1987). The theory of institutional change. *Journal of Economic Issues, 21,* 1075-1115.

Caiden, G. E. (1984). In search of an apolitical science of American public administration. In J. Rabin & J. S. Bowman (eds.), *Politics and administration: Woodrow Wilson and American public administration* (pp. 51-76). New York: Marcel Dekker.

Caldwell, B. (1982). *Beyond positivism: Economic methodology in the twentieth century.* London: Allen & Unwin.

Caldwell, L. K. (1968). Methodology in the theory of public administration. In J. C. Charlesworth (ed.), *Scope of public administration* (pp. 205-222). Philadelphia: American Academy of Political and Social Science.

Caldwell, L. K. (1976). Novus ordo seclorum: The heritage of American public administration. *Public Administration Review, 36,* 476-488.

Caldwell, L. K. (1980). Biology and bureaucracy: The coming confrontation. *Public Administration Review, 40,* 1-12.

Caldwell, L. K. (1990). The administrative republic: The contrasting legacies of Hamilton and Jefferson. *Public Administration Quarterly, 13,* 470-493.

Campbell, C. (1986, February 9). The tyranny of the Yale critics. *New York Times Magazine,* p. 23.

Campbell, D. C. (1986). Science's social system of validity-enhancing collective belief change and the problem of the social sciences. In D. W. Fiske & R. A. Schweder (eds.), *Metatheory in social science* (pp. 108-135). Chicago: University of Chicago Press.

Campbell, D. C. (1988). *Systems theory and social experimentation.* Paper presented at USSR-US Conference on Systems Theory and Management, Moscow.

Campbell, D. C., & Stanley, J. C. (1963). *Experimental and quasi-experimental designs for research.* Chicago: Rand McNally.

Carter, L. H. (1984). *Reason in law.* Boston: Little, Brown.

Casanova, P. G. (1981). *The fallacy of social science research: A critical examination and a new qualitative model* (S. B. Kapilian & G. Weller, trans.). Elmsford, NY: Pergamon.

Catalano, R., Dooley, D., & Jackson, R. (1985). Economic antecedents of help seeking: A reformulation of the time-series tests. *Journal of Health and Social Behavior, 26,* 141-152.

Catron, B. L., & Harmon, M. M. (1981). Action theory in practice: Toward theory without conspiracy. *Public Administration Review, 41,* 535-541.

Chandler, R. C. (ed.). (1987). *A centennial history of the American administrative state.* New York: Free Press.

Churchman, C. W. (1968). *The systems approach.* New York: Delacorte.

Churchman, C. W. (1971). *The design of inquiring systems: Basic concepts of systems and organization.* New York: Basic Books.

Cicourel, A. (1973). *Cognitive sociology.* London: Penguin.

Cleary, R. E. (1992). Revisiting the doctoral dissertation in public administration: An examination of the dissertations of 1990. *Public Administration Review, 52,* 55-61.

Cleveland, H. (1988). Theses of a new reformation: The social fallout of science 300 years after Newton. *Public Administration Review, 48,* 681.

Clifford, J. (1986). Introduction: Partial truths. In J. Clifford & G. E. Marcus (eds.), *Writing culture: The poetics and politics of ethnography* (pp. 1-26). Berkeley: University of California Press.

Collingwood, R. G. (1956). *The idea of history.* New York: Oxford University Press.

Colson, H. (1990). Citation rankings of public administration journals. *Administration and Society, 21,* 452-471.

Cooper, T. L. (1991). *An ethic of citizenship for public administration.* Englewood Cliffs, NJ: Prentice-Hall.

Corning, P. A. (1983). *The synergism hypothesis: A theory of progressive evolution.* New York: McGraw-Hill.

Coser, L. A. (1971). *Masters of sociological thought.* Orlando, FL: Harcourt Brace Jovanovich.

Council of Graduate Schools (1991). *The role and nature of the doctoral dissertation.* Washington, DC: Council of Graduate Schools.

Crease, R. P., & Mann, C. C. (1986). *The second creation.* New York: Macmillan.

Crenson, M. A. (1975). *The federal machine: Beginnings of bureaucracy in Jacksonian America.* Baltimore, MD: Johns Hopkins University Press.

Croly, H. (1909). *The promise of American life.* New York: Macmillan.

Cronbach, L. J. (1982). Prudent aspirations for social inquiry. In W. Kruskal (ed.), *The social sciences: Their nature and uses* (pp. 125-131). Chicago: University of Chicago Press.

Crosby, R. (1987). Toward a classification of complex systems. *European Journal of Operational Research, 30,* 291-293.

Cuff, R. D. (1978). Wilson and Weber: Bourgeois critics in an organized age. *Public Administration Review, 38,* 240-244.

Dahl, R. A. (1947). The science of public administration: Three problems. *Public Administration Review, 7,* 1-11.

Dallmayr, R. R. (1986). Critical theory and public policy. In W. Dunn (ed.), *Policy analysis: Perspectives, concepts and methods* (Vol. 6, pp. 46-68). Greenwich, CT: JAI.

Dallmayr, R. R., & McCarthy, T. A. (eds.). (1977). *Understanding and social inquiry.* South Bend, IN: University of Notre Dame Press.

Daly, H. E. (1989). A. N. Whitehead's fallacy of misplaced concreteness: Examples from economics. *Contemporary Philosophy, 12,* 22-25.

Daneke, G. A. (1984). The philosophical crisis in the policy sciences. *Contemporary Philosophy, 10,* 10-13.

Daneke, G. A. (1990a). A science of public administration? *Public Administration Review, 50,* 383-392.

Daneke, G. A. (1990b). Evaluation in an evolving world: Towards an advanced systems perspective. In S. Nagel & W. Dunn (eds.), *Policy theory and policy evaluation* (pp. 43-59). New York: Greenwood.

Das, T. H. (1983). Qualitative research in organizational behavior. *Journal of Management Studies, 20,* 301-314.

Deetz, S. (1973). An understanding of science and a hermeneutic science of understanding. *Journal of Communication, 23,* 154-155.

de Haven-Smith, L. (1988). *Philosophical critiques of policy analysis: Lindblom, Habermas, and the Great Society.* Gainesville: University of Florida Press.

deLeon, P. (1992). The democratization of the policy sciences. *Public Administration Review, 52,* 125-129.

Denhardt, R. B. (1981a). *In the shadow of organization.* Lawrence: Regents Press of Kansas.

Denhardt, R. B. (1981b). Toward a critical theory of public organization. *Public Administration Review, 41,* 628-636.

Denhardt, R. B. (1984). *Theories of public organization.* Belmont, CA: Brooks/Cole.

Denhardt, R. B. (1990). Public administration theory: The state of the discipline. In N. B. Lynn & A. Wildavsky (eds.), *Public administration: The state of the discipline* (pp. 4372). Chatham, NJ: Chatham House.

Denhardt, R. B, & White, J. D. (1982). Beyond explanation: A methodological note. *Administration and Society, 14,* 163-169.

Denhardt, R. B., & White, J. D. (1986). Integrating theory and practice in public administration. In D. J. Calista (ed.), *Bureaucratic and governmental reform* (pp. 311-320). Greenwich, CT: JAI.

Derrida, J. (1973). *Speech and phenomena, and other essays on Husserl's theory of signs.* Evanston, IL: Northwestern University Press.

Derrida, J. (1976). *Of grammatology.* Baltimore, MD: Johns Hopkins University Press.

Derrida, J. (1978). *Writing and difference.* London: Routledge & Kegan Paul.

Diamond, M. A. (1984). Bureaucracy as externalized self-system: A view from the psychological interior. *Administration and Society, 16,* 195-214.

Doron, G. (1986). A comment: Telling the big stories—Policy responses to analytical complexity. *Journal of Policy Analysis and Management, 5,* 798-803.

Douglas, M., & Wildavsky, A. (1982). *Risk and culture: An essay on the selection of technical and environmental dangers.* Berkeley: University of California Press.

Duncan, W. J. (1978). *Organizational behavior.* Boston: Houghton Mifflin.

Dunn, D. D. (1984). Blinders on research in public sector performance. *Public Administration Quarterly, 8,* 315-324.

Dunn, E. S. (1971). *Economic and social development: A process of social learning.* Baltimore, MD: Johns Hopkins University Press.

Dunn, W. N. (1981). *An introduction to public policy analysis.* Englewood Cliffs, NJ: Prentice-Hall.

Dunn, W. N. (1982). Reforms as arguments. *Knowledge: Creation, utilization, diffusion* (Vol. 3, pp. 293-326).

Dunn, W. N. (1988). Methods of the second type: Coping with the wilderness of conventional policy analysis. *Policy Studies Review, 7,* 720-737.

Dunn, W. N., & Fozouni, B. (1976). *Toward a critical administrative theory.* Beverly Hills, CA: Sage.

Dynes, R. R., Quarantelli, E. L., & Kreps, G. A. (1972). *A perspective on disaster planning.* Columbus: Ohio State University, Disaster Research Center.

Eichner, A. S. (1985). *Towards a new economics: Essays in post-Keynesian and institutionalist theory.* Armonk, NY: M. E. Sharpe.

Ellul, J. (1954). *The technological society.* New York: Vintage.

Ely, R. (1982). Report of the organization of the American Economic Association, 1886. In M. B. Levy (ed.), *Political thought in America* (pp. 282-285). Homewood, IL: Dorsey.

Engelen, G. (1988). The theory of self-organization and modelling of complex urban systems. *European Journal of Operational Research, 37,* 42-57.

Faulconer, J. E., & Williams, R. N. (1985). Temporality in human action: An alternative to positivism and historicism. *American Psychologist, 40,* 1179-1188.

Fay, B. (1976). *Social theory and political practice.* Boston: Allen & Unwin.

Feigl, H. (1956). Some major issues and developments in the philosophy of logical positivism. In H. Feigl & M. Scriven (eds.), *Minnesota studies in the philosophy of science* (Vol. 1, pp. 3-38). Minneapolis: University of Minnesota Press.

Feigl, H. (1970). The orthodox view of theories: Remarks in defense as well as criticism. In M. Radner & S. Winokur (eds.), *Minnesota studies in the philosophy of science* (Vol. 4, pp. 3-16). Minneapolis: University of Minnesota Press.

Feldman, M. S. (1989). *Order without design: Information production and policy making.* Stanford, CA: Stanford University Press.

Ferguson, K. E. (1984). *The feminist case against bureaucracy.* Philadelphia: Temple University Press.

Ferris, J. M., & Stallings, R. A. (1988). Sources of reputation among public administration and public affairs programs. *American Review of Public Administration, 18,* 309-325.

Feyerabend, P. (1975). *Against method: Outline of an anarchistic theory of knowledge.* London: NLB.

Fischer, F. (1987). Policy expertise and the "new class": A critique of the neoconservative thesis. In F. Fischer & J. Forester (eds.), *Confronting values in policy analysis: The politics of criteria* (pp. 94-126). Newbury Park, CA: Sage.

Fischer, F. (1990). *Technology and the politics of expertise.* Newbury Park, CA: Sage.

Follett, M. P. (1918). *The new state.* New York: Longman.

Forester, J. (1983). What analysts do. In N. Dunn (ed.), *Values, ethics and the practice of policy analysis* (pp. 47-62). Lexington, MA: D. C. Heath.

Forester, J. (1989). *Planning in the face of power.* Berkeley: University of California Press.

Frederickson, H. G. (1980). *The new public administration.* University: University of Alabama Press.

Furner, M. O. (1975). *Advocacy and objectivity: A crisis in the professionalization of social science.* Lexington: University Press of Kentucky.

Gadamer, H.-G. (1975). *Truth and method* (G. Barden & J. Cumming, eds. & trans.). New York: Seabury.

Garson, G. D., & Overman, S. E. (1983). *Public management research in the United States.* New York: Praeger.

Gaus, J., White, L., & Dimock, M. (1936). *The frontiers of public administration.* Chicago: University of Chicago Press.

Gawthrop, L. C. (1984). *Public sector management, systems and ethics.* Bloomington: Indiana University Press.

Gazell, J. A. (1973). Empirical research in American public administration and political science: Is the estranged relative outstripping the rest of its former household? *Midwest Review of Public Administration, 7,* 229-244.

Geertz, C. (1973). *The interpretation of culture.* New York: Basic Books.

Gendlin, E. T. (1967). Analysis. In M. Heidegger, *What is a thing?* (pp. 247-296) (W. B. Barton & V. Deutsch, trans.). South Bend, IN: Regnery/Gateway.

Gendlin, E. T. (1973). Existential phenomenology. In M. Natanson (ed.), *Phenomenology and the social sciences.* Evanston, IL: Northwestern University Press.

Geuss, R. (1981). *The idea of a critical theory: Habermas and the Frankfurt School.* Cambridge, UK: Cambridge University Press.

Giles, M. W., & Wright, G. C., Jr. (1985). Political scientists' evaluation of sixty-three journals. *PS, 8,* 254-256.

Gillespie, J. A., & Zinnes, D. A. (eds.). (1982). *Missing elements in political inquiry: Logic and levels of analysis.* Beverly Hills, CA: Sage.

Glaser, B. G., & Strauss, A. L. (1967). *The discovery of grounded theory: strategies for qualitative research.* Hawthorne, NY: Aldine.

Gordon, G., et al. (1974). A contingency model for the design of problem-solving research programs: A perspective on diffusion research. *Health and Society, 52,* 185-220.

Gould, S. J. (1989). *Wonderful life: The Burgess shale and the nature of history.* New York: W. W. Norton.

Graebner, W. (1987). *The engineering of consent: Democracy and authority in twentieth century America.* Madison: University of Wisconsin Press.

Green, R. T. (1990). Alexander Hamilton and the study of public administration. *Public Administration Quarterly, 13,* 494-519.

Grizzle, G. A. (1985). Essential skills for financial management. *Public Administration Review, 45,* 840-844.

Gruchy, A. G. (1987). *The reconstruction of economics: An analysis of the fundamentals of institutional economics.* Westport, CT: Greenwood.

Guba, E. G. (1985). The context of the emergent paradigm research. In Y. S. Lincoln (ed.), *Organizational theory and inquiry: The paradigm revolution* (pp. 76-98). Beverly Hills, CA: Sage.

Guba, E. G., & Lincoln, Y. S. (1987). The countenances of fourth-generation evaluation: Description, judgment and negotiation. In D. J. Palumbo (ed.), *The politics of program evaluation* (pp. 202-234). Newbury Park, CA: Sage.

Guerreiro-Ramos, A. (1981). *The new science of organization.* Toronto: University of Toronto Press.

Gulick, L. (1937). Science, values, and public administration. In L. Gulick & L. Urwick (eds.), *Papers on the science of administration* (pp. 191-195). New York: Institute of Public Administration.

Gulick, L., & Urwick, L. K. (eds.). (1937). *Papers on the science of administration.* New York: Institute of Public Administration.

Gunnell, J. G. (1975). *Philosophy, science, and political inquiry.* Morristown, NJ: General Learning Press.

Guy, M. E. (1989). Minnowbrook II: Conclusions. *Public Administration Review, 49,* 219-220.

Haber, S. (1964). *Efficiency and uplift: Scientific management in the Progressive Era, 1890-1920.* Chicago: University of Chicago Press.

Habermas, J. (1970). *Toward a rational society.* Boston: Beacon.

Habermas, J. (1971). *Knowledge and human interests* (J. J. Shapiro, trans.). Boston: Beacon.

Habermas, J. (1983). *The theory of communicative action. Vol. 1: Reason and the rationalization of society.* Boston: Beacon.

Habermas, J. (1987). *The theory of communicative action. Vol. 2: Lifeworld and system: A critique of functionalist reason.* Boston: Beacon.

Hale, M. L. (1983). *A structured observation study of the nature of city manager's work.* Unpublished doctoral dissertation, University of Southern California, Los Angeles.

Hanson, R. L. (1985). *The democratic imagination in America: Conversations with our past.* Princeton, NJ: Princeton University Press.

Hardin, R. (1988). *Morality within the limits of rationality.* Chicago: University of Chicago Press.

Harmon, M. M. (1981). *Action theory for public administration.* New York: Longman.

Harmon, M. M. (1989). Decision and action as contrasting perspectives in organization theory. *Public Administration Review, 49,* 144-152.

Harris, B. (1981). Policy-making, programming and design. In J. P. Crecine (ed.), *Research in public policy analysis and management: Basic theory, methods and perspectives* (Vol. 1, pp. 275-295). Greenwich, CT: JAI.

Haskell, T. L. (1977). *The emergence of professional social science.* Urbana: University of Illinois Press.

Hawkesworth, M. E. (1988). *Theoretical issues in policy analysis.* Albany: State University of New York Press.

Hechter, M. (ed.). (1983). *The microfoundations of macrosociology.* Philadelphia: Temple University Press.

Hedge, D. M., & Mok, J. W. (1987). The nature of policy studies: A content analysis of policy journal articles. *Policy Studies Journal, 16,* 49-62.

Hegel, G. W. F. (1965). Preface to the *Phenomenology of Mind.* In W. Kaufmann (ed. & trans.), *Hegel: Texts and commentary* (pp. 1-112). South Bend, IN: Notre Dame University Press. (Original work published 1807)

Heidegger, M. (1967). *What is a thing?* South Bend, IN: Regnery/Gateway.

Heidegger, M. (1976). *Sein und zeit.* Tuebingen: Max Niemeyer.

Heidegger, M. (1977). *Basic writings* (D. Krell, trans.). New York: Harper & Row. (Original work published 1926)

Hempel, C. (1965). *Aspects of scientific explanation.* New York: Free Press.

Henry, N. (1990). Root and branch: Public administration's travail toward the future. In N. Lynn & A. Wildavsky (eds.), *Public administration: State of the discipline* (pp. 3-26). Chatham, NJ: Chatham House.

Hesse, M. (1980). *Revolutions and reconstructions in the philosophy of science.* Brighton, UK: Harvester.

Higgs, R. (1987). *Crisis and leviathan: Critical episodes in the growth of American government.* New York: Oxford University Press.

High, L. A. (1990). What are you going to be when you grow up? *The Bureaucrat, 19,* 68-71.

Hirsch, E. D. (1967). *Validity and interpretation.* New Haven, CT: Yale University Press.

Hirsch, E. D. (1976). *The aims of interpretation.* Chicago: University of Chicago.

Hofstadter, R. (1955). *The age of reform.* New York: Vintage.

Honey, J. C. (1957). Research in public administration: A further note. *Public Administration Review, 17,* 238-243.

Hoogenboom, A. A. (1961). *Outlawing the spoils: A history of the civil service reform movement.* Urbana: University of Illinois Press.

Horkheimer, M. (1947). *The eclipse of reason.* New York: Oxford University Press.

Houston, D. J., & Delevan, S. M. (1990). Public administration research: An assessment of journal publications. *Public Administration Review, 50,* 674-681.

Howard, R. J. (1982). *Three faces of hermeneutics: An introduction to current theories of understanding.* Berkeley: University of California Press.

Hughes, E. C. (1960). The professions in society. *Canadian Journal of Economics and Political Science, 26,* 54-61.

Hult, K. M., & Walcott, C. (1990). *Governing public organizations: Politics, structure, and institutional design.* Belmont, CA: Brooks/Cole.

Hummel, R. P. (1977). *The bureaucratic experience.* New York: St. Martin's.

Hummel, R. P. (1985, September). *Bottom-up knowledge in organizations.* Paper presented at Conference on Critical Perspectives in Organization Theory.

Hummel, R. P. (1987a). Behind quality management: What workers and a few philosophers have always known and how it adds up to excellence in production. *Organizational Dynamics, 16,* 71-78.

Hummel, R. P. (1987b). *The bureaucratic experience* (3rd ed.). New York: St. Martin's.

Hummel, R. P. (1988). A curriculum for the thinking manager: The MPA in the next fifty years. *Dialogue, 10*(4), 1-17.

Hummel, R. P. (1990). Uncovering validity criteria for stories managers hear and tell. *American Review of Public Administration, 20,* 303-314.

Hummel, R. P. (1991). Stories managers tell: Why they are as valid as science. *Public Administration Review, 51,* 31-41.

Hunter, J. E., Schmidt, F. L., & Jackson, G. B. (1982). *Meta-analysis: Cumulating research findings across studies.* Beverly Hills, CA: Sage.

Husserl, E. (1965). *Phenomenology and the crisis of philosophy.* New York: Harper & Row.

Husserl, E. (1970). *The crisis of European sciences and transcendental phenomenology* (D. Carr, trans.). Evanston, IL: Northwestern University Press.

Independent Panel to Review the Causes of the Teton Dam Failure (1976, December). *Report to the U.S. Department of the Interior and the State of Idaho.* Washington, DC: Government Printing Office.

Interagency Committee on Dam Safety (1979, June 25). *Federal guidelines on dam safety.* Washington, DC: Federal Coordinating Committee for Science, Engineering and Technology.

Isaac, S., & Michael, W. B. (1981). *Handbook in research and evaluation.* San Diego: Edits Publishing.

James, W. (1932). *The meaning of truth.* New York: Longman.

Jameson, F. (1984). Postmodernism and the cultural logic of capital. *New Left Review, 146* pp. 56-71.

Jameson, F. (1985). *The political unconsciousness: Narrative as a socially symbolic act.* New York: Methuen.

Jantsch, E. (1980). *The self-organizing universe.* Elmsford, NY: Pergamon.

Jantsch, E. (1981). Introduction. In E. Jantsch (ed.), *The evolutionary vision: Toward a unifying paradigm of physical, biological, and sociocultural evolution* (pp. 1-17). Boulder, CO: Westview.

Jennings, B. (1987). Interpretation and the practice of policy analysis. In F. Fischer & J. Forester (eds.), *Confronting values in policy analysis: The politics of criteria* (pp. 128-152). Newbury Park, CA: Sage.

Joreskog, K.G., & Sorbom, D. (1981). *LISREL V: User's guide.* Chicago: National Educational Resources.

Kant, I. (1965). *Critique of pure reason* (N. K. Smith, trans.). New York: St. Martin's. (Original works published 1781, 1787)

Kanter, R. M. (1977). *Men and women of the corporation.* New York: Basic Books.

Kaplan, A. (1964). *The conduct of inquiry.* San Francisco: Chandler.

Karl, B. D. (1974). Charles E. Merriam and the study of politics. Chicago: University of Chicago Press.

Karl, B. D. (1976). Public administration and American history: A century of professionalism. *Public Administration Review, 36,* 489-504.

Karl, B. D. (1987). The American bureaucrat: A history of a sheep in wolves' clothing. *Public Administration Review, 47,* 26-34.

Kass, H. D., & Catron, B. L. (1990). *Image and identity in public administration.* Newbury Park, CA: Sage.

Kaufman, H. A. (1960). *The forest ranger: A study in administrative behavior.* Baltimore, MD: Johns Hopkins University Press.

Kaufman, H. A. (1985). *Time, change, and organization.* Chatham, NJ: Chatham House.

Keller, E. F. (1983). *A feeling for the organism: The life and work of Barbara McClintock.* New York: W. H. Freeman.

Keller, E. F. (1985). *Reflections on science and gender.* New Haven, CT: Yale University Press.

Kelly, M., & Maynard-Moody, S. (1993). Policy analysis in the postpositivist era: Engaging stakeholders in evaluating the economic development district's program. *Public Administration Review, 53,* 135-142.

Kerlinger, R. N. (1986). *Foundations of behavioral research* (3rd ed.). New York: Holt, Rinehart & Winston.

Kidder, L. H. (1981). *Research methods in social relations* (4th ed.). New York: Holt, Rinehart & Winston.

Kiel, L. D. (1989). Nonequilibrium theory and its implications for public administration. *Public Administration Review, 49,* 544-551.

Kisiel, T. (1972). Scientific discovery: Logical, psychological, or hermeneutical? In D. Carr & E. Casey (eds.), *The phenomenological horizon* (pp. 50-78). Chicago: Quadrangle.

Kolakowski, L. (1968). *The alienation of reason: A history of positivist thought.* Garden City, NY: Doubleday.

Kolko, G. (1963). *The triumph of conservatism: A reinterpretation of American history, 1900-1916.* New York: Free Press.

Kraemer, K. L., & Perry, J. L. (1989). Institutional requirements for academic research in public administration. *Public Administration Review, 49,* 9-16.

Kronenberg, P. S. (1971). The scientific and moral authority of empirical theory of public administration. In F. Marini (ed.), *Toward a new public administration: The Minnowbrook perspective* (pp. 190-225). Scranton, PA: Chandler.

Kuhn, T. S. (1970). *The structure of scientific revolutions* (2nd ed.). Chicago: University of Chicago Press.

Kuhn, T. S. (1977). *The essential tension: Selected studies in scientific tradition and change.* Chicago: University of Chicago Press.

Labovitz, S., & Hagedorn, R. (1981). *Introduction to social research* (3rd ed.). New York: McGraw-Hill.

Lacan, J. (1977). *Ecrits: A selection.* London: Tavistock.

Lacan, J. (1978a). *The language of the self: The function of language in psychoanalysis.* Baltimore, MD: Johns Hopkins University Press.

Lacan, J. (1978b). *The four fundamental concepts of psychoanalysis.* London: Hogarth.

Landau, M. (1973). On the concept of a self-correcting organization. *Public Administration Review, 33,* 533-542.

Larson, M. L. (1977). *The rise of professionalism.* Berkeley: University of California Press.

Lasswell, H. D. (1951). The policy orientation. In D. Lerner & H. D. Lasswell (eds.), *The policy sciences: Recent developments in scope and method* (pp. 3-15). Stanford, CA: Stanford University Press.

Lasswell, H. D. (1956). Impact of psychoanalytic thinking on the social sciences. In L. D. White (ed.), *The state of the social sciences* (pp. 84-115). Chicago: University of Chicago Press.

Lasswell, H. D. (1961). The qualitative and the quantitative in political and legal analysis. In D. Lerner (ed.), *Quantity and quality* (pp. 103-116). New York: Free Press.

Lasswell, H. D. (1962). The public interest: Proposing principles of content and procedure. In C. J. Friedrich (ed.), *The public interest* (pp. 54-79). New York: Atherton.

Lasswell, H. D. (1971). *A preview of policy sciences.* New York: American Elsevier.

Latour, B. (1987). *Science in action.* Cambridge, MA: Harvard University Press.

Lester, J. P., & Webber, D. J. (1990). *The utilization of policy analysis by state agency officials: A comparative analysis.* Paper presented at annual meeting of the Southwestern Political Science Association, March 28-31, Ft. Worth, TX.

Lester, J. P., & Wilds, L. J. (1990). The utilization of public policy analysis—A conceptual framework. *Evaluation and Program Planning, 13.*

Lieberson, S. (1985). *Making it count: The improvement of social research and theory.* Berkeley: University of California Press.

Lincoln, Y. S. (ed.). (1985). *Organizational theory and inquiry: The paradigm revolution.* Beverly Hills, CA: Sage.

Lincoln, Y. S., & Guba, E. G. (1985). *Naturalistic inquiry.* Beverly Hills, CA: Sage.

Lindblom, C. E. (1990). *Inquiry and change: The troubled attempt to understand and shape society.* New Haven, CT: Yale University Press.

Lindblom, C. E., & Cohen, D. K. (1979). *Usable knowledge: Social science and social problem solving.* New Haven, CT: Yale University Press.

Linder, S. H., & Peters, B. G. (1988). The analysis of design or the design of analysis. *Policy Studies Review, 7,* 738-750.

Lindsay, A. D. (1936). *Kant.* London: Oxford University Press.

Lindstone, H. A. (1984). *Multiple perspectives for decision making: Bridging the gap between analysis and action.* New York: Elsevier North-Holland.

Link, A. S. (1964). *Woodrow Wilson and the Progressive Era 1910-1917.* New York: Harper & Row.

Lofland, J. (1971). *Analyzing social settings: A guide to qualitative observation and analysis.* Belmont, CA: Wadsworth.

Lofland, J., & Lofland, L. H. (1984). *Analyzing social settings: A guide to qualitative observation and analysis.* Belmont, CA: Wadsworth.

Louch, A. R. (1966). *Explanation and human action.* Berkeley: University of California Press.

Lustig, R. J. (1982). *Corporate liberalism: The origin of modern American political theory, 1890-1920.* Berkeley: University of California Press.

Lynn, L. E., Jr. (1987). *Managing public policy.* Boston: Little, Brown.

Lynn, N. B., & Wildavsky, A. (eds.). (1990). *Public administration: The state of the discipline.* Chatham, NJ: Chatham House.

Lyotard, J.-F. (1984). *The postmodern condition: A report on knowledge.* Manchester, UK: Manchester University Press.

MacIntrye, A. (1977). Epistemological crisis, dramatic narrative, and the philosophy of science. *Monist, 60,* 453-472.

MacIntyre, A. (1984). *After virtue* (2nd ed.). South Bend, IN: University of Notre Dame Press.

Mannheim, K. (1940). *Man and society in an age of reconstruction.* New York: Harcourt, Brace & World.

March, J. G., & Olsen, J. P. (1984). The new institutionalism: Organizational factors in political life. *American Political Science Review, 78,* 738-749.

Marini, F. (ed.). (1971). *Toward a new public administration.* Scranton, PA: Chandler.

Marini, F. (1992). Introduction. In M. T. Bailey & R. T. Mayer (eds.), *Public management in an interconnected world* (pp. 1-9). Westport, CT: Greenwood.

Marshall, G. S., & White, O. F., Jr. (1990). The Blacksburg manifesto and the postmodern debate: Public administration in a time without a name. *American Review of Public Administration, 20,* 61-76.

Martin, D. W. (1989). *The guide to the foundations of public administration.* New York: Marcel Dekker.

May, W. F. (1980). Professional ethics: Setting, terrain, and teacher. In D. Callahan (ed.), *Ethics teaching in higher education* (pp. 205-241). New York: Plenum.

Maynard-Moody, S., Burress, D., Ambrosius, M., & Weisenburger, R. (1991). *Economic development districts: Policy issues and choices.* Lawrence: Kansas Center for Community Economic Development.

Mazmanian, D. A., & Nienaber, J. (1979). *Can organizations change?* Washington, DC: Brookings Institution.

McClintock, C. C., Brannon, D., & Maynard-Moody, S. (1979). Applying the logic of sample surveys to qualitative case studies: The case cluster method. *Administrative Science Quarterly, 24,* 612-629.

McCurdy, H. E. (n.d.). The dismal quality of public administration research. *Discussion Pieces of the Barnard Society, U.S.A., 4.*

McCurdy, H. E. (1984). A call for "appropriate methods." *Public Administration Review, 44,* 553-554.

McCurdy, H. E. (1986). *Public administration: A bibliographic guide to the literature.* New York: Marcel Dekker.

McCurdy, H. E., & Cleary, R. E. (1984). Why can't we resolve the research issue in public administration? *Public Administration Review, 44,* 49-55.

McLuckie, B. F. (1973). *The warning system: A social science perspective.* Washington, DC: National Oceanic and Atmospheric Administration.

McMillen, L. (1991, 3 April). Mellon foundation plans to spend $50 million over 5 years to improve doctoral education. *Chronicle of Higher Education,* pp. 29-30.

Merkle, J. A. (1980). *Management and ideology.* Berkeley: University of California Press.

Merton, R. K. (1971). Insiders and outsiders: A chapter in the sociology of knowledge. *American Journal of Sociology, 78,* 13, 28-29.

Michael, D. M. (1973). *On learning to plan and planning to learn.* San Francisco: Jossey-Bass.

Miles, M. B. (1979). Qualitative data as an attractive nuisance. *Administrative Science Quarterly, 24,* 590-601.

Mileti, D. S. (1975). *Natural hazard warning systems in the United States: A research assessment.* Boulder: University of Colorado, Institute of Behavioral Science.

Miller, J. C. (1978). *Living systems.* New York: McGraw-Hill.

Miller, P., & O'Leary, T. (1989). Hierarchies and American ideals 1900-1940. *Academy of Management Review, 14,* 250-265.

Miller, T. C. (1984). Conclusion: A design science perspective. In T. C. Miller (ed.), *Public sector performance* (pp. 251-268). Baltimore, MD: Johns Hopkins University Press.

Miller, T. C. (1989a). *Design science as a unifying paradigm, or political power as a variable.* Paper presented at American Political Association meeting, Atlanta, GA.

Miller, T. C. (1989b). The operation of democratic institutions. *Public Administration Review, 49,* 511-521.

Mills, C. W. (1959). *The sociological imagination.* London: Oxford University Press.

Mintzberg, H. (1973). *The nature of managerial work.* New York: Harper & Row.

Mintzberg, H. (1975). *Impediments to the use of management information.* Study for National Association of Accountants and the Society of Industrial Accountants of Canada. New York: National Association of Accountants.

Mitroff, I. I., & Kilmann, R. (1975). Stories managers tell. *Academy of Management Review,* pp. 18-28.

Morgan, D. R., & Meier, K. J. (1982). Reputation and productivity of public administration/affairs programs: Additional data. *Public Administration Review, 42,* 171-173.

Morgan, D. R., Meier, K. J., Kearney, R. C., Hays, S. W., & Birch, H. B. (1981). Reputation and productivity among U.S. public administration and public affairs programs. *Public Administration Review, 41,* 666-673.

Mosher, F. C. (1956). Research in public administration: Some notes and suggestions. *Public Administration Review, 16,* 169-178.

Mosher, F. C. (1968). *Democracy and the public service.* New York: Oxford University Press.

Nachmias, D., & Nachmias, C. (1987). *Research methods in the social sciences* (3rd. ed.). New York: St. Martin's.

Nagel, E. (1961). *The structure of science.* Orlando, FL: Harcourt Brace Jovanovich.

National Association of Schools of Public Affairs and Administration. (1987). *Final report of the task force on the status of research in public administration* (mimeograph). Washington, DC: Author.

Nelson, M. (1982). A short ironic history of American national bureaucracy. *Journal of Politics, 44,* 747-778.

Nelson, W. E. (1982). *The roots of American bureaucracy, 1830-1900.* Cambridge, MA: Harvard University Press.

Neustadt, R. E., & May, E. R. (1986). *Thinking in time: The uses of history for decision-makers.* New York: Free Press.

Nietzsche, F. (1956). *The birth of tragedy and genealogy of morals* (F. Golffing, trans.). Garden City, NY: Doubleday. (Original work published 1872)

Noble, D. F. (1958). *The paradox of progressive thought.* Minneapolis: University of Minnesota Press.

Noble, D. F. (1970). *The progressive mind, 1890-1917.* Chicago: Rand McNally.

Office of Science and Technology Policy. (1978). *Federal dam safety; Report of the independent review panel.* Washington, DC: Government Printing Office.

Ostrom, E. (1982). Synthesis: The benefits of coherence and precision. In J. A. Gillespie & D. A. Zinnes (eds.), *Missing elements in political inquiry: Logic and levels of analysis* (pp. 78-98). Beverly Hills, CA: Sage.

Ostrom, V. (1974). *The intellectual crisis in American public administration* (rev. ed). University: University of Alabama Press.

Ostrom, V., Feenyr, D., & Picht, H. (eds.). (1988). *Rethinking institutional analysis and development.* San Francisco: International Center for Economic Growth.

O'Sullivan, E., & Rassel, G. R. (1989). *Research methods for public administrators.* New York: Longman.

O'Toole, L. J., Jr. (1984). American public administration and the idea of reform. *Administration and Society, 16,* 141-166.

O'Toole, L. J., Jr. (1987). Doctrines and developments: Separation of powers, the politics-administration dichotomy, and the rise of the administrative state. *Public Administration Review, 47,* 17-25.

Outhwaite, W. (1975). *Understanding and social life: The method called Verstehen.* London: Allen & Unwin.

Overman, E. S. (ed.). (1988). *Methodology and epistemology in the social sciences.* Chicago: University of Chicago Press.

Palmer, R. (1969). *Hermeneutics.* Evanston, IL: Northwestern University Press.

Park, R. E. (1928). Human migration and the marginal man. *American Journal of Sociology, 33,* 892.

Park, R. E. (1931). Mentality of racial hybrids. *American Journal of Sociology, 36,* 534-551.

Parsons, T. (1937). *The structure of social action.* New York: McGraw-Hill.

Pearce, J. L., Stevenson, W. B., & Perry, J. L. (1985). Managerial compensation based on organizational performance: A time-series analysis of the impact of merit pay. *Academy of Management Journal, 28,* 261-278.

Pepper, S. C. (1966). *Concept and quality: A world hypothesis.* La Salle, IL: Open Court.

Perrow, C. (1984). *Normal accidents: Living with high-risk technologies.* New York: Basic Books.

Perry, J. L. (ed.). (1990). *Handbook of public administration.* San Francisco: Jossey-Bass.

Perry, J. L., & Kraemer, K. L. (1986). Research methodology in the public administration review 1975-1984. *Public Administration Review, 46,* 215-226.

Peters, T. J., & Waterman, R. H., Jr. (1982). *In search of excellence: Lessons from America's best run companies.* New York: Harper & Row.

Petr, J. L. (1984). Fundamentals of an institutionalist perspective of economic policy. In M. R. Tool (ed.), *An institutionalist guide to economics and public policy* (pp. 1-18). New York: M. E. Sharpe.

Poister, T. H., & McGowan, R. P. (1984). The use of management tools in municipal government: A national survey. *Public Administration Review, 44,* 215-223.

Popper, K. (1959). *The logic of scientific discovery.* New York: Harper & Row.

Popper, K. (1966). *The open society and its enemies* (2 vols.) (5th ed. rev.). London: Routledge & Kegan Paul.

Popper, K. (1972). *Conjectures and refutations. The growth of scientific knowledge* (4th ed. rev.). London: Routledge & Kegan Paul.

Pressman, J., & Wildavsky, A. (1984). *Implementation* (3rd ed.). Berkeley: University of California Press.

Proctor, R. N. (1991). *Value-free science? Purity and power in modern knowledge.* Cambridge, MA: Harvard University Press.

Quarantelli, E. L. (1985). *The functioning of the local emergency services offices in disasters.* Newark: University of Delaware, Disaster Research Center.

Rabin, J., & Bowman, J. S. (eds.). (1984). *Politics and administration: Woodrow Wilson and American public administration.* New York: Marcel Dekker.

Rabin, J. W., Hildreth, B., & Miller, G. (eds.). (1989). *Handbook of public administration.* New York: Marcel Dekker.

Rabinbach, A. (1990). *The human motor: Energy, fatigue and the origins of modernity.* New York: Basic Books.

Rabinow, P., & Sullivan, W. M. (eds.). (1979). *Interpretive social science: A reader.* Berkeley: University of California Press.

Redford, E. S. (1969). *Democracy in the administrative state.* New York: Oxford University Press.

Reich, R. B. (ed.). (1987). *The power of public ideas.* Cambridge, MA: Ballinger.

Reichenbach, H. (1963). *The rise of scientific philosophy.* Berkeley: University of California Press.

Rein, M. (1976). *Social science and public policy.* New York: Penguin.

Rogers, E. M., & Agarwala-Rogers, R. (1976). *Communication in organizations.* New York: Free Press.

Rohr, J. A. (1985). Professionalism, legitimacy and the constitution. *Public Administration Quarterly, 8,* 401-418.

Rohr, J. A. (1986). *To run a constitution.* Lawrence: University of Kansas Press.

Rorty, R. (1982). *Consequences of pragmatism.* Minneapolis: University of Minnesota Press.

Rorty, R. (1991). *Objectivity, relativism, and truth.* Cambridge, UK: Cambridge University Press.

Rosenbloom, D. H. (1971). *Federal service and the constitution.* Ithaca, NY: Cornell University Press.

Rosenbloom, D. H. (1983). *Public administration and law.* New York: Marcel Dekker.

Rosenbloom, D. H. (1989). *Public administration: Understanding management, politics and law in the public sector* (2nd ed.). New York: McGraw-Hill.

Rossi, P. H. (1971). Evaluating educational programs. In F. G. Caro (ed.), *Readings in evaluation research* (pp. 97-99). New York: Russell Sage.

Samuels, W. (ed.). (1982). *The methodology of economic thought.* New Brunswick, NJ: Transaction Books.

Saussure, F. (1974). *Course in general linguistics.* London: Fontana.

Schmidt, M. R. (1993). Grout: Alternative forms of knowledge and why they are ignored. *Public Administration Review, 53.*

Schneider, A., & Ingram, H. (1988). *Filling empty boxes: A framework for the comparative analysis of policy designs.* Paper presented at Western Political Science Association meeting, San Francisco.

Schon, D. A. (1983). *The reflective practitioner: how professionals think in action.* New York: Basic Books.

Schuman, D. (1982). *Policy analysis, education, and everyday life.* Lexington, MA: D. C. Heath.

Schutz, A. (1944). The stranger: An essay in social psychology. *American Journal of Sociology, 49,* 499-507.

Schutz, A. (1967). Common-sense and scientific interpretation of human action. In A. Schutz, *Collected works. Vol. 1: The problem of social reality* (pp. 3-47). The Hague: Martinus Nijhoff.

Schwartz, P., & Ogilvy, J. (1979). *The emergent paradigm: Changing patterns of thought and belief.* Menlo Park, CA: SRI International.

Scriven, M. (1962). Explanations, predictions, and laws. In H. Feigl & G. Maxwell (eds.), *Minnesota studies in the philosophy of science* (Vol. 3). Minneapolis: University of Minnesota Press.

Searle, J. R. (1969). *Speech acts: An essay in the philosophy of language.* London: Cambridge University Press.

Sedgwick, J. L. (1986). Executive leadership and administration: Founding versus progressive views. *Administration and Society, 17,* 411-432.

Sedgwick, J. L. (1987). Of centennials and bicentennials: Reflections on the foundations of American public administration. *Administration and Society, 19,* 285-308.

Selznick, P. (1949). *TVA and the grass roots: A study in the sociology of formal organization.* Berkeley: University of California Press.

Shangraw, R. F., & Crow, M. M. (1989). Public administration as a design science. *Public Administration Review, 49,* 153-159.

Shieve, W. C., & Allen, P. M. (eds.). (1982). *Self organization and dissipative structures: Applications in the physical and social sciences.* Austin: University of Texas Press.

Simmel, G. (1909). The problem of sociology. *American Journal of Sociology, 15,* 289-320.

Simon, H. A. (1947). A comment on the "science of public administration." *Public Administration Review, 7,* 200-203.

Simon, H. A. (1976). *Administrative behavior: A study of decision-making processes in administrative organization* (3rd ed.). New York: Free Press.

Simon, H. A. (1981). *The sciences of the artificial.* Cambridge: MIT Press.

Simon, H. A. (1983). *Reason in human affairs.* Stanford, CA: Stanford University Press.

Skowronek, S. (1982). *Building a new American state: The expansion of national administrative capacities, 1877-1920.* Cambridge, UK: Cambridge University Press.

Small, A. (1916). Fifty years of sociology. *American Journal of Sociology, 21,* 724-731.

Smith, P. (1990). *Killing the spirit: Higher education in America.* New York: Viking.

Snow, C. P. (1964). *The two cultures and a second look.* New York: Mentor.

Stallings, R. A. (1986). Doctoral programs in public administration: An outsider's perspective. *Public Administration Review, 46,* 235-240.

Stallings, R. A., & Ferris, J. A. (1988). Public administration research: Work in PAR 1940-1984. *Public Administration Review, 48,* 580-587.

Steiss, A. W., & Daneke, G. A. (1980). *Performance administration.* Lexington, MA: D. C. Heath.

Stever, J. A. (1986). Mary Parker Follett and the quest for pragmatic public administration. *Administration and Society, 18,* 159-177.

Stever, J. A. (1988). *The end of public administration: Problems of the profession in the post-Progressive Era.* Dobbs Ferry, NY: Transnational.

Stever, J. A. (1990). The dual image of the administrator in progressive administrative theory. *Administration and Society, 22,* 39-57.

Stillman, R. J. (1987). *The American bureaucracy.* Chicago: Nelson Hall.

Stillman, R. J. (1991). *Preface to public administration: A search for themes and directions.* New York: St. Martin's.

Stivers, C. (1993). *Gender images in public administration.* Newbury Park, CA: Sage.

Stone, D. A. (1988). *Policy paradox and political reason.* Glenview, IL: Scott, Foresman.

Stone, D. A. (1989). Causal stories and the formation of policy agendas. *Political Science Quarterly, 104,* 281-300.

Taylor, C. (1971). Interpretation and the sciences of man. *Review of Metaphysics, 13,* 3-51.

Taylor, S. J., & Bogdan, R. (1984). *Introduction to qualitative research methods: The search for meaning.* New York: John Wiley.

Thayer, F. C. (1972). General systems theory: The promise that could not be kept. *Academy of Management Journal, 15,* 481-493.

Thayer, F. C. (1980). Organization theory as epistemology: Transcending hierarchy and objectivity. In C. J. Bellone (ed.), *Organization theory and public administration* (pp. 113-139). Boston: Allyn & Bacon.

Thayer, F. C. (1984). Understanding research. *Public Administration Review, 44,* 552-553.

Thomas, N. C. (1983). Case studies. In G. C. Edwards III & S. J. Wayne (eds.), *Studying the presidency* (pp. 50-78). Knoxville: University of Tennessee Press.

Thompson, J. B. (1981). *Critical hermeneutics.* Cambridge, MA: Harvard University Press.

Toffler, A. (1984). Foreword. In I. Prigogine & I. Stengers, *Order out of chaos* (pp. vi-xx). New York: Bantam.

de Tocqueville, A. (1945). *Democracy in America.* New York: Knopf. (Original work published 1856)

Torgeson, D. (1985). Contextual orientation in policy analysis: The contribution of Harold D. Lasswell. *Policy Sciences, 18,* 241-261.

Toulmin, S. (1953). *The philosophy of science.* London: Hutchinson.

Toulmin, S. (1958). *The uses of argument.* Cambridge, UK: Cambridge University Press.

Turner, B. S. (ed.). (1990). *Theories of modernity and postmodernity.* London: Sage.

U.S. Congress, House Committee on Government Operations. (1976). *Teton dam disaster.* Report of subcommittee hearings. Washington, DC: Government Printing Office.

U.S. Congress. (1982). *Evaluation of the authorities and programs of the Economic Development Administration.* Washington, DC: Government Printing Office.

U.S. Corps of Army Engineers. (1976). *National program of inspection of dams.* Washington, DC: Government Printing Office.

U.S. Department of Commerce. (1981). *Annual report: The Economic Development Administration.* Washington, DC: Government Printing Office.

U.S. Department of the Interior, Teton Dam Failure Review Group. (1976). *Failure of Teton Dam: A report of findings.* Washington, DC: Government Printing Office.

Uveges, J. A., Jr. (1985, October 23-25). *Identifying the impacts of NASPAA's MPA standards and peer review process on education for the public service: 1975-1985.* Paper presented at Southeast regional ASPA meeting, Charleston, SC.

Vanderburg, W. H. (1985). *The growth of minds and cultures: A unified theory of the structure of human experience.* Toronto: University of Toronto Press.

Van Dyke, V. (1960). *Political science: A philosophical analysis.* Stanford, CA: Stanford University Press.

Van Maanen, J. (ed.). (1979). Symposium on qualitative methodology. *Administrative Science Quarterly, 24,* 519-671.

Van Riper, P. P. (1958). *A history of the U.S. civil service.* Evanston, IL: Row, Peterson.

Van Riper, P. P. (1983). The American administrative state: Wilson and the founders—An unorthodox view. *Public Administration Review, 43,* 477-490.

Van Riper, P. P. (1990). *The Wilson influence on public administration: From theory to practice.* Washington, DC: American Society for Public Administration.

Ventriss, C. (1987). Two critical issues of American public administration. *Administration and Society, 19,* 25-47.

Ventriss, C., & Luke, J. (1988). *Organizational learning and public policy* (working paper). Burlington: University of Vermont.

Vickers, G. (1965). *The art of judgment.* New York: Basic Books.

Vickers, G. (1970). *Value systems and social process.* New York: Penguin.

Vickers, G. (1973). *Making institutions work.* New York: John Wiley.

Vickers, G. (1984). The art of judgment. In D. S. Pugh (ed.), *Organization theory* (2nd ed., pp. 183-201). New York: Penguin.

Vocino, T., & Elliott, R. H. (1982). Journal prestige in public administration: A research note. *Administration and Society, 14,* 5-14.

Vocino, T., & Elliott, R. H. (1984). Public administration journal prestige: A time series analysis, *Administrative Science Quarterly, 29,* 43-51.

Vogel, D. R., & Wetherbe, J. C. (1984). MIS research: A profile of leading journals and universities. *Data Base, 16,* 3-14.

von Mises, L. (1949). *Human action: A treatise on economics.* New Haven, CT: Yale University Press.

Waldo, D. (1948). *The administrative state: A study of the political theory of public administration.* New York: Ronald.

Waldo, D. (1953). *Ideas and issues in public administration.* New York: McGraw-Hill.

Waldo, D. (1955). *The study of public administration.* New York: Doubleday.

Waldo, D. (1966). Editorial. *Public Administration Review, 26,* 237.

Waldo, D. (1980). *The enterprise of public administration: A summary view.* Novato, CA: Chandler & Sharp.

Waldo, D. (1984). *The administrative state* (2nd ed.). New York: Holmes & Meier.

Walker, L. N. (1990). Woodrow Wilson, progressive reform and public administration. In P. P. Van Riper (ed.), *The Wilson influence on public administration* (pp. 83-98). Washington, DC: American Society for Public Administration.

Wamsley, G. L. (1990). *Refounding public administration.* Newbury Park, CA: Sage.

Weber, M. (1949). *The methodology of the social sciences.* New York: Free Press.

Weber, M. (1958). *The Protestant ethic and the spirit of capitalism.* New York: Scribners. (Original work published 1905)

Weber, M. (1968). Roscher und Knies und die logischen Probleme der historischen Nationaloekonomie. In J. Winckelmann (ed.), *Gesammelte Aufsaetze zur Wissenschaftslehre* (pp. 1-145). Tuebingen: J. C. B. Mohr. (Original work published 1922)

Weber, M. (1979). *Economy and society* (2 vols.). Berkeley: University of California Press.

Weinstein, J. (1968). *The corporate ideal in the liberal state 1900-1918.* Boston: Beacon.

Weiss, C. H. (ed.). (1991). *Organizations for policy advice: Helping government think.* Newbury Park, CA: Sage.

Weiss, J. A., & Gruber, J. E. (1984). Using knowledge for control in fragmented policy arenas. *Journal of Policy Analysis and Management, 3,* 225-247.

Weiss, R. S., & Rein, M. (1970). The evaluation of broad-aim programs: Experimental design. *Administrative Science Quarterly, 15,* 98-109.

White, E., & Losco, J. (eds.). (1986). *Biology and bureaucracy.* Lanham, MD: University Press.

White, J. D. (1986a). On the growth of knowledge in public administration. *Public Administration Review, 46,* 15-24.

White, J. D. (1986b). Dissertations and publications in public administration. *Public Administration Review, 46,* 227-234.

White, J. D. (1987, November). Action theory and literary interpretation. *Administration and Society,* pp. 346-366.

White, J. D. (1990). Images of administrative reason and rationality. In H. D. Kass & B. L. Catron (eds.), *Images and identities in public administration* (pp. 132-150). Newbury Park, CA: Sage.

White, J. D. (1992). Taking language seriously: Toward a narrative theory of knowledge for administrative research. *American Review of Public Administration, 22,* 75-88.

White, L. D. (1926). *Introduction to the study of public administration.* New York: Macmillan.

White, L. D. (1948). *The Federalists.* New York: Macmillan.

White, L. D. (1951). *The Jeffersonians.* New York: Macmillan.

White, L. D. (1954). *The Jacksonians.* New York: Macmillan.

White, L. D. (1958). *The Republican era.* New York: Macmillan.

White, M. (1957). *Social thought in America.* Boston: Beacon.

White, O. F., Jr., & McSwain, C. J. (1990). The Phoenix project. In H. D. Kass & B. L. Catron (eds.), *Images and identities in public administration* (pp. 23-59). Newbury Park, CA: Sage.

Whitehead, A. N. (1925). *Science and the modern world*. New York: Macmillan.

Whitehead, A. N. (1929). *Process and reality*. New York: Harper & Row.

Whitehead, A. N., & Russell, B. (1910). *Principia mathematica*. Oxford, UK: Oxford University Press.

Wiebe, R. H. (1967). *The search for order, 1877-1920*. New York: Hill & Wang.

Williams, H. B. (1964). Human factors in warning-and-response systems. In G. H. Grosser, H. Wechsler, & M. Greenblatt (eds.), *The threat of impending disaster: Contributions to the psychology of stress* (pp. 79-104). Cambridge: MIT Press.

Wilson, D. E. (1980). *The national planning idea in public policy*. Boulder, CO: Westview.

Wilson, E. O. (1975). *Sociobiology: The new synthesis*. Cambridge, MA: Harvard University Press.

Wilson, W. (1887). The study of administration. *Political Science Quarterly, 2,* 481-507.

Wimsatt, W. C. (1986). Heuristics and the study of human behavior. In D. W. Fiske & R. A. Shweder (eds.), *Metatheory in social sciences* (pp. 279-301). Chicago: University of Chicago Press.

Winch, P. (1958). *The idea of a social science and its relation to philosophy*. London: Routledge & Kegan Paul.

Winkler, K. J. (1985, June 26). Questioning the science in social science, scholars signal a "turn to interpretation." *Chronicle of Higher Education,* pp. 5-6.

Witkin, H. A. (1976). Cognitive style in academic performance and in teacher-student relations. In S. Messick (ed.), *Individuality in learning* (pp. 25-54). San Francisco: Jossey-Bass.

Witkin, H. A., Dyk, R. B., Faterson, H. F., Goodenough, D. R., & Karp, S. A. (1962). *Psychology differentiation*. New York: John Wiley.

Wittgenstein, L. (1922). *Tractatus logico-philosphicus*. New York: Harcourt, Brace & World.

Wittgenstein, L. (1953). *Philosophical investigations*. New York: Macmillan.

Wolff, K. H. (1950). *The sociology of Georg Simmel*. New York: Free Press.

Yin, R. K. (1981a). The case study as a serious research strategy. *Knowledge, 3,* 97-114.

Yin, R. K. (1981b). The case study crisis: Some answers. *Administrative Science Quarterly, 26,* 58-65.

Yin, R. K. (1990). *Case study research: Design and methods* (rev. ed.). Newbury Park, CA: Sage.

Yin, R. K., & Heald, K. A. (1975). Using the case survey method to analyze policy studies. *Administrative Science Quarterly, 20,* 371-381.

Zaner, R. (1970). *The way of phenomenology*. New York: Pegasus.

Author Index

Abel, T., 17, 59
Adams, G. B., 7, 13, 21, 34, 39
Adams, R. N., 74
Agarwala-Rogers, R., 95, 96, 123
Agor, W. A., 243
Aguilar, F. J., 226
Aldrich, H., 64
Allaire, Y., 59
Allen, P. M., 74
Allen, W. H., 33
Allison, G. T., 193
Ambrosius, M., 211
American Society for Public Administration, 166
Apel, K.-O., 59
Arendt, H., 5, 30, 55
Argyris, C., 46
Aronson, S. H., 27
Asher, W., 65
Association of American Universities, 157
Axelrod, R., 71

Babbie, E. R., 112, 122
Backoff, R. W., 67
Bailey, M. T., 10, 12, 20
Barley, S. R., 39, 59
Barnard, C. A., 47
Barrett, W., 26, 32
Bauman, Z., 25
Bell, D., 2
Bellah, R. N., 21
Bendix, R., 4, 30, 32
Berger, B., 2
Berger, P. L., 2, 21, 179, 123, 173, 244
Berlinski, D., 72

Bernstein, R. J., 16, 25, 43, 53, 54, 55, 56, 58, 74, 149, 156, 198
Biller, R. P., 108, 173
Birch, H. B., 101, 122
Blalock, Jr., H. M., 132
Blankenship, V. L., 108, 124
Bobrow, D. B., 64
Bogdan, R., 114
Boulding, K., 66
Bowerman, P. V., 21, 34
Bowman, J. S., 34
Box, R. C., 10, 13, 25
Bozeman, B., 64, 211
Brannon, D., 106
Brodbeck, M., 51
Brown, R. E., 67
Brunner, R. D., 65
Buckley, W., 66, 68, 69
Burke, J. P., 193
Burrell, G., 46
Burress, D., 211
Bush, P. D., 66

Caiden, G. E., 28, 34, 121, 135
Caldwell, B., 27, 74
Caldwell, L. K., 12, 27, 96, 123, 124
Campbell, C., 15
Campbell, D. C., 60, 72, 96
Carter, L. H., 58, 59
Casanova, P. G., 189
Catalano, R., 107
Catron, B. L., 12, 37, 46, 95, 125
Chandler, R. C., 27, 28
Churchman, C. W., 64, 74
Cicourel, A., 58, 59

Subject Index

About the Authors

Jay D. White is professor of public administration at the University of Nebraska at Omaha. His primary research interests are in the philosophical foundations of administrative research. He is the author of many articles on knowledge acquisition and use in public administration that have appeared in several books and in journals such as the *Public Administration Review, Administration and Society, American Review of Public Administration,* and *Public Administration Quarterly.*

Guy B. Adams is associate professor and director of graduate studies in the department of public administration at the University of Missouri-Columbia. His research has focused on organizational symbolism and culture, as well as on public administration history and ethics. He is coauthor of *The Tacit Organization* (1992) and coeditor of *Policy Making, Communication, and Social Learning: Essays of Sir Geoffrey Vickers* (1987). He has published widely in such scholarly journals as the *Public Administration Review, American Review of Public Administration, Administration and Society,* and *Organization Studies.*

Mary Timney Bailey is associate professor of political science and director of the MPA program at the University of Cincinnati. Her research focuses on public administration theory and environmental policy. She is the coeditor (with Richard T. Mayer) of *Public Management in an Interconnected World* (1992).

Richard C. Box (Ph.D., University of Southern California) is assistant professor in the graduate school of public affairs at the University of Colorado at Colorado Springs. His doctoral completion in 1990 followed more than a decade of service as a professional planner and administrator in local government. His current research focuses on the impact of community politics on administrative behavior and the boundaries of administrative discretion.

Robert E. Cleary is professor of public affairs at American University, where he was dean of the College of Public Affairs from 1980 to 1987. He is a past president of the National Association of Schools of Public Affairs and Administration. His research focuses on the areas of administrative politics and public administration education.

Gregory A. Daneke is a professor of public affairs, business, and environmental studies at Arizona State University. He also has held appointments at Virginia Polytechnic Institute, the University of Michigan, and Stanford University. He has written extensively and is currently completing a research monograph that applies nonlinear dynamics (e.g., chaos and complexity theory) to the problems of practical management.

Sybil M. Delevan is assistant to the dean for the School of Social Work at Arizona State University. Her research interests include the fields of organization theory, methodology, and public policy, specifically health and human services. Her research focuses primarily on alternative organizational arrangements for the delivery of public goods and services and research and knowledge development in public administration. She is a contributing editor to *Transferring Technology in the Public Personal Social Services* and has published in *Public Administration Review, Administration and Society, Review of Public Personnel Administration, Journal of Public Health Policy,* and *Administration in Social Work.*

James M. Ferris is Professor in the Public Policy program in the School of Public Administration at the University of Southern California. His research interests include the political economy of service delivery, the economics of the nonprofit sector, and education and health policy.

David J. Houston is assistant professor of political science at the University of Tennessee, Knoxville. His research interests include public administration theory, social welfare policy, and responses to bureaucratic discretion. His most recent research has appeared in the *Public Administration Review, the International Journal of Public Administration,* and the *Review of Public Personnel Administration.*

Ralph P. Hummel is associate professor of political science and public administration at the University of Oklahoma. He is author of the first phenomenology of bureaucracy, *The Bureaucratic Experience* (1976, 1982, 1987, 1994) and coauthor (with Robert A. Isaak) of the first phenomenology of politics, *Politics for Human Beings* (1975, 1981).

Kenneth L. Kraemer is director of the Center for Research on Information Technology in Organizations and Professor in the Graduate School of Management and the Department of Information and Computer Science at the University of California, Irvine. His research focuses on the use, impact, and management of computers and information systems in organizations, as well as on assessing national policies toward the international production and use of information technologies. He is coauthor of *Wired Cities* (1987), *Datawars* (1987), and *Managing Information Systems* (1989), and is currently working on a book on global information technology and competition.

Marisa Kelly (Ph.D., University of Kansas) is is an assistant professor in the Department of Political Science at the University of the Pacific. Her work on postpositivist policy analysis and public administration has appeared in the *Public Administration Review* and the *Journal of Public Administration Research and Theory.*

Steven Maynard-Moody is associate professor of public administration and research fellow at the Institute for Public Policy and Business Research, University of Kansas. He is currently finishing *Fall from Grace: The Story of Fetal Research and Its Moral Politics* (in press). He and Marisa Kelly recently published "Stories Public Managers Tell About Elected Officials: Making Sense of the Defunct Dichotomy" in *Public Management: The State of the Art* (Barry Bozeman, editor) (1993).

Chester A. Newland is a teacher at the University of Southern California, where he is the Frances R. and John J. Duggan Distinguished Professor of Public Administration. He is the past national president of the American Society for Public Administration and a member of the National Academy of Public Administration. He was editor-in-chief of the *Public Administration Review* from 1984 to 1990.

James L. Perry is a professor in the School of Public and Environmental Affairs, Indiana University, Bloomington. His research focuses on public management and public personnel administration. Perry's research has appeared in such journals as the *Academy of Management Journal, Administrative Science Quarterly, American Political Science Review,* and *Public Administration Review.* He has coauthored or edited four books, including the *Handbook of Public Administration* (1989).

Mary R. Schmidt (Ph.D., Massachusetts Institute of Technology) is a planning consultant in Cambridge, Massachusetts. She has developed organizational and educational programs on urban design, air and water quality, and urban energy problems. She is currently working on organizational development for nonprofit groups with environmental concerns.

Robert A. Stallings is associate professor in the School of Public Administration at the University of Southern California in Los Angeles. His current research focuses on the interplay among collective behavior, social problems, and public policy, particularly in toxic waste and other environmental controversies. He is currently completing a book on the social construction of the earthquake threat.